teaching as treatment

robert r. carkhuff, ph. d.
&
bernard g. berenson, ph. d.

carkhuff
institute
of human
technology

american
international
college

Human
Resource
Development
Press

Human
Resource
Development
Press

Box 863, Dept. M31, Amherst, Massachusetts 01002
1-413-253-3488

International Standard Book Number: 0-914234-84-6
Library of Congress Number: 75-40865

First Printing — February 1976
Second Printing — July 1977
Third Printing — July 1978

Designed and Illustrated by Tom Capolongo
Consulting Art Director, Eileen Donovan

2.5, 1.5, 1

teaching as treatment

Table of Contents

About the Authors

Dr. Robert R. Carkhuff is Chairman, Board of Directors Carkhuff Institute of Human Technology, Amherst, Mass. He has directed graduate training programs in psychology and research at the state universities of New York, Massachusetts, Kentucky and Wisconsin. Dr. Carkhuff has devoted his life to operationalizing the process of human, educational and community resource development. He is the father of the human technology movement. He has written more than 100 articles on education, psychology and social change. His books include the now-classic **Helping and Human Relations** and **The Development of Human Resources** published by Holt, Rinehart & Winston and the **Life Skills Series**, the **Learning Skills Series** and the **Working Skills Series** published by Human Resource Development Press.

Dr. Bernard G. Berenson is Executive Director, Carkhuff Institute for Human Technology, Amherst, Mass. and Director of Graduate Training, Department of Human Relations and Community Affairs, American International College, Springfield, Mass. He has directed clinical training programs in counseling centers at the state universities of New York, Maryland and Massachusetts. Dr. Berenson has been a working partner of Dr. Carkhuff's over the past decade. As such, they have shared in the development of a human technology: systematic programs leading to humanistic outcomes. Dr. Berenson has collaborated with Dr. Carkhuff on the books **Sources of Gain in Counseling and Psychotherapy** and **Beyond Counseling and Therapy** published by Holt, Rinehart & Winston. His most recent works include **Confrontation — For Better or Worse** and **Belly to Belly, Back to Back — The Militant Humanism of Robert R. Carkhuff**, both published by Human Resource Development Press.

Preface

We come to bury therapy and give birth to "teaching as the preferred mode of treatment." Human needs are expanding at such a geometric rate that we can no longer afford the luxury of the traditional modes of counseling and psychotherapy. They have not delivered. They cannot deliver. Those of us who are too tired to change so that we can do the things that will deliver must simply move over and allow those who are not too tired to make the changes.

In this context, the reasons this book was written are several fold:

1. to sound a requiem for traditional counseling and therapeutic practices once and for all because they do not make a difference in terms of human benefits;

2. to sound a reveille for teaching and training practice because they do make a difference in terms of human benefits;

3. to detail the numerous models and correct the numerous distortions of the concepts of teaching or training as treatment because the concept is much more complex than the reviewers seem to understand, and

4. to take credit for the concepts of teaching and training as treatment in order to exert a continuing influence upon the development of the teaching models as they are extended fully into treatment.

Briefly, **Teaching as Treatment** not only provides the empirical base for its own evolution but also teaches the outcomes, processes, skills, training and systems involved in its implementation. In addition, it points to the future with a human technology for human effectiveness.

i

This book is meant for all people who are concerned with helping and human services including functional or paraprofessionals, parents, teachers, employers and community workers as well as credentialed professionals in guidance and rehabilitation, counseling and clinical psychology, psychiatry and social work, and nurses and members of the allied health sciences. If you are such a person, this book is for you. Its aim is to teach you how to make your own treatment programs effective.

We wish to acknowledge the continuing stimulation and support of our colleagues in the Carkhuff Institute of Human Technology, *Dr. William A. Anthony, Dr. David N. Aspy, Dr. George Banks, Dr. David H. Berenson, Dr. David H. Bland, Dr. John R. Cannon, Dr. Tom Collingwood, Dr. Ted W. Friel, Dr. Andrew H. Griffin, Dr. Richard M. Pierce and Dr. Flora Roebuck.*

In addition, we wish to acknowledge the continuing support and stimulation of our colleagues at the National Foundation for the Improvement of Education, *Dr. James W. Becker, Dr. Peg Jones and Dr. Shirley McCune.*

The concept of "teaching as treatment" is a new one. It replaces all other therapeutic practices because it contributes measurably and immeasurably more to helping effectiveness.

The distance from traditional counseling and psychotherapy to "teaching as treatment" is the distance between life and death itself—for helpers as well as for their helpees.

R.R.C.
B.G.B.

Amherst, Massachusetts
January, 1976

Section One—Introduction

Chapter One

Moving Upstream

Times change but people do not.

People do not change because they do not know what they want to be.

People cling to the illusion that they know what they want the world around them to be. They attempt to design their world so that they themselves will no longer need to adapt, to change, to grow.

Our present, all-too-obvious failures are tied to our effort to build a world that leaves a place for us as we **are** rather than as we **can be.**

In the past decade we have made hope something grim. Our promises have mocked noble dreams and have made a hollow ritual of human contact. We have numbed ourselves to the agony of being alone, fearful, angry and hateful. We are unaware of human experience beyond our own skins. We compulsively feed our vanity with our ignorance.

We have produced a terrible world in the process (Carkhuff, 1976).

In the near future almost 80% of our children will be sufficiently maladjusted to add to the statistics of delinquency and crime, emotional instability and vocational maladjustment, marital unhappiness and many other expressions of profound failure.

And still we persist in making false promises to ourselves and to others.

Our children's energy levels will never be as high as they are now—whatever their age. Few of them will ever translate their physical drives into productivity as well as they do right now.

Our children are currently more sensitive to others than they will ever be as adults—whatever their current limitations. They will only learn how to increase distance and cruelty, not intimacy and compassion. Our children are six times more likely to commit crimes and/or have crimes committed against them than were previous generations.

Our children will significantly deteriorate in inquisitiveness, spontaneity, originality and creativity—however restricted their present efforts. Two-thirds of our children in inner-city schools will be functionally illiterate and one out of four of our children who enter the fifth grade will not graduate from high school. These are simply numbers fulfilling the prediction of an intellectual regression curve that may well be irreversible.

Our children will never develop the planning and working habits of previous generations. Our children's per-man-hour productivity will fall to last place among the industrialized nations of this world—this in a nation whose human growth and development was predicated upon the production of goods and materials.

Because we build our world with the twisted hope that we will not have to change, our children choose to leave it.

Through it all, our children will feel less and less in control of their destinies because the people running the country leave them out and do not care what they think and will not help them to achieve the American dream.

For them, the American dream is a nightmare.

Three million of our children will attempt suicide. Fifty thousand will succeed and make suicide the second leading killer of young people in this country.

Downstream

We in the helping professions wait downstream to fish the bodies out.

We persist in fabricating and clinging to complex theories of personality and therapy while we have yet to insist upon basically decent behaviors from one another. We interpret dreams, condition, touch, feel, scream and confront while we deny each other a pleasant disposition. We deny each other any external recognition of existence. We share words about commitment and regard while we knowingly withhold nourishment.

We know a great deal about losers yet still we plot to divert the winners. We insist upon being intellectual, while failing to be intelligent. We insist upon attacking complex problems while we make insane decisions. We insist upon ignoring basics while we undermine systematic solutions.

We generate our own insanity. Within the ranks of counseling and psychotherapy we have empathy specialists, genuineness specialists, confrontation specialists and many other kinds of psychopathy. Each specialist makes the insane assumption that her or his specialty is necessary and sufficient for constructive human resource development.

We choose to respond without following our responses with initiative; or we initiate without first responding. Both are insane.

In their desperation, clients and patients continue to seek out treatment in ever-increasing numbers because we have failed to train skillful helpers. The desperation of our clients comes from their inability to get outside of their own skins. They are afraid of learning, angry at the emptiness, starving for contact and hating those who have more. The clients and patients are, in one way or another, the broken and disabled products of a social system which has disallowed their emergence as constructive and potent persons by supporting destructive educational experiences, by denying them the interpersonal skills they need to communicate with others and by withholding the strategies these clients and patients need to operationalize goals and achieve them.

The "more knowing" roles prescribed by society, those of parent, teacher, minister, guidance counselor, coach and perhaps even spouse, while supposedly dedicated to the provision of human nourishment, have obviously left their principle functions undischarged. Most of these people have left their "less knowing" counterparts impotent and unfulfilled. They have ceded their own special voids to their children, students and partners, for they themselves have very little to offer.

Moving Upstream

We have the potential yet we choose not to use it.

We have the people yet we refuse to free them.

We have the programs yet we neglect to implement them.

We choose instead to wait downstream to fish the bodies out rather than to move upstream to where they are being thrown in.

We choose to make a living off the misery of others rather than to make a life of sharing the beauty of others.

Nowhere is this seen more clearly than in two contrasting studies of poor Black children. Our inability to rise to face the challenge of the poor, the Black and Brown and the needy is epitomized in this work.

In the first study, the American Association for the Advancement of Science (AAAS) sent a team of psychologists and nutritionists into the rural South to study the developmental I.Q.s of Black infants. Now, developmental I.Q.s are based primarily upon physiological responsiveness or the responsiveness of the individual's neurological system to stimuli. This physiological responsiveness is the basis for intelligence. It is what the child brings with him or her to be stimulated and reinforced in the learning situation.

We all know that the mean I.Q. is 100 for American children, a group which is predominantly white.

What do you suppose these AAAS field researchers found when they evaluated the I.Q.s of 500 Black infants selected at random in rural Mississippi?

Would an estimate of 100 be reasonable? Or are your biases toward the Black and the rural showing? Less? Much less?

They found the I.Q.s of the Black infants to be 117. Amazing!

Then how come, you ask, there seems to be so much racial difficulty with regard to education and other human service areas? How is it that the U.S., a nation built upon the contributions of each successive wave of European-born immigrants, does not capitalize on the rich potential of our own African Americans? Put another way, how come we deny these people their emergence?

How come we don't even want to hear about the movement for human rights and human dignity anymore?

Could it be because we have constructed our world so that we no longer need grow in it? Could it be because we have built our roles so that no one else can emerge from them?

Clearly, children with I.Q.s of 117 are superior children. The prognosis for such children should be good. They should live rich and rewarding lives. Right? Wrong!

By the time these children are school age, they are already functioning at inferior levels. Their I.Q.s have dropped to 86. Upon entering school, then, the Black children are already relatively inferior in intellectual terms to other children.

Yet they began with superior neurological systems.

How could this happen?

Obviously, the environment did not stimulate and support the initially superior resources of these children.

Their parents did not know how to do so because no one had ever taught them how to do so. They could not teach their children because no one had ever taught them. They could not support their children's learning because no one had ever supported their own learning.

This group of 500 Black children, then, while initially superior in intellectual resources, was destined to live with minds and bodies enslaved by intellectual limitations just as surely as the children's ancestors had been enslaved by chains. These children were to subsist at below poverty levels on their poor farms. Or they were to move to the city and join the ranks of the unemployed. Or they were to become less than full persons because of financial dependence on the welfare system. Or they were to opt for a criminal career ladder, itself far more efficiently developed than conventional vocational·routes, and end up in prison or the morgue.

All because we did not help them to actualize their superior potential.

And no amount of guidance will serve to guide them down the path to education. And no amount of rehabilitation counseling will help them to actualize their potential. And no amount of psychotherapy will help them to emerge as full human beings. And no amount of correctional counseling will give them back their freedom.

Because we are not ready for our own fulfillment, our own actualization, our own emergence, our own freedom, we will not give these children theirs.

Until we do, we are but part of the same slave mentality that enslaves the master as well as the servant.

Upstream

Some few people rise above their bonds to demand justice. Perhaps they are moved by little more than a vague concept having to do with right and wrong. But they know it is wrong for their children to be unachieving or under-achieving in school, unemployed or under-employed at work and unrepresented or under-represented in government.

Fewer people still have paid the price to translate their protests into programs. Part of this price is the realization that opportunity alone does not operationalize justice. People must have skills to take advantage of any opportunity.

Skills alone define freedom, for if we do not have the responses in our repertoire, we are not even aware of our options.

Skills alone define development, for there is no other

6

way of increasing and measuring human resource development.

Skills alone define fulfillment, for the actualization of our potential is a direct function of the quantity and quality of responses that enable us to take advantage of both our resources and the opportunities that the environment affords us.

Some people rise above their bonds to study the effects of a human environment upon little human beings. This brings us to the second of those two studies mentioned above.

Dr. Rick Heber and his associates, in studying the relationship between poverty and mental retardation, divided the children of retarded Wisconsin welfare mothers into two groups. In the experimental group, they carefully selected teachers and trained them to work with the infants of retarded mothers on welfare. The teachers, in turn, trained the mothers of the Black infants to respond sensitively to the children and to stimulate and reinforce their learning activities.

In other words, all parties involved worked together to maximize the impact of the environment at the point where the child was going through the greatest growth. And they did this through skills training. Skills for the teachers. Skills for the parents. Skills for the children.

We already have the evidence from the AAAS study: an average I.Q. drop of 31 points in five years.

What do you suppose the difference was between the experimental and control infants in the Wisconsin study after three-and-one-half years?

Ten points? Twenty points? Thirty points?

The differences between the children who were nourished intellectually and those who were not was 33 points.

Think of it! One group includes children who, in the absence of continuous responsiveness and stimulation, are destined to live out their lives as rural share-croppers or city slum dwellers at best—and at worst, may have no lives at all!

7

The children in the other group, in the presence of continuous responsiveness and stimulation, may exercise their superior abilities to rise above their places of origin.

The difference?

The enslaved group was abandoned to the benign neglect of the play pen and the TV set.

The free group was saved by committed and disciplined people who put the human being back into the learning equation.

But most of all, the free group was saved by skilled people who taught skills to people who, in turn, taught skills to other people.

In the one instance, the AAAS study, the unattended child drops by more than thirty I.Q. points over a period of several years. In the other instance, Dr. Heber's study, the attended child gains more than thirty points over a period of several years.

The difference between the infants in the two studies is the difference between life and death itself. And it is the use—or the absence—of skills that makes all the difference!

Coming Home

What does all of this have to do with counseling and psychotherapy you ask?

Everything and nothing!

If we define the helping professions as being dedicated, like other professions, only to their own survival and perpetuation, then helping has nothing to do with Black infants in Mississippi and Milwaukee. Professional livelihoods are paramount and little children are irrelevant.

If, on the other hand, we define the helping professions as being dedicated to doing everything within their power to help other people to live, learn and work effectively in their own worlds, then the relevancy becomes obvious. And we see that it is traditional counseling theories and practices which are irrelevant!

The difference in our definition of the helping professions is the difference between human goals that demand new human programs and irrelevant processes that demand more irrelevant outcomes.

This difference cuts to the very heart of—not counseling accountability—but human accountability.

Let us elaborate.

The children who go to school—whether in Mississippi, Milwaukee or anywhere else—go to schools that will increase the gap between themselves and their potential. For the minority group children, the gap will increase even more severely between themselves and their white counterparts.

We in the helping professions, if we do nothing about it, will inherit these children to guide them, counsel them, therapize them, rehabilitate them, correct them, re-correct them and eventually bury them. And our numbers will swell in proportion to the victims we allow to be produced.

Because the system in which we function cannot service the children.

The system cannot meet the basic principles of learning.

Our schools and their teachers and counselors do not enter the frame of reference of the learner. Yet **all learning begins with the learner's frame of reference.** How else can we hope to hook up our learning programs with the learner?

Most children can go through an entire schooling experience without ever having had a teacher or counselor respond once to their frame of reference. While the frame of reference may be assumed for some middle class children, the absence of an accurate response does nothing to facilitate their achievement. For lower class and minority children, the learning process may never begin. We can listen to thousands of hours of classroom interactions without hearing a feeling word, let alone a feeling word that is interchangeable with the experience expressed by the learner.

Yet Dr. David Aspy can go into a school system in Florida and teach basic interpersonal skills to the teachers and get differences in I.Q.s of ten or more points with each year of schooling. He can do this simply by ensuring that the teacher has the skills to respond to each student's own frame of reference.

Our schools and their teachers and counselors do not bring their programs to skills conclusions. Yet, **all learning culminates in a skills objective.** How else can we leave the learner with something to use after we have gone?

Most children are exposed only to vague concepts of learning skills so that their actual achievement deteriorates. Our children will learn 30% of what they are capable of learning and forget 80% of that. Perhaps it does not matter, since most of what they do learn does not lend itself to practical usage.

Yet Dr. David Berenson can teach learning-to-learn skills to inner-city youth in Massachusetts who do not even go to regular school during the day; and, by teaching these skills, he can get years of achievement in weeks of teaching.

Our schools and their teachers and counselors do not teach students skills that are transferable to real-life situations. Yet **all learning is transferable.**

Most children do not learn skills which they can use in their everyday worlds. Between 60% and 80% of what our children learn will be unrelated to the lives they live. Two out of three of our children will hold jobs that do not even exist right now; yet we do not even prepare them for the jobs which do exist.

Yet Dr. Ted Friel can enter a Michigan school system and set up programs that produce elementary school students who have more career development skills than career specialists in the State Department of Education.

Our outcome is, to be sure, the children. The means to this outcome is ourselves and the skills programs which we develop.

Whether we are guidance counselors, mental health counselors, rehabilitation counselors, correctional counselors or psychotherapists by identification, we are all helpers. And all helpers are teachers of skills.

Our first and foremost function is to teach our helpees —our children, students, counselees and patients—the skills which they need to live, learn and work effectively in their worlds.

Our first and foremost need is to learn the skills which we need to be effective helpers.

The thesis of this book is to address this need—to respond to the challenge of our unchanging time—to change—to re-orient the helping and teaching professions to do the things that they are paid to do, transform learners into teachers and, by so doing, to train themselves out of their jobs.

Times may change and people with them. Because the people know what they want to be. And they are willing to pay the price to get there (Berenson, 1975).

Whatever the price, it is not too high when the alternative is dying.

References

Berenson, B. G. **Belly-to-belly and back-to-back: The militant humanism of Robert R. Carkhuff.** Amherst, Mass.: Human Resource Development Press, 1975.

Carkhuff, R. R. **The promise of America.** Amherst, Mass.: Human Resource Development Press, 1976.

Section Two—Toward Effective Helping

Chapter Two

Toward a Helping Model

When I left the Wisconsin Psychiatric Institute in the early 1960's* I had a closing interview with Dr. Carl Rogers, someone who has influenced the tradition of counseling and therapeutic practice as much as anyone since Freud. As I think back upon this interview, I remember myself as young and intellectually aggressive. I remember Rogers as slow and stolid but still sharp intellectually.

Our exchange went something like this:

"Dr. Rogers, you can open your position up and account for many if not most of the ingredients of therapeutic effectiveness."

"I'm not interested in opening the position up. The ingredients I have postulated are necessary and sufficient for therapeutic personality change."

"But Dr. Rogers, there are going to be many more ingredients added before we fill out the equation of therapeutic effectiveness."

"I am interested only in demonstrating the effectiveness of client-centered techniques with schizophrenic patients."

"But Dr. Rogers, potentially there are much more efficient ways of being effective with any patient population."

"I am interested only in providing the experiential conditions which help the client to change. The clients evolve in their own unique ways."

"But Dr. Rogers, training the clients in the dimensions which we have found to be effective would seem to be the most efficient and effective way to change people."

*Senior Author

"I am interested only in helping the clients to achieve what they want."
"But Dr. Rogers, they want so little."

Research Studies

At any given point in time, we are either growing or dying—as individuals, families, communities and nations.

We can only be vigilant as to whether our development and that of our loved ones is facilitated or retarded.

We can only discern and operationalize the ingredients of the facilitative processes in order to insure that we are growing.

These are our conclusions after nearly two decades of practice and research. They are conclusions which have been paid for by thousands of hours of counseling and therapy and thousands more of analyzing the recorded sessions of counselors and therapists, the masters as well as the beginners, and studying effects of these sessions.

It all began with challenges to the helping professions that were at once acute in their discriminations and profound in their implications.

In the early 1960's, a number of challenges were issued to the helping professions (Eysenck, 1965; Levitt, 1963; Lewis, 1965). These challenges were posed by our increasing recognition that, for both adults and children, professional psychological treatment did not make a difference. In other words, persons who were in control groups that were not assigned professional practitioners fared as well **on the average** as people assigned professional counselors and therapists. There were several important answers to these challenges, the first coming from some of the early research studies of counseling and psychotherapy.

Based upon the early naturalistic studies of counseling and therapy, a number of predictive studies were conducted and generalizations were made to other areas of helping and teaching. In addition, studies extending and refining the relevant dimensions were conducted.

14

These research studies laid the base for the models for human resource development.

The early naturalistic studies which examined the helping process as it flowed naturally were the source of the most significant findings. A number of studies were conducted to assess the relationship of certain therapist characteristics and the outcomes of their therapy. Two major areas of findings emerged from these studies.

Helpee Effects

The first of these findings was that professional counseling and psychotherapy may be **"for better or for worse"** (Rogers, et al, 1967; Truax and Carkhuff, 1967). This was a finding that was acknowledged only reluctantly; until that time we had assumed that, while helping could be helpful, it could in no way be harmful. Indeed, the early findings led to the comment that some patients were improved while others were "test deteriorated" (see Figure 2-1).

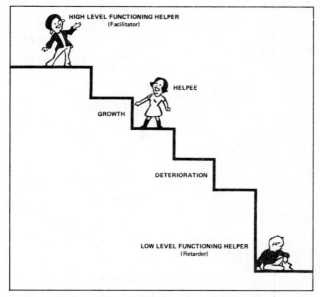

Figure 2-1: Helping may be "for better or for worse"   15

What all this meant was that when professional counselors and therapists were introduced into the lives of their clients and patients, they tended to have a greater range of effects upon the indices of change than when they were not introduced. Thus, while there were no differences **on the average** between professionally treated and untreated groups, there was significantly greater variability in the change indices of the treated groups when compared to the untreated groups.

These early studies led to a reassessment of all helping and human relationships. What was found was consistent with the early findings. While the evidence was greater in some areas than in others, the results were similar. At every point where the helpers (parents, teachers, counselors, therapists) intervened in the lives of their helpees (children, students, counselees, patients), the effects could be "for better or for worse" (see Figure 2-2).

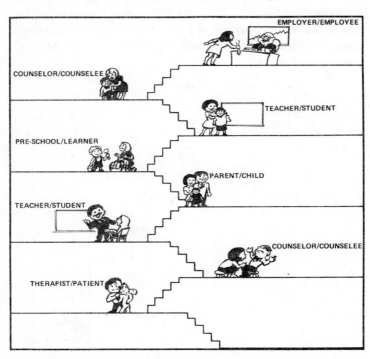

Figure 2-2: All helping may be
"for better or for worse"

The findings of these early naturalistic studies indicated that all helping and human relationships could have constructive or deteriorative consequences. The problem, then, became one of discerning those dimensions while accounting for the helpful or harmful effects. Primarily concerned with the therapeutic personality change of the helpee, we could study the outcomes and determine what processes led to these outcomes.

Helpee Outcomes
Therapeutic
Personality
Change *(TPC)*

With the advent of audio and audio-visual recording devices, it became possible to observe the constructive or deteriorative outcomes and trace back through the process to determine the effective ingredients of helping.

Helping Dimensions

The second significant finding was that we could account, in part, for the two-edged "better or worse" effects by examining the helper's level of functioning on certain emotional and interpersonal dimensions (Rogers, et al, 1967; Truax and Carkhuff, 1967). That is, helpees whose helpers functioned at relatively high levels of certain interpersonal dimensions demonstrated constructive change or gain while helpees of helpers functioning at relatively low levels of these dimensions demonstrated either no change or deteriorated change.

In order to understand the interpersonal dimensions, we must return to some of the original formulations of Rogers (1951). He put his early emphasis upon empathy *(E)* as the source of client involvement leading to therapeutic personality change *(TPC)*. This dimension emphasized entering the feelings of the client. It remains the cornerstone of all helping equations leading to helpee benefits.

17

Helper Skills	Helpee Outcome
E	TPC

In addition, Rogers and others (Shaffer and Shoben, 1956) increasingly came to emphasize dimensions such as "unconditional positive regard" *(UPC)* or "non-retaliatory permissiveness" as sources of therapeutic change or gain.

Helper Skills	Helpee Outcome
E + UPR	TPC

This dimension emphasized respect for the client without any conditions upon his or her behavior.

Finally, Rogers (1957) brought his formulations concerning the effective ingredients of client growth together in his postulates concerning the "necessary and sufficient conditions of therapeutic personality change." The major addition in this equation, influenced by the work of more existentially oriented therapists like Whitaker and Malone, was congruence *(Cg)*.

Helper Skills	Helpee Outcome
E + UPR + Cg	TPC

Congruence, in the original formulations, emphasized a kind of responsive genuineness, where the therapist was genuine where he needed to be genuine for the client's benefit.

At this point of development, the scales employed to measure the interpersonal dimensions were gross measures of functioning. The dimensions that were measured emphasized empathy, unconditional regard and congruence. These dimensions were later to be modified (Truax and Carkhuff, 1967) to emphasize non-possessive warmth and genuineness; but they remained essentially the same dimensions. In addition, client involvement in the therapeutic process leading to therapeutic change was also measured by experiential indices *(Ex)* developed by

Gendlin (Rogers, et al, 1967). The equation remained.

Helper Skills	Helping Process	Helpee Outcome
E + UPR + Cg	Ex	TPC

In summary, the findings of the early naturalistic studies indicated 1) that helping may be "for better or for worse"; and that 2) these effects can be accounted for in part by the level of the helper's functioning on certain interpersonal dimensions. The implications for counseling were both consoling and distressing. In answer to the challenges to the helping professions, these findings suggest that we do indeed have an effect. However, this effect may be constructive or destructive, depending upon the specific interpersonal skills which we can bring to bear.

The results of these naturalistic studies led directly to a number of studies of the skills of the helper, the helpee outcomes which he or she reflects and the helping process by which the helper's skills effect the helpee outcomes.

Helper Skills

A number of predictive studies were conducted to assess the differential effects of high- and low-functioning helpers upon indices of helpee outcome. But before these were done, the ingredients of helper skills were extended to include a variety of additional helper dimensions. These included helper self-disclosure *(SD)* and concreteness *(Ct)* or specificity of expression as well as, later on, confrontation *(Cn)* and immediacy of experience *(IE)* (Carkhuff, 1967). These new dimensions marked the beginnings of a systematic helping model for helper skills development.

Helper Skills

E + UPR + Cg + SD + Ct + Cn + IE

In addition, a number of helper skills were refined. Accurate empathy *(AE)* was defined operationally in terms of the helper's ability to make responses that were interchangeable with the feeling and the meaning expressed by the helpee. Unconditional positive regard was expanded to emphasize respect *(R)* which allowed for unconditional regard at the lowest level and differential regard at the highest level. Also, congruence was modified to emphasize externalized genuineness *(G)* rather than an internalized convergence of experiencing and behavior (Carkhuff, 1967, 1969).

Helper Skills

AE + R + G + SD + Ct + Cn + IE

Next, the process of operationalizing and thus collapsing the helper skills was begun. It was found that empathy accounted for the variance of respect; and genuineness accounted for the variance of self-disclosure (Carkhuff, 1969).

Helper Skills

$$AE_R + G_{SD} + Ct + Cn + IE$$

In addition, the different helping skills were factor analyzed to determine the sources of effect. It was found that there were essentially two helper factors: responsiveness *(R)* which subsumed empathy and respect; and initiative *(I)* which incorporated confrontation and immediacy. Genuineness and concreteness were given dimensions which loaded on both factors (Berenson and Mitchell, 1974; Carkhuff, 1969).

Helper Skills

$$R_{AE,R_{G,Ct}} + I_{Cn,IE_{G,Ct}}$$

Finally, the helper skills were found to require preliminary or transitional skills. Thus, it was found that attending skills *(A)* preceded the responding skills *(R)* and personalizing skills *(P)* provided a transition from the responding skills to the initiative skills *(I)* (Carkhuff, 1969, 1972).

Helper Skills
A + R + P + I

So far, while we had studied the effects of the helper's emotional and interpersonal skills, we had not studied the programs which they used. It now became appropriate to study the differential effects of he' 'er functioning and systematic programs.

In path-finding research on the differential effects of people and programs, Vitalo (1970) found that both the helper's level of functioning on the interpersonal dimensions and the systematic program were significant sources of effect in verbal conditioning of personal pronoun emissions by the subject. Examination of the interaction effects revealed that the presence of conditioning was dependent upon the level of the experimenter's functioning. Only the high-functioning experimenters elicited learning rates from the experimental group that were different from those produced by the control group.

In an extension of this work, Mickelson and Stevic (1971) investigated the effects of verbal reinforcement counseling as a preferred method for increasing high school students' acquisition of information relevant to their educational and/or vocational goals. The investigators found that high-level functioning helpers produced a significantly greater amount of helpee information-seeking behavior than low-functioning helpers. For our purposes, perhaps the most significant result was the finding that, while the verbal reinforcement program was effective at the beginning of the sessions for the helpees of the low-functioning helpers, as the sessions went on these non-facilitative helpers had turned off "their helpee's information-seeking behavior."

This means, then, that we must add program development *(PD)* dimensions to the initiative skills which the helper uses to effect helpee benefits.

21

Helper Skills
$$A + R + P + I_{PD}$$

The addition of program development includes the more cognitive problem-solving, decision-making and program development and implementation skills that are necessary to help the helpee to achieve his or her goal. In addition, these skills add an intellectual dimension to the helper's skills repertoire.

Collingwood and his associates (1972) found that the helper's physical functioning adds still another requisite for helping effectiveness. They have emphasized physical fitness as a necessary but not sufficient condition for helping effectiveness. The helper must have a high level of physical energy if she or he is to discharge the demanding responsibilities of helping.

Together, then, these helper dimensions defined the skills which the helper needed to bring about change or gain on the part of the helpee. They also necessitated a greater understanding of the helpee outcomes effected by these helper skills.

Helpee Outcomes

A number of outcome studies were conducted to assess the differential effects of high- and low-functioning helpers upon different indices of helpee outcome. These indices included physical and intellectual indices as well as emotional and interpersonal. As such, the new indices marked the replacement of the therapeutic personality change model by the human resource development model *(HRD)*.

Helper Skills	Helpee Outcome
$A + R + P + I$	HRD

In one series of studies, the effects of the emotional-interpersonal functioning of the helper upon the emotional-interpersonal functioning of the helpee were investigated (Carkhuff, 1969). Helpee outcomes were assessed by the exact same emotional and interpersonal skills that the helper was assessed by.

Helper Skills	Helpee Outcome
A + R + P + I	HRD *(E)*

With both outpatient neuropsychiatric patients and college student counselees, the results were similar. In general, the helpees moved in the direction of the level of functioning of their helpers. The clients and patients of high-functioning helpers demonstrated positive changes in their levels of emotional and interpersonal skills. The clients and patients of low-functioning helpers demonstrated no change or deteriorative change. Indeed, the helpee of the helper functioning at the highest levels was functioning after treatment at levels higher than all other helpers in the project.

In summary, these studies suggested that the heart of helping involved the emotional and interpersonal changes in the helpee that were brought about differentially by the helper's emotional and interpersonal skills. The work suggested a number of new studies generalizing the effects to other areas of helpee functioning.

The earliest of these generalization studies was done by Aspy (1969) in the educational realm. Aspy selected teachers functioning at high and low levels of emotional and interpersonal skills and assessed their effects on the intellectual achievement of elementary school students. Thus, he studied the helper-teacher dimensions and their effects upon the helpee-learner's intellectual functioning.

Helper Skills	Helpee Outcome
A + R + P + I	HRD *(E + I)*

What Aspy found was consistent with previous work. In general, students of high-functioning teachers achieved at significantly higher levels than students of low-functioning teachers on a variety of language communication

23

and computation skills. In addition, in their on-going research, Aspy and Roebuck (1972, 1975) have added a number of additional indices including tardiness, absenteeism, truancy and discipline as well as the emotional and interpersonal skills of the teacher.

In their work, Aspy and Roebuck have found discrepancies as great as two years between the students of high-functioning teachers and those of low-functioning teachers. This has led them to conclude that it takes two facilitative teachers to wash out the effects of one retarding teacher and only one retarding teacher to wash out the effect of two facilitative teachers.

Pierce and his associates (1967, 1969, 1970, 1971) extended the work of Aspy by studying the trainer supervision of trainee skills development where the subject matter was helping skills. His findings were consistent with the earlier evidence: trainees move in the direction of their trainer's level of functioning; and these effects are most pronounced when the subject matter is emotional and interpersonal skills development.

In generalizing to the physical area, Collingwood and his associates (1972) conducted a number of research projects establishing the relationship of the helpee's physical fitness to his or her emotional and intellectual functioning. Physical fitness, he concluded, was a necessary condition of emotional and intellectual functioning. He also found that physical fitness was influenced by the physical training programs of the helper.

Helper Skills **Helpee Outcome**
$A + R + P + I$ $HRD\ (P + E + I)$

Together, the helper skills and helpee outcomes define the cause and the effect of helping. They also point up the need to understand the process by which the outcomes are achieved.

Helping Process

The very early predictive studies of helpee process movement involved the experimental manipulation of helper skills and the study of their effect upon the helping process. Helpee exploration *(E)* was the first process variable studied. It involved the helpee's exploration of personally relevant material.

Helper Skills	Helping Process	Helpee Outcome
A + R + P + I	E	HRD *(P + E + I)*

A series of studies yielded results that may be divided according to both helper and helpee level of functioning. In general, helpees of high-functioning helpers moved over the course of helping toward higher levels of exploration (Carkhuff, 1969). There were several important qualifications related to this work.

When high-functioning helpers experimentally lowered their level of responsiveness, low-functioning helpees continued to explore themselves. When moderate-functioning helpers experimentally lowered their responsiveness, both low- and high-functioning helpees moved to lower levels of exploration.

These findings mean that the helpee's level of exploration is, in part, a function of the helper's level of responsiveness. The implications for helpee outcome over time and with crises are important. If helpees tend to explore themselves differentially according to the level of functioning of their helpers, then over time they will tend to move in the direction of their helper's level of functioning.

The effects are also reciprocal. When high-functioning clients experimentally lower their levels of exploration, high-functioning counselors continue to upgrade their levels of interpersonal skills, while low-functioning counselors lower their levels of skills. Ultimately, the helpees of high-functioning helpers raise their levels of exploratory behavior. Thus, the helpee is helped to explore by a high-functioning helper, whether or not the helpee is engaged in exploratory behavior.

We know the beginning point, then, in the helping process. The helping process is initiated by the helper's attentiveness and responsiveness which elicits and reinforces the helpee's exploratory behavior.

We also know the termination point of the helping process. We know that human resource development involves some kind of behavioral demonstration of change or gain in physical, emotional or intellectual functioning. This means that the helpee must act in some way to demonstrate the behavior. Acting *(A)* then, is the final phase of the helping process (Carkhuff, 1969).

Helper Skills	Helping Process	Helpee Outcomes
A + R + P + I	E + A	HRD *(P + E + I)*

It remains only to develop the transition from exploration to action. In order to act, the helpee must have some kind of accurate understanding of his or her world. Understanding *(U)* then, is the mediating process that links experiential exploration with effective action (Carkhuff, 1972).

Helper Skills	Helping Process	Helpee Outcomes
A + R + P + I	E + U + A	HRD *(P + E + I)*

Understanding was explored in the early predictive studies assessing the effects of helper's skills upon helpee's skills. It was found that the helpee developed understanding according to the level of accurate understanding offered by the helper. Thus, helper understanding leads to helpee understanding.

Indeed, all behaviors exhibited by the helper tend to lead to similar behaviors by the helpee. The sources of learning emphasize the modeling or initiative sources along with the experiential and the direct didactic teaching.

Together, then, the helper's skills, the helping process and the helpee outcomes serve to define the helping model. It becomes essential that we operationalize these ingredients so that we can learn and then transmit them in the most efficient and effective manner.

In summary, effectiveness in human resource development (HRD) is a function of the helper's skills which enable him or her to involve the helpee in a helping process leading to desirable outcomes for the helpee. The desirable outcomes involve physical, emotional and intellectual growth on the part of the helpee. The process by which the helpee grows is exploration, understanding and action. And the skills which the helper requires to involve the helpee in the helping process are attending, responding, personalizing and initiating.

The implications for our own personal HRD efforts are important. In order to accomplish our HRD tasks, we must insure our own personal development. We must be helped before we can help ourselves. We must acquire helping skills before we can help others.

At any given point in time, we are indeed either growing or dying and, thus, causing others to grow or die. Everything depends upon our helping skills and our understanding of how to use them.

References

Aspy, D.   The effect of teacher-offered conditions of empathy, positive regard and congruence upon student achievement. **Florida Journal of Educational Research**, 1969, **11**, 39-48.

Aspy, D.   **Toward a technology for humanizing education.** Champaign, Illinois: Research Press, 1972.

Aspy, D. and Roebuck, F.   **Affective ingredients of a human education.** Amherst, Mass.: Human Resource Development Press, in press, 1976.

Berenson, B. G. and Mitchell, K. M.   **Confrontation.** Amherst, Mass.: Human Resource Development Press, 1974.

Carkhuff, R. R.   **Helping and human relations. Vols. I and II.** New York: Holt, Rinehart and Winston, 1969.

Carkhuff, R. R.   **The development of human resources.** New York: Holt, Rinehart and Winston, 1971.

Carkhuff, R. R.   **The art of helping.** Amherst, Mass.: Human Resource Development Press, 1972.

Collingwood, T.   HRD model and physical fitness. In **HRD Model in Education,** D. W. Kratochvil, Ed. Baton Rouge, La.: Southern University, 1972.

Eysenck, H. J.   The effects of psychotherapy. **International Journal of Psychiatry,** 1965, **1**, 99-178.

Levitt, E. E.   Psychotherapy with children: A further evaluation. **Behavior Research and Therapy,** 1963, **1**, 45-51.

Lewis, W. W.   Continuity and intervention in emotional disturbance: A review. **Exceptional Children,** 1965, **31**, 465-475.

Mickelson, D. J. and Stevic, R. R. Differential effects of facilitative and non-facilitative behavioral counselors. **Journal of Counseling Psychology,** 1971, **18,** 314-319.

Pierce, R. M., Carkhuff, R. R. and Berenson, B. G. The differential effects of high- and low-functioning counselors upon counselors-in-training. **Journal of Clinical Psychology,** 1967, **23,** 212-215.

Pierce, R. M. and Drasgow, J. Teaching facilitative interpersonal functioning to psychiatric inpatients. **Journal of Counseling Psychology,** 1969, **16,** 295-298.

Pierce, R. M. and Schauble, P. Graduate training of facilitative counselors: The effects of individual supervision. **Journal of Counseling Psychology,** 1970, **17,** 210-215.

Pierce, R. M. and Schauble, P. Study on the effects of individual supervision in graduate school training. **Journal of Counseling Psychology,** 1971, **18,** 186-187.

Rogers, C. R. **Client-centered therapy.** Boston: Houghton Mifflin, 1951.

Rogers, C. R. The necessary and sufficient conditions of therapeutic personality change. **Journal of Consulting Psychology,** 1957, **22,** 95-103.

Rogers, C. R., Gendlin, E. T., Kiesler, D. and Truax, C. B. **The therapeutic relationship and its impact.** Madison, Wisconsin: University of Wisconsin Press, 1967.

Schaffer, L. F. and Shoben, E. J. Common aspects of psychotherapy. From Psychotherapy: Learning new adjustments, chapter in **The psychology of adjustment.** Boston: Houghton Mifflin Co., 1956.

Truax, C. G. and Carkhuff, R. R. **Toward effective counseling and psychotherapy.** Chicago: Aldine, 1967.

Vitalo, R. The effects of facilitative interpersonal functioning in a conditioning paradigm. **Journal of Counseling Psychology,** 1970, **17,** 141-144.

29

Chapter Three

Toward a Training Model

Thelma is a Black woman.

Her future got lost somewhere before her past.

Her present bubbled in a bottle.

To say that she—without a street address—was unemployed would be an understatement.

She could not believe her eyes the first day of her New Careers class. There before her, teaching her class, was a black man, "off the streets" just as she was! Imagine—someone who just a few months before was as lost as she was had now been suddenly transformed into her teacher. She looked at this teacher and wondered.

"Maybe there is hope."

To many people, poor Black and Brown and Red, hope has been the greatest lie. Over and over, each hope has lied. Hope, and nothing happens.

But now Thelma hoped again. She hoped against hope that maybe, maybe she could turn out like the teacher in front of her.

This time there was something different. There in front of her was another Black. There was a new ingredient.

Maybe, maybe!

The Black man in front of the New Careers class was named Jay. He and the other staff members had been selected from a group of volunteers from a Concentrated Employment Program Project. They had received over one hundred hours of rigorous life skills training before they were de-selected, i.e., those who were not utilizing the training experience at the highest levels were dropped.

Jay and the other staff members were then given an intensified program in teaching the life skills that they themselves had been learning.

Jay and the other staff members had been trained by the co-director of the Center for Human Relations and Community Affairs. His name was Andy. Andy was a professional teacher and community worker by training.

Andy, in turn, had received "on-the-job" training from Bob, a creator of the life skills technology.

And here we have the point of the entire story. Hope need not be a lie. The human technologist trains the credentialed professional who trains the functional professional who trains the people indigenous to the population being serviced to become an indigenous functional professional.

The indigenous functional professional is trained so that he or she can pass on the training directly to the population being serviced. Ultimately, the population being serviced learns the skills they need to service themselves.

Now Thelma works at Welfare as a Welfare Technician.

She used to go there as a recipient. She still could.

But instead she works there, teaching people the things that people teach to other people if they really want to help.

Applications

The most important point is not whether a model works but whether it is useful and practical. Most models can be made to work under controlled circumstances. Only those which operate in the absence of these controls flourish over time. There are several conditions which useful models meet.

The first condition is that useful models are congruent with human experience. They converge, so to speak, with human truth or, more basically, with common sense. Given this convergence, useful models have a lasting effect.

The second condition is that all practical models keep the human being in the human equation. They contribute to his potency by teaching him how to contribute rather than promoting his impotency by critiquing his shortcomings.

The third condition is that the practical model is alive and growing. It incorporates new learnings and recycles old. Most importantly, it teaches what it has learned; and people use what they have learned.

A human model serves human beings. It delivers to people the skills which they need to live effectively in their worlds. It delivers these skills through people. It trains the people to deliver the skills and constantly upgrades and updates the skills with the feedback which people get from the helpees they serve.

A human model is a skills training model.

A number of studies were conducted in which experimental training was introduced and its effects studied in the resultant helping efforts. These studies moved naturally from studies of credentialed and functional professionals, including those indigenous to the community being serviced, to studies involving the training of entire communities seeking help in the implementation of the concept of "teaching as a preferred mode of treatment."

Credentialed Professionals

A series of studies of the training of credentialed professionals and the assessment of their effects served to introduce applications in this area. In general, the results suggested that credentialed professionals could be trained systematically within limited periods of time to demonstrate effective HRD efforts with the helpee population whom they serve (see Figure 3-1).

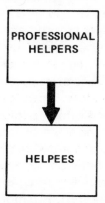

Figure 3-1. Professional helpers help people

32

Counseling Personnel

The first of the series of training applications with professional counselors and therapists (Carkhuff, 1969) demonstrated that these individuals could be trained to function at levels commensurate with outstanding practitioners (Truax and Carkhuff, 1967) or above (Carkhuff, 1969). In the later series, it was established that credentialed professionals could, in the brief time of 100 hours or less, learn to function above minimally effective and self-sustaining levels of interpersonal skills, criteria not met by most outstanding practitioners (Carkhuff, 1969). Perhaps most importantly, trained counselors were able to involve their counselees in the helping process at levels of self-exploration and self-understanding that led to constructive change or gain. In one demonstration study in guidance, against a very low base rate of success, the counselors were able to demonstrate success rates of between 74 and 91% with the introduction of systematic training in interpersonal skills, problem-solving skills and other specialty area skills (Carkhuff, 1972).

Teaching Personnel

A series of training applications in teaching soon followed (Carkhuff, 1971). In one of these, Hefele (1971) found student achievement to be a function of systematic training of teachers in interpersonal skills. In addition, he found that the trained group not only succeeded in communicating at higher levels with their students than did the control group but that it was possible to select those teacher supervisors who could best teach others the specific methodologies involved. The finding that teachers and trainees subsequently exerted a reciprocal impact upon one another in providing a basis for the relationship between subsequent student academic achievement and the interpersonal skills of the teacher was of equal interest. In a more extensive design,

33

Berenson (1971) found that experimentally trained teachers were rated significantly higher in interpersonal skills and competency in the classroom and that they scored significantly higher on a situation-reaction test and utilized significantly more positive reinforcing behaviors in their teaching than did others under a variety of control conditions including a training control group, a Hawthorne Effect control group and a control group proper.

The implications for the selection and training of credentialed professionals in the helping profession are both obvious and profound. HRD efforts may be improved enormously by the introduction of systematic interpersonal and specialty area program skills.

The success in training credentialed professionals led directly to attempts at training lay personnel.

Functional Professionals

It is clear that dimensions such as interpersonal skills are not the exclusive province of credentialed professionals. In this context, a number of studies utilizing lay personnel were conducted. These studies dealt with both staff personnel and indigenous personnel. In general, the results suggest that trained lay personnel may serve as functional professionals in effecting significant HRD (see Figure 3-2).

Figure 3-2. Functional professionals help people

34

Staff Personnel

In a series of studies, lay staff personnel such as nurses, hospital attendants, prison guards, dormitory counselors and community volunteers were trained and their effects in treatment studied (Carkhuff, 1971). The success of the programs was dramatic in terms of the gains in interpersonal skills of the trainees. In terms of outcome, the trainees were able to elicit significant changes in work behavior, being discharged from and staying out of the hospital and changes in a variety of areas including self-reports, significant-other reports and expert reports. Against a backdrop of a dramatic crisis in corrections, the results of the implementation of the training model in Atlanta Federal Penitentiary (McGathlin and Porter, 1969) might serve as a timely illustration. In this project, prison guards were systematically trained in interpersonal skills and 12 of them were appointed as correctional officers to counsel and develop courses of action for the inmates. Where the prison had been reported to have been in a state of anarchy and at the mercy of the inmates before the model was implemented, reports by Hall (1970) indicated a success rate of between 80 and 90% depending upon what questions were asked of the inmates. In addition, work attendance and productivity went up and sick leave and work transfers went down significantly. As a consequence, two national correctional counseling institutes have been conducted and have served to demonstrate further that much can be done with systematic selection and training of staff in interpersonal skills even against a backdrop of violence. Quite a contrast with Attica!

Whereas the utilization of lay personnel initially involved staff members and volunteers, there were implications for direct utilization of members of the community being serviced.

35

Indigenous Personnel

The difference between functional professional staff and indigenous functional professional personnel is the difference between the attendant and the patient, the guard and the inmate, the teacher and the student, the policeman and the community member. That is, the use of indigenous personnel involves persons who are part of the community being serviced. It is a natural extension of the earlier work to train indigenous personnel as well as staff personnel in the kinds of skills involved (see Figure 3-3).

Figure 3-3. Indigenous functional professionals help people

Here the emphasis upon selection and training appear particularly critical—although certainly no more critical than for credentialed and functional professionals. However, not just anybody, particularly from the ranks of the physically, emotionally and intellectually immobilized, can serve as helpers. Nevertheless, with selection and training, studies of the use of indigenous functional professionals indicated that such individuals could work effectively with the populations from which they were drawn. A few of the many programs conducted in this area might be mentioned here. In one program, human relations specialists were selected systematically from the black community on the basis of their functionality for service in a crisis-ridden school system. They were trained to function in treatment, training and teaching (Black History) capacities and demonstrated significantly positive results in assessments of their work (Carkhuff, 1971). In another program, New Careers teachers were systematically selected from the black community and trained and supervised in the kinds of skills which they needed to teach and guide the development of hard core unemployed people from their community. In two programs, six teachers were able to help hundreds of people previously considered hard core unemployed hold human service work positions in the community (Carkhuff, 1971).

In summary, lay personnel, whether staff or indigenous, may be selected and trained as functional professional helpers. In these roles, they can effect any human resource development that professionals can—and more!

There were direct implications of the success of this work for training entire helpee populations.

Helpee Populations

The final logical extension of the HRD model involved cutting out the middle man and training the helpee populations directly in the kinds of skills which they need to function effectively in their worlds. Whether for individuals (HRD) or entire communities in general, we have found that teaching (see Figure 3-4) is "the preferred mode of treatment."

Figure 3-4. Helpee-learners help people

Individuals

A number of studies have been conducted with the aim of servicing individuals. In one series, parents of emotionally disturbed children were systematically trained in the kinds of skills which they needed to function effectively with themselves and with their children. In one such program (Carkhuff, 1971), this approach was found to be significantly more effective than all other forms of traditional parental counseling groups. In another series, hospitalized neuropsychiatric patients were trained in the kinds of skills which they needed to function effectively in their wards and, ultimately, in the communities to which they returned. In several of these programs (Pierce and Drasgow, 1969) the systematic training was found to be significantly more effective than all other forms of treatment, whether individual psychotherapy, group psychotherapy, drug treatment or "total push" treatment involving a combination of all other forms of treatment. In general, then, helpees may be trained directly in the kinds of skills which they need to service themselves.

The concept of "training as a preferred mode of treatment" led directly to the development of programs to train entire communities.

Communities

The notion of training entire communities stems from the need to train those persons in a helpee's environment who are necessary to sustain her or his functioning. Such an endeavor culminates in the training of entire institutions from top to bottom. For example, an extension of the aforementioned correctional work and an outgrowth of the national correctional counseling institutes culminated in one program at the Federal Adult Correctional Center in Lompoc, California where staff and inmates at all levels were trained in the kinds of skills necessary to work effectively with each other (Carkhuff, 1971). A great deal of evidence supports the success of this program; perhaps the most significant evidence involves those instances in which such training was brought to bear to prevent the occurrence of riots such as those at Attica. In another project, the Rhode Island Training School's programs were systematically transformed from custodial to treatment orientations (Carkhuff, 1974). Staff at all levels, beginning with the superintendent, were trained in interpersonal, problem-solving, program development and specialty program skills. In the area of program development alone, the staff developed over 80 programs ranging from cottage maintenance through field trips to individual and group counseling programs. in addition, students and parents were trained in interpersonal skills and such specialty skills as study methods.

The results indicated that runaways and recidivists were down significantly and that percentile levels for physical, emotional-interpersonal and intellectual functioning were up significantly.

In summary, teaching is the preferred mode for HRD. When we train people in the kinds of skills which they need to function effectively in their worlds, we increase the probability that they will, in fact, begin to live, learn and work in increasingly constructive ways.

Summary

Research studies of helping relationships developed and validated the helping model: in general, helpees move toward their helpers' level of functioning. The results led readily to large scale applications in HRD with both credentialed and functional professionals.

In general, effectiveness in HRD is largely a function of two primary factors: the skills with which the helpers relate to other people (interpersonal skills); and the skills which helpers have in their specialty areas (program skills). The implications for professional HRD efforts are important. With systematic selection and equally systematic training, helping personnel may effect significant and constructive change in individuals or communities of people.

The implications for personal HRD efforts are even more important. In order to accomplish these HRD tasks, we must insure our own effective development and systematically translate our own offerings into effective programs. The most effective modality for developing our own effectiveness as well as that of our helpees is training.

The HRD model meets the tests of usefulness. The effective ingredients of this model have been born in human experience, modeled after human effectiveness and recycled with human feedback. The HRD model is a human model.

References

Berenson, D. H. The effects of systematic human relations training upon the classroom
performance of elementary school
teachers. **Journal of Research and
Development in Education**, 1971, **4,**
70-85.

Carkhuff, R. R. **Helping and human relations. Vols.
I and II.** New York: Holt, Rinehart
and Winston, 1969.

Carkhuff, R. R. **The development of human resources.**
New York: Holt, Rinehart and
Winston, 1971.

Carkhuff, R. R. **The art of helping.** Amherst, Mass.:
Human Resource Development Press,
1972.

Carkhuff, R. R., **Cry twice!** Amherst, Mass.: Human
et al. Resource Development Press, 1974.

Collingwood, T. HRD model and physical fitness. In
HRD Model in Education, D. W.
Kratochvil, Ed. Baton Rouge, La.:
Southern University, 1972.

Hall, R. **Atlanta correctional and industrial
counseling: First annual report.**
Washington, D.C.: Federal Bureau of
Prisons, 1970.

Hefele, T. J. The effects of systematic human relations training upon student achievement. **Journal of Research and Development in Education,** 1971, **4,**
52-69.

McGathlin, W. **The effects of facilitation training
and Porter, T. provided correctional officers stationed at the Atlanta Federal Penitentiary.** Washington, D.C.: U.S.
Justice Department, 1969.

41

Truax, C. G. and Carkhuff, R.R.　**Toward effective counseling and psychotherapy.** Chicago: Aldine, 1967.

Section Three—Helping in Transition

Chapter Four

Requiem for Therapy

Consciously or unconsciously chosen, ignorance feeds evil cowards who have given up.

There is no evidence that the major techniques of traditional therapies translate to constructive therapeutic outcomes:

There is no evidence that the superficial reflections of the client-centered helper make a constructive contribution to the helpee.

There is no evidence that the existential helper's awareness that "man is alone in an essentially artificial world " translates to a constructive contribution to the helpee.

There is no evidence that the stereotyped interpretations of the psychoanalyst make a constructive contribution to the helpee.

There is very little evidence that the conditioning techniques of the behavioral therapist make a constructive contribution to the helpee beyond the stimulus complex within which the conditioning takes place.

There is little evidence that the interpretation of "objective" data and test results of the trait-and-factor helper translates to a constructive contribution to the helpee.

Effective Helping

There is ample evidence that many, many persons spend many, many hours engaged in these traditional therapies: their experiences are, for the most part, deleterious if for no other reason than they cost the client precious progress time and precious funds.

43

Effective helping draws upon those dimensions of interpersonal relationships which blend subjective experience
with objective reality. The traditionally trained helper
scores scandalously low on all dimensions of helping that
make a constructive difference.

Effective helping succeeds in blending subjective experience and objective reality by creating a higher order
reality within which the individual is equipped to achieve
growth goals (skills). The traditionally trained helper
creates the conditions for insanity by boxing the helpee
into a system which limits the helper's learning as well
as the helpee's growth.

Effective helping creates a reality within which efficient
action is possible because goals and means to achieve
goals are based upon the high level skills of a helpee
turned teacher. The traditionally trained helper is unable
to achieve any growth goals because traditional systems
do not transmit skills needed to learn; at best, such traditional systems put the helpee through a limited conditioning experience for limited goal achievement.

Effective helping creates a higher order reality that
enables the individual to gauge and plan his or her next
act in tune with the feedback received from the previous
action. Traditionally trained helpers act (when they do
act) from their own limited frame of reference; hence
they are unaware of the potentially useful feedback
offered by the helpee.

Effective helping creates a high order reality because
effective helping, considered in its cyclical sense, begins
and ends with responding. Traditionally trained helpers
are limited in their own lives because they have only
responded to their own inner experiences. Such helpers
cannot respond to another person because they cannot
escape their own selfish preoccupation with their own
needs.

Effective helping creates a higher order reality because it equips helpers to escape the boundaries of their own skin and, in so doing, creates the conditions which make learning possible. Traditionally trained helpers, like others who cannot break free of their own limited inner experiences, cannot learn and can only be conditioned. The inability to learn because of limited and distorted input makes such helpers ugly.

Effective helping creates a higher order reality because it prepares the individual to attend to what is relevant by giving the helpee the skills needed to operationalize goals. The traditionally trained helper demands a preoccupation with non-functional dichotomies and other irrelevancies. This preoccupation with irrelevancies is more than merely self-destructive; it is an operational definition of insanity.

Effective helping creates a higher order reality when it blends subjective experience with objective reality because it makes individual sanity possible and promotes a just social consensus. The traditionally trained helper actually promotes insanity by explaining away either objective reality or subjective experience.

Effective helping, indeed effective living, creates a higher order reality because effective helping translates to effective teaching. Effective teaching experientially and objectively responds to the learner's experience of disarray, organizes that experience and then gives that organization meaning. The helpee is transformed into a learner by the method **and** the experience.

The traditionally trained helper is still debating whether learning is possible, whether there is such a thing, and whether or not methods can be found to use learning.

When systems are not built upon effective teaching and

learning, they invariably produce individuals who attempt to **defeat** their helpees. Effective helping-teaching produces individuals who are motivated to win for their helpees and themselves without the need to humiliate anyone. The effective teacher-helper works only to defeat the enemies of learning and growth.

All the traditional therapies limit learning. All therapies limit learning. Only teaching leads to learning.

A History of Tragedy

The entire history of the human condition reflects the development and implementation of limited conditioning techniques with very little practice or encounter with learning. Espousing one extreme or the other, each therapy used simple-minded conditioning, marketing it's dogma in different packages and always claiming uniqueness. In reality, each therapy pathologically distorted **both** subjective experience **and** objective reality into a scheme to assist therapists in their efforts to avoid honest labor.

The therapist's real technique was and is charm, or some "idiosyncratic variation" like confrontation, sincerity, concern, caring, reinforcing, warmth, controversiality, reflections, thoughtfulness and seduction.

What therapists may or may not realize is that stupidity is the product of knowing something about conditioning and little or nothing about learning.

Traditionally trained therapists neither help nor teach.

Therapies deserve no credit for producing their own brand of insanity. The insanity they produce, mostly by neglect, twists and distorts not only basic human experience but, more tragically, human potential. Any approach not based upon teaching skills is simply a cruel and contemptuous display of pathology in the name of a "stance" represented by highly resistant learners. The resistant learner offers his or her techniques in as charming a way as possible to avoid learning while at the same time delaying exposure. Public reali- zation that the resistant learner (therapist) produces nothing but vanity, ignorance and psychopathology reflects, in sharp relief, the fact that these individuals take much, much more than they earn. *Therapists earn nothing because they produce nothing of constructive (growth) consequence.*

Initially, most new movements engage in bold explora- tion based in some measure of strength. Past therapeutic movements became formal and institutionalized training programs for psychopaths when their promulgators failed to look beyond how little they needed to do. The fo- lowers and often the leaders turned to seduction and charm and away from substance and system when they realized how little people asked for and how little patients settled for. Effective helping is designed to make the helpee less vulnerable, not more vulnerable, because the effective teacher-helper looks for the extra step and tapes it. *When therapists take more than they earn, their potential love for their patients turns to contempt for themselves as well as for their patients.*

"Contributions" and "Differences" and Similarities

To some, the development of a systematic approach to helping and teaching becomes an end in itself. To others, the development of a systematic approach to the solu- tion of problems and the implementation of those solu- tions frees them to raise more and more critical ques- tions and pursue their answers. The solution of one issue may become the first step in a program to achieve a higher level goal.

A technology guided by human values will, in fact, free us all to be more ethical and moral by supplying the means to develop, describe, expand and evaluate our working models. The alternative is to join the benign game played by the psychotherapies for decades. All traditional therapists (and their therapies) alternate between explaining away objective reality and/or sub- jective experience, depending upon the current fad.

Psychoanalysis explains away both subjective experience and objective reality and thus contributes the least. Existential therapies come close to explaining away both but settle for some recognition of subjective experience. The client-centered counselor explains away objective reality while recognizing only superficial subjective experience. The behavior modification therapies explain away subjective experience with a very limited use of objective reality. The trait-and-factor counselor functions in a similar fashion.

The major traditional approaches to helping explain away one or the other (external reality or subjective experience) because, in the end, there is nothing else to do when trapped in a system which denies learning. Moving away from one position and then back to it is a constant, durable source of seemingly penetrating insights for those who wish to appear wise but who are unwilling or unable to work hard enough to learn and continue to learn.

The helping professions have been free of accountability long enough to have lost their direction and grown stupid enough to have to do a wide variety of things that do not make a constructive difference. Many of the practices are destructive, depressive and disastrous.

The helping professions have tolerated and even housed the twisted cruelty of psychoanalysis.

The helping professions have tolerated and even housed the hatefulness of client-centered permissiveness.

The helping professions have tolerated and even housed the impotence of many philosophical "approaches" to therapy.

The helping professions have tolerated and even housed blatant insanity and the rantings of psychopaths as they touched, confronted, trusted, fornicated and screamed.

The effective teacher-helper is committed to learning and growing. The teacher-helper grows as a result of increasing the quality and quantity of his or her physical, emotional and intellectual skills. The teacher-helper employs her skills to explore, understand and act upon the world and, in so doing, organizes what was once in disarray and gives meaning to what is now organized.

Teacher-helpers increase their chances to maintain their growth by contributing to the growth of others, teaching the latter to increase their physical, emotional and intellectual skills. While they turn to existing bodies of knowledge and systems in order to determine the contributions of each (see Figure 4-1), effective teacher-helpers focus upon constructive initiative by creating new functional models for teaching.

Psychoanalysis:	Interprets pathology as Freud interpreted pathology.
Existential Therapy:	Focuses on individual responsibility and the impotence of philosophy without initiatives.
Client-Centered:	Gets the helper's foot in the door by superficially responding to the client's expressed frame of reference.
Behavior Modification:	Develops systematic programs for observable, measurable and repeatable behavioral change within the helper's program repertoire.
Trait-and-Factor:	Involves systems for identifying and defining goals based upon a technology for organizing and transforming data into information.

Figure 4-1: The essential contribution of the Major Psychotherapies

On the surface, each of the major approaches to psy-chotherapy appears to be offering different experiences (see Figure 4-2). Each approach is designed to elicit

Patient
Behavior | **Superficial** | **Narrow** | **Limited**
| **Exploration** | **Understanding** | **Action**
| Client-Centered | Trait-and-Factor | Behavior
| Existential | Psychoanalysis | Modification

Figure 4-2. Apparent Differences:
Major Traditional Approaches to Psychotherapy

superficial and narrow patient exploration **or** under-standing **or** action. Only the effective teacher-helper provides the conditions for a complete learning experi-ence: responding to elicit learner exploration; person-alizing the exploration to elicit learner understanding; **and** initiating to elicit learner action.

The superficial reflections of the client-centered coun-selor may provide the conditions necessary for superfi-cial client exploration that does not make a constructive difference.

The limited philosophical stance of the existential thera-pist may provide the conditions necessary for superficial and narrow patient exploration that does not make a constructive difference.

The stereotyped interpretations of the psychoanalyst may provide the conditions necessary for narrow but compulsive patient exploration and a **psychoanalytic** understanding that does not make a constructive differ-ence.

The objective data and the interpretation of that objec-tive data may provide the conditions necessary for an intellectually limited client understanding that makes a limited constructive difference.

The conditioning and counter-conditioning techniques of the behavior modification therapist may provide the conditions necessary for narrow and limited patient action that makes a limited and often questionable difference.

The implications of offering helper conditions that provide the helpee with the opportunity to "explore" **or** "understand" **or** "act" are profound (see Figure 4-3).

Psychoanalysis promises **understanding** by a helper who knows only about how losers lose.

Client-Centered helping promises freedom to **explore** by a helper who is a prisoner of his or her own technique.

Existential helping promises an **exploratory** encounter by a helper who can only feel alone.

Behavior Modification promises **action** by a helper who acts without choices.

Trait-and-Factor helping promises **understanding** for goal definition by a helper who does not understand learning or acting.

Figure 4-3. The major approaches offer exploration or understanding or action

Action without understanding may not only be limited to a specific stimulus complex; it is also likely to be inappropriate for learning and therefore, destructive.

Understanding without exploration may not only be incomplete; it is also faulty to the point of insanity.

Exploration not followed by understanding **and** action based upon that understanding may not only be an intellectual exercise; it is also likely to be completely impotent.

The helper who does not provide accurate responding to facilitate helpee exploration, who does not provide conditions that personalize that exploration to facilitate helpee understanding and who fails to suggest initiatives to facilitate helpee action *simply creates or recreates the conditions that generated the problem in the first place; such a helper also insures that the therapy approach will be less than minimally helpful.*

It is the patient's limited exploration **or** understanding **or** action that renders psychoanalysis cruel, existentialism crazy, client-centered efforts hateful and sad, behavior modification stupid and rigid, and trait-and-factor approaches absurdly impersonal.

In an effective teaching-helping system, potentially preferred modes of treatment are those personalized systematic programs which emerge from the teacher's skills and which facilitate the learner's exploration, understanding and action.

In spite of their protests, all the major psychotherapies are conditioning systems. Knowingly or unknowingly, all the major psychotherapies equate conditioning with learning when conditioning is the production of a behavior within a specific stimulus complex and learning is the reproduction of behaviors under a wide variety of circumstances that lead to goal achievement.

Systematic programs designed to achieve goals assist in the development of subprograms to appropriately alter the learner's metabolic state and sensory/perceptual processes as well as the individual's choice of symbols and language employed to describe his or her perceptions and experience.

Goals operationalized and based upon the learner's frame of reference place the learner's repertoire of responses under the control of the learner and constitute the reproduction of behavior. In sharp contrast, the production of behavior via the presentation of conditioned stimuli is essentially unconscious and not under the control of the learner.

Any approach to teaching or helping that relies on exploration **or** understanding **or** action can only provide a conditioning, not a learning, experience.

Each of the major psychotherapies compete with one another to be the most impotent.

At one extreme, existential therapies are bound by words about empty and artificial people in empty and artificial worlds; at the other extreme, behavior modification is bound by its own rigidity and limited input. In between, other philosophical systems and psychoanalysis represent impotence, depression and the inevitable cruelty that emerges from empty and meaningless lives.

If, in fact, such approaches did deliver what they promised, they would create nothing but disaster.

Psychotherapies: Insane Systems

Sane systems, like sane people, pinpoint the contributions of effective people and effective programs and the interaction between such people and programs. Insane systems, like insane people, trap their users with inflexible assumptions about irrelevancies.

Sane systems, like sane people, understand that learning must start with the learner's frame of reference. Insane systems, like insane people, never start with the learner's frame of reference and always culminate in conditioning.

Sane systems, like sane people, operationalize subjective experience by responding to the learner's frame of reference. Insane systems, like insane people, cannot operationalize subjective experience because insane people do not have the skills to respond to the learner's frame of reference.

Sane systems, like sane people, blend subjective experience with external reality by operationalizing achievable physical, emotional and intellectual goals through personalizing the learner's frame of reference. Insane systems, like insane people, dichotomize subjective experience and external reality because insane people are caught up in pseudo-dichotomies that preclude responding to the learner's frame of reference.

Sane systems, like sane people, deem it necessary to make a difference. Insane systems, like insane people, deem it necessary and sufficient not to make a difference and run away from anything that does.

Sane systems, like sane people, fulfill their own growth by expanding their learning experiences. Insane systems, like insane people, bring about their own demise by limiting and resisting learning experiences and rejecting effective teacher-helpers.

Sane systems, like sane people, seek influence because they know they can make a constructive difference. Insane systems, like insane people, are non-productive and seek the limelight for much the same reasons that people who find their days empty seek satisfaction from their TV sets during the wee hours of the morning.

Sane systems, like sane people, find the meaning of their values in what they produce. Insane systems, like insane people, are destructive because they are always looking for meaning which has the appearance but not the substance of reality.

Sane systems, like sane people, value and strive for truth and excellence. Insane systems, like insane people, experience truth and excellence as products of the enemy.

Sane systems, like sane people, increase their maturity by expanding their exploration and, hence, their understanding of what is relevant. Insane systems, like insane people, remain immature by limiting their exploration and, hence, are only aware of what is irrelevant.

The sane seek associations that demand their best while they work and learn to achieve physical, emotional and intellectual goals. They succeed because they move in a world beyond their own skin. The insane seek associations in search of a soul in the desperate hope that a soul will bring them freedom from their empty experience of an ever-ebbing life. The insane know that they can only turn life into an empty experience because they are locked within their own skin.

Selected Additional Conclusions

Patients can expect to have helpers who are not influenced by the patient's experience or, for that matter, by his or her (the therapist's) own experience.

The therapist's inability to crawl out of his or her own skin to fully respond to another person's experience reflects more than scandalously poor training. It means that the therapist must stunt the patient's growth before the patient moves beyond the therapist and exposes the fraud.

The inability to fully and constructively respond is attributable to a wide variety of therapist deficits: lack of discipline, energy, basic decency responses, vigilance, helping-teaching skills and high level responding and initiative skills. In many instances, the inability to respond is attributable to dysfunctional metabolism and sensory-perceptual processes as well as to faulty language skills— as if the therapist was insane.

Therapists are trained to ignore the patient's frame of reference. Teachers, on the other hand, are trained to formulate methods which reflect the learner's experience.

All the major traditional therapies operate to disregard the patient's experience. Their practice and outcomes repeatedly suggest that the helpee's case could have been described without the therapist ever meeting the individual patient. As a consequence, therapists tend to prolong their activity beyond any point where the activity is even apparently useful.

Only those who produce something know when to rest or stop their activity. Therapists tend to persist out of fear that, if they stop playing their psychopathic game, the game will be exposed.

Without the basic skills to make a difference, therapists attribute behavior to constructs or concepts such as: conditioning, the unconscious, loneliness, guilt, anxiety or any combination of these and other concepts. When therapists do this, they apparently make it impossible to hold any person or any system responsible for outcomes because they rarely fill in the objectives and strategies necessary to achieve objectives. With few exceptions, the objectives are rarely behavioral. When therapists leave their patients with only concepts and a few limited insights, we hold the therapist responsible! There is no evidence that concepts and/or insights make a constructive difference to the therapists or the patients.

The teacher-helper makes a difference because concepts are translated into principles which help to operationalize objectives that, in turn, determine strategies to achieve concrete objectives. In addition, the effective teacher-helper takes the process an additional step by teaching the learner to develop his or her own transferable strategies.

Subscribing to limited points of view based only on concepts may reflect an individual's wish to remain trapped by her or his limited inner experiences; most of all, however, such a subscription reflects a firm resolve never to learn any more than what one already knows.

Therapy has become an interlude of self-indulgence frequently marked with temper tantrums by cowards who live in fear of learning, of learners, of the responsibilities of teaching, of their own ignorance and, most of all, in fear of truth.

In their infancy, all psychotherapies attempted to organize some aspect of human experience for the therapist and the patient. Some approaches have simply been more broadly based and/or more systematic than others. All the therapeutic approaches attempted directly or indirectly to give whatever organization they fabricated some kind of meaning. Students of some approaches concentrated on technique while others concentrated on assumptions or philosophy. Whether the approach was or is relatively broadly based and/or selectively systematic is, in fact, irrelevant because all of them fail. The traditional therapies fail because they do not accurately begin with the patient's (learner's) frame of reference and, as a consequence, never accurately and fully respond to the patient's (learner's) experience of disarray. They all fail because they do not and cannot recycle what they know through the use of finely-tuned responding skills and rarely act upon others constructively because they do not have the skills they need to define goals and achieve them.

When adherents of any system or approach to helping fail to equip their patients with the skills the patients **and** helpers need to make it at home, school and work, we call them therapists.

Psychotherapy fails for several additional reasons:

Therapists confuse conditioning with learning.

Therapists learn to lie about what they can do and what they really do.

Therapists ignore their own experience as well as their patient's experience because they avoid truth.

Therapists do not have the training to **functionally** diagnose, prescribe and treat.

Therapists maintain their ignorance by vigorously avoiding learning.

Therapists communicate a hopelessly contemptuous view of human potential (client-centered notwithstanding) as well as the quality of their own thinking when they call what they do therapeutic.

57

Therapists tend to lack pride because they have lied so much and because they have given up.

Therapists know but choose to ignore the fact that they **and** their systems deserve no real credit; yet how can they cheer their broken promises, especially when they knew all along they could not keep these promises.

Therapists often resemble the distorted female who withholds the real nourishment people need not only to grow but merely to survive.

Therapists grow lazy, often maintain their apparency with little more than their "stupid question" technique and their alphabet soup credentials.

Therapists know that if they really believe they can make a constructive difference with only insights and a few concepts then they are crazy: crazier than any patient they may encounter.

Therapists know that when they sell their limited concepts, they grow cruel; and if they learn no more than that, they become cowards.

Therapists, most of all, know that they cannot escape the tragedy of not being able to learn.

Therapists know that if their meager efforts succeeded, their patients, like the therapists themselves, would be doomed to an early childhood level of maturity.

Finally, therapists know that the continued study of psychopathology only justifies more psychopathology under a new name: psychotherapy.

From our point of view, the psychological cripple only develops strategies to lose and die. The psychological cripple invites others to do the same.

The psychological cripple has nothing to contribute to human resource development as a patient or as a psychotherapist.

We do not have the right to attempt to help others unless we at least wish them well and reflect our wish with diligent, decent behaviors.

We can move beyond the broken promises and broken lives left behind by psychotherapy if we focus our energies on testing the limits of a constructive environment made up of the only two ingredients that are relevant: effective people and effective programs guided by a system of human values.

Human technology will move us from technique to person to programs.

References

Carkhuff, R. R.
and
Berenson, B. G.

Chapters in **Beyond Counseling and Therapy.** New York: Holt, Rinehart and Winston. First Edition, 1967; Second Edition, 1976.

Chapter 4 Apparency in search of a person (client-centered)

Chapter 5 Man for each other (existential)

Chapter 6 The illusive suicide (psychoanalytic)

Chapter 7 Chance, not choice or change (trait-and-factor)

Chapter 8 To act or not to act (behavior modification)

Chapter Five

HRD: Reveille for Teaching

If it is requiem for therapy, it is reveille for teaching: teaching involving healthy people who learn from their experience and then transmit it to others.

If therapy fails, it does so because it fails to enter fully the helpee's frame of reference, to understand that there are things missing in his or her life. The teaching process emphasizes that the teacher must enter the learner's frame of reference in order to hook up the teaching program because **all learning begins with the learner's frame of reference.**

If therapy fails, it does so because it fails to deliver to the helpee the skills which the helpee needs to make it effectively in his or her world. The teaching process emphasizes the delivery of skills objectives because **all learning culminates in a skills objective.**

If therapy fails, it does so because it fails to prepare the helpee for the everyday world. The teaching process emphasizes skills that can be used by the learner in his or her everyday life because **all learning is transferable.**

Training Helpees

During the past several years, there has been growing recognition within the helping professions of the role of teaching as treatment. In 1964, we initiated a program of **training as treatment.** Through it, we attempted to teach our helpees the skills which they needed to make it effectively in their world (Carkhuff and Berenson, 1967; Carkhuff, 1969).

Helping Themselves

The first of these studies involved training helpees first to help themselves and second to help others. With regard to teaching helpees to help themselves, Pierce and Drasgow (1969) taught a group of psychiatric inpatients who were rejected from traditional individual and group therapeutic treatment. The patients ranged in age from 21 to 55 years and had been hospitalized from one to five times. Several of the patients were diagnosed schizophrenics; others were diagnosed as having difficulties associated with chronic brain syndrome. The group met for one and one-half to two hours a day for several weeks.

The purposes of the program were several. First, it was hoped that an improvement in interpersonal functioning would lead to improvement in other areas of functioning: in particular, functioning with significant others both within and outside the hospital. Accordingly, the patient's chances for discharge, staying out of the hospital and retaining his or her job would be increased. Second, according to the **helper therapy principle** the patient might eventually benefit other patients. Equipped with high-level interpersonal skills, he or she might become a patient-helper to other persons in need of help.

Since these patients were so severely disabled as to be unable to conduct a pre-training interview, an index of functioning was obtained from responses to standard helpee stimulus expressions designed expressly for these individuals. The patients were functioning at such a low level that the trainers began with some very fundamental steps. In response to spontaneous helpee expressions the patients cast in the helping role were simply asked whether the helpee felt happy, sad, angry and so on. If the patient accurately perceived sadness, for example, he or she was directed to construct a response beginning "You feel...": thus, the response "You feel sad."

The trainees were reinforced for such accurate single-statement responses. Gradually, trainee responses were built into two-statement interactions, then three, and so on until they were able to sustain 15- to 20-minute interactions as "talkers" and "listeners." The group clearly demonstrated an ability to function at more than a single level higher than initially after little more than 20 hours of intensified training; over a three-week period two of the patients were finally functioning above level 3 on 5-point scales.

In addition, **the training group demonstrated significantly higher levels of interpersonal functioning than a pre-post-tested time control group as well as a control group under drug treatment and a control group under individual psychotherapeutic treatment.**

Finally, all but the brain damaged patients were discharged by staff who had no knowledge of the training program. The brain damaged patients were given weekend privileges as a result of their improved levels of functioning. The discharged patients have remained discharged for several years and all patients have maintained their post-training levels of functioning.

Of course, the focus of the groups was not exclusively on training and shaping behavior. In the context of a facilitative atmosphere established by high-level functioning helpers, the patients came to ask many of the questions which were of life and death urgency for them. First they wanted to know "What's in it for me?," because they had so little interest and had to be sure of their return. Second, the whole process of focusing upon someone else was alien to them. With these critical challenges, the program could not have been implemented successfully without the most effective leadership; the patients could not have gone on to demonstrate for themselves the answers to these questions.

Helping Others

In another study, a group of parents on the waiting list of a child psychiatric clinic were directed toward a training group that met two nights a week for three weeks, one night a week for three additional weeks and one night two weeks later—a very workable schedule for most clinic staffs (Carkhuff & Bierman, 1970). The group was comprised of five couples ranging in age from their 30's to their 50's. They were from many walks of life and included a truck driver, a sanitation worker, a small businessman, a production manager and a professional counselor. The common bond among them was that their children had been diagnosed as emotionally disturbed.

A set of step-by-step training procedures was developed to meet the particular needs of this group. The method involved several early instructions concerning formulating responses to helpees: 1) listen for at least one minute (something that most people cannot do); 2) formulate your initial responses in terms of "You feel..."; 3) make no more than a single statement initially. Modifications in the formulation and the number of responses were incorporated as the trainees moved toward higher levels of functioning. Assuming that the child's difficulties were a function at least in part of the interpersonal process 1) between parents and 2) between parents and children, the following stages were implemented: a) a parent of one sex in one family unit and a parent of the other sex from another family unit served alternately as helper and helpee with the focus upon problems in general; b) in a similar manner, a parent of one sex in one family unit and a parent of the other sex from another family unit were alternately helper and helpee with the focus on problems dealing with the child specifically; 3) parents from the same family unit served alternately as helper and helpee with the focus upon their own interpersonal problems; 4) parents from the same family unit served alternately as parent and child with the focus upon the difficulties between parent and child; 5) the children were brought in and parents and children interacted in play therapy situations and/or on common problems. Between sessions, homework which involved the child and the parent and which led to the next stage of training was assigned; the assumption was that whatever really significant happens will happen between and after the termination of the training sessions. While the emphasis throughout training was upon communication practice, the trainer and the other trainees not only provided feedback on ratings of level of functioning but also attempted to enable the trainee involved to achieve new levels of understanding the problem area involved. The groups were extremely successful, achieving an improvement in functioning with each other of nearly a level and a half. However, the changes in functioning were not nearly as great for individual parents in relation to their own children, thus underscoring the need to incorporate more practice sessions directly involving the children: for example, the promising training specific to the child's play which grew out of this project.

Again, there were problems to be worked through other than those involved directly with the training structure. On the one hand, there was active resistance on the part of the parents to the notion that their children's problems were in large part due to their own problems. The burning question for the parents was whether they could surrender the defensive maneuvers they had incorporated as a way of life and replace them with more constructive behaviors. On the other hand, the trainer had a hold on them—their children. The question could be put to the reluctant—as it was—of whether they would maintain their neurotic modes of behavior at the expense of their children's welfare. **The group members found that, just as the trainer must act in relation to them, they must go all the way in relation to their children.**

One of the most important experiences took place during the fifth stage of training when the children were brought in and the interaction between parents and children was observed through a two-way observation room by the remaining parents. There was a clear absence of pathology. **There were no emotionally disturbed children!** Indeed, the parents with other children at home felt that these other children now presented more problems than the child with the original problem. In order to change their behavior patterns, the parents had to recognize themselves as a major source of their child's problems. They had to face themselves and work out their own conflicts, conscious or unconscious, or observe the repercussions of these conflicts in their children.

It must be emphasized that of all the training programs for which extensive data are available, these groups, trained with a behavioral emphasis upon practice, demonstrated the most constructive change in interpersonal functioning. Indeed, they tended to demonstrate the greatest change in that which they had practiced most, communication between spouses. It must be further emphasized that these groups were considered "patients" rather than professional or even subprofessional trainees. Contrary to our earlier expectations and orientations, then, we found that what was most critical was practice leading up to the goal which we wished to achieve. Rather than discrimination leading to communication, we assumed and found that, with these groups of people, discrimination followed rather than led to communication; that is, insight followed action. Of course, the training sessions were conducted in a highly therapeutic atmosphere and many of the conditions of group therapy as well as psychodrama were present. However, the discrete, step-by-step procedures involving practice at every stage appeared to be significantly more effective than the earlier training orientation of stressing discrimination in order to promote communication.

Results from other areas have lent support to the consideration of training or teaching as the preferred mode of psychological treatment. Certainly the early social learning theorists interpreted counseling and psychotherapy as interpersonal learning or relearning processes (Dollard and Miller, 1950; Mowrer, 1950; Murray, 1945; Rotter, 1954; Shoben, 1949). Also, those espousing the early behavior modification approaches growing out of learning theory conceived of the helpee as learner (Eysenck, 1960; Franks, 1964; Krasner and Ullman, 1965; Lang and Lazovik, 1963; Lazarus, 1960; Ullman and Krasner, 1966; Wolpe, 1958). Outgrowths of these early works have gone on to involve extensive use of dimensions of teaching in psychotherapeutic practices: didactic teaching; modeling; self-control content; homework assignments. However, none of these learning-oriented theorists made the direct translation to the counselor or therapist as teacher in daily psychotherapeutic interactions. In addition, these theorists were not broadly based in terms of the needs of the clients whom they serviced, for the most part channeling the clients' needs into the theorists' own counter- or instrumental conditioning specialty.

More recently, the counselor or therapist has been conceived of globally in terms of teaching specific skills that helpees need to live effectively in their lives. Thus, the counselor has been conceived of as a tutor of individuals (Ivey, 1971), a small group instructor employing group training as a preferred mode of treatment (Carkhuff, 1969) and a consultant to community based programs (Carkhuff, 1974). However, the rights, responsibilities and role functions (the 3 R's of helping) were not always clearly delineated in the movement from counselor to teacher. In this context, a number of dimensions of learning and teaching were not sufficiently specified: the learning outcomes and the learning processes which lead to those outcomes; the teaching programs that facilitate the learner's movement through the learning processes to the outcomes; the teacher-training programs which produce the teaching skills; and the teaching-learning systems in which the teaching and learning processes took place.

However, what convinced us in the end of teaching as a preferred mode of treatment was our extensive learnings from our daily experiences in counseling and psychotherapeutic practices. Never separating research from practice, we began our research and demonstration programs oriented toward learning and concerned with applying the effective ingredients of counseling and psychotherapy. Increasingly, we learned from the results of our research in hundreds of projects that the more systematically we went about helping, the more helpful we were in terms of affecting constructive changes or gains in our helpee populations. We moved quite readily from traditional counseling and psychotherapy to facilitative helpee gains as change agents to trainers and finally teachers of the skills that people need to live effectively in their worlds. We moved in the late 1960's to setting up teaching-as-treatment centers.

It was simply a matter of realizing that, in all instances, teaching or training was several times more effective in achieving helpee benefits than were the traditional modes of treatment (Carkhuff, 1966, 1969, 1971). We realized that no one person or group of researchers or practitioners has a final say on what will ultimately prove most effective. We are, at best, only researching the tips of icebergs. However, the tip of the teaching-as-treatment iceberg loomed giganticly in comparison to the tip of the psychotherapeutic iceberg, suggesting to us that it has much greater support under the surface. We have moved to it. It seemed stupid to us to stay where we were.

All this had led us to refinements in the Human Resource Development (HRD) model.

Teaching as Treatment

The results have also convinced others. Patterson in his Forward to **Helping and Human Relations** (Carkhuff, 1969) reinforced our notion of educational training:

> Perhaps therapy is not necessary! What we may need is direct training or education of everyone in the conditions of good human relations—not only normal people and children but the emotionally disturbed as well (p. ix).

Many supporters have followed suit:

Most often the area of the psychological practitioner's teaching includes not only symbolic and cognitive processes but also instruction in overt behavior, expecially interpersonal behavior. Indeed, it is the affective behavioral-interpersonal nature of what he teaches that sets the psychological practitioner teacher apart from the typical classroom teacher. Such an approach, of course, of necessity forces the psychological practitioner to be more concerned with questions of personal and cultural ethics and moral values than most other teachers. His area of instruction is generally tied closely to the self-concept and the emotions of his client. It is because of these factors that his endeavors require all the knowledge and skill that have been acquired through experience and research in the area called psychotherapy (Authier, et al., 1975), pp. 31-32).

The Learning Outcomes

Unfortunately, there are many limitations to this view of psychological education. There are several dimensions of any teaching delivery in any system. The first of these is the outcome. The outcome questions are "What are we going to achieve?" and "What are we going to deliver in order to achieve?" While problems and goals in the affective-behavioral-interpersonal realm may dominate treatment, they may not dominate the people who walk our streets. In other words, we may be emphasizing treatment in the emotional-interpersonal realm simply because teaching programs have been developed in the emotional-interpersonal realm (Carkhuff, 1969, 1971; Carkhuff and Berenson, 1967; Truax and Carkhuff, 1967).

The basic question which we must ask ourselves concerns outcome: "What are the helpee outcomes which we and/or the helpees wish to effect?" The answer in

69

terms of any model for human resource development involves the development of the physical, emotional and intellectual resources of the helpee.

The means to this human resource development is skills. Living skills emphasizing physical fitness skills help to develop physical resources. Living skills emphasizing interpersonal skills to facilitate the development of emotional resources. Learning and working skills emphasizing learning to learn and planning skills to expedite the development of intellectual resources. Of course, each of the living, learning and working skills dimensions interacts with each other and with each of the physical, emotional and intellectual resources.

Living skills or life skills are, to be sure, critical. Basically, the projects training helpees to help themselves and others were demonstrations of skills in the living area. Other living skills include problem-solving, decision-making, program-development and program implementation skills. So the skills products to be delivered to the helpees should not be exclusively interpersonal in nature.

Living or life skills is the single area of skills which troubled and untroubled people need. Our recent research, however, has led us to the conclusion that, in many respects, learning skills may be as important in our social system or more important. For example, children who have the learning skills to stay in school do not tend to be delinquent, while children who do not have the learning skills to stay in school do tend to be delinquent or criminal in their behavior (Carkhuff, 1976). Indeed, if children have learning skills at the highest levels, they tend to be designated as "outstanding" by others in the respect that they excel in one or more areas of endeavor. These learning skills include the skills the learner needs to explore, understand and act upon his or her world.

Finally, skills in working are also critical to the learner's future. Two out of three jobs which our children will have do not even exist right now. Our children must be prepared with the career development planning and preparation skills which they need to make it effectively in their future worlds. Our research indicates that we can teach children the career development skills which they need to compete and cooperate effectively in the world of work (Carkhuff and Friel, 1974). These planning and working skills include the skills the learners need to expand and narrow career alternatives, make career decisions and prepare themselves to find, acquire, hold and get promoted on jobs (Carkhuff, Pierce, Friel and Willis, 1975).

The learning outcomes, then, must be expanded from the affective-behavioral-interpersonal realm to include all of the skills which the helpee-learner needs to live, learn and work effectively in his or her world.

The Learning Process

Another limitation of the view of the psychological educator is the view of the teaching process:

> Most of the advocates of such an approach agree that the educational model means psychological practitioners seeing their function not in terms of abnormality (or illness) → diagnosis → prescription → therapy → cure; but rather in terms of client dissatisfaction (or ambition) → goal setting → skill teaching → satisfaction or goal achievement (Authier, et al, 1975, p. 31).

Unfortunately, it appears that the psychological practitioner is out of her field when she enters the area of education because she does not understand the educational process. To suggest that diagnosis and prescription are separate and distinct from goal setting and skill teaching is to misunderstand the compound nature of taking on the task of teaching in addition to the task of helping.

First of all, the failure of therapy was not that it diagnosed illness and prescribed therapy but rather that it

71

did not diagnose illness and prescribe therapy. There was no differential diagnosis leading to differential treatment.

Second, education is not simply a goal-setting process leading to skill teaching. It is much more; and that much more involves diagnosis in terms of the content area to be delivered.

The confusion of the functions and skills of psychological education can only lead to the same confusion that resulted in the demise of therapy. In order to learn how to teach, we must first learn how to learn and, then, we must master the skills which we need to facilitate this learning.

What, then, is the learning process? True learning is reflected in some kind of observable and measurable behavior. This means that the learner has acted in some way to demonstrate a significant change or gain in his or her behavior. In other words:

Outcome = Action = Behavior = Learning

Whether we begin with the "shaping" of this behavior or with the insight or understanding which leads to this behavior is not critical. What is critical is that the learner learns to make the discriminations necessary to act effectively in the future. And in order to have promoted our own accurate understanding of his or her world, the learner must have explored himself or herself.

Exploration → Understanding → Action

It is important to understand that many learning activities are subsumed within these phases of learning. In addition, it is important to recognize the teaching skills which facilitate the learner's movement through the phases of learning.

The tasks of helping are one thing. The tasks of teaching are another. We are asking our helpers to become helper-teachers. Let us separate out the functions and skills involved.

The helping tasks involve giving attention to the helpee, entering the helpee's frame of reference, personalizing the helpee's experience and initiating with the helpee to achieve his or her goals. In terms of learning, attending to the helpee involves him or her in the helping process. Responding to the helpee facilitates her exploration. Personalizing his exploration facilitates his understanding. Initiating with the helpee facilitates her action behavior. These tasks may be summarized in terms of the helper skills involved.

Attending → Responding → Personalizing → Initiating

Now the teaching tasks may be added to those of the helping tasks. They may be instigated by the products of the helping tasks. Or they may occur simultaneously with the helping tasks. That is, initiating to help the helpee to act to get to his or her goal may stimulate a recognition of the need for certain skills in order to achieve the goal. Alternatively, the helper-teacher may employ the teaching skills simultaneously with the helping skills in order to facilitate the helpee's movement through the learning phases of exploration, understanding and action.

The teaching tasks involve developing the content to a skills objective, diagnosing the helpee's level of functioning in terms of a skills objective, setting goals in terms of the diagnosis and delivering to the helpee-learner the skills which he needs to achieve his learning goals. In terms of learning, the content development constitutes the reason for involving the learner in learning. The diagnosis helps both teacher and learner to explore the learner's level of functioning in terms of content. The goal-setting helps both to understand the goals for learning based upon the diagnosis. The teaching delivery insures that the learner receives the skills which he or she needs in order to achieve his or her learning goals. These tasks may be summarized in terms of the teaching skills involved:

Content Development → **Diagnosis** → **Goal-Setting** → **Teaching Delivery**

The teaching process, then, is more difficult than the helping process because the teacher must use teaching skills as well as helping skills. In this regard, the skills needed in teaching are more closely identified with those of the therapies abandoned by the psychological educator than they are with those promulgated by the psychological educator. The teaching process simply puts the learner and the delivery together through the welding of helping skills and teaching skills.

We know what our learning outcomes are and how they are learned. We know the skills which we need to learn. It remains for us to learn these skills.

Teacher-Training Programs

Teachers learn in the exact same way that their learners learn. In order to learn new behaviors, teachers must first explore and understand themselves.

Exploration → **Understanding** → **Action**

In other words, utilize the exact same skills in facilitating their own movement through the phases of learning that they will ultimately utilize for their learners. Their teacher-trainers will use their helping skills to relate the teacher's frame of reference to the learning program:

Helping Skills:
Attending → **Responding** → **Personalizing** → **Initiating**

The helping skills which the teachers must learn, then, are the skills which they will use. The helping skills include learning to attend in order to involve; learning to respond for exploration; learning to personalize for understanding; and learning to initiate for action.

Subsequently, teacher-trainers will also use their teaching skills to deliver the learning program:

Teaching Skills:

Content Development → **Diagnosis** → **Goal-Setting** → **Teaching Delivery**

The teaching skills which the teacher must learn, then, involve developing content for skills; diagnosing for exploring; goal-setting for understanding, and delivering for action.

These helping and teaching skills may operate simultaneously to facilitate the learner's movement through the phases of learning

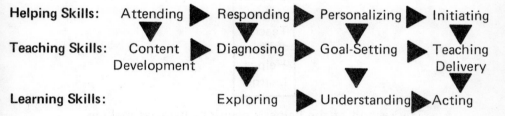

Each of the helping and teaching skills serves to facilitate movement through the phases of learning. Each of the helping and teaching skills to be learned by the teacher is guided by the learner's level of exploration, understanding and action.

All that remains is to set up a teaching system to deliver the learning products through the learning process using the teaching skills which the teachers have learned in their teaching-training programs.

Teaching Systems

Having dealt with the acquisition of teaching skills, the only question which remains concerns the system by which we deliver our learning products. With the

75

learner as our outcome population in helping, we must determine whether we teach the learners directly or teach the people who work with them directly.

The teaching system is really a series of personal systems, each one calculated to make the final delivery to the learner. The helpee-learner, then, is the primary recipient of the teaching delivery system.

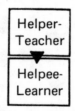

The question is "Who is the primary delivery component?" Here the helper must make several decisions, none of which excludes the others. The first of these includes the idea that the helper becomes the primary delivery component for the primary recipient population.

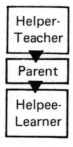

The second of the helper's decisions involves making the delivery to those other potential helpers who come in greatest contact with the helpee-learner. Thus, at different times the helper-teacher may teach the parent how to deliver living skills in the home.

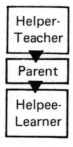

Or at different times and on different occasions, the helper-teacher may teach the school teacher how to deliver learning skills in the school.

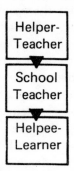

Finally, the helper-teacher may, under still different conditions, teach the employer how to deliver working skills at work.

Again, none of these teaching delivery systems precludes any of the others. In addition, each of these potential primary delivery populations may function as support components for another of these delivery populations. Thus the parents may support the educational delivery in school and the vocational delivery at work. The school teachers may support the human delivery in the home and the vocational delivery at work. The employer may support the human delivery at home and the educational delivery in school.

And the helper-teacher may support all of these functions.

Summary and Conclusions

Therapeutic practices have failed because they have

not left their recipient populations with the skills which the latter need to service themselves.

Educational practices can succeed because they can and do leave their recipient populations with the skills which the latter need to service themselves.

But these educational practices must incorporate the broadest possible learning products, understand the most inclusive learning process, deliver the most functional learning skills, develop the most effective teaching personnel and organize the most efficient teaching system.

We have our learning products: physical, emotional and intellectual resource development.

We understand the learning process: exploration, understanding and action.

We can deliver the learning skills: living, learning and working.

We can develop the skills of teaching personnel: helping, teaching and planning.

We can organize the teaching systems: the products, the delivery and support components.

We have the human goals and the human technology for change.

It remains for us only to commit ourselves to change.

References

Authier, J., Gustafson, K., Guerney, B. and Kasdorf, J. A.
The psychological practitioner as a teacher. **Counseling Psychologist,** 1975, 5, 31-50.

Carkhuff, R. R.
Training in counseling and psychotherapy: Requiem or reveille? **Journal of Counseling Psychology,** 1966, **13,** 360-367.

Carkhuff, R. R.
Helping and human relations. Vol. I. Selection and training. New York: Holt, Rinehart & Winston, 1969.

Carkhuff, R. R.
The development of human resources. New York: Holt, Rinehart & Winston, 1971.

Carkhuff, R. R., et al.
Cry twice! Amherst, Mass.: Human Resource Development Press, 1974.

Carkhuff, R. R.
Everything is education. Amherst, Mass.: Human Resource Development Press, 1976.

Carkhuff, R. R. and Berenson, B. G.
Beyond counseling and therapy. New York: Holt, Rinehart and Winston, 1967.

Carkhuff, R. R. and Bierman, R.
The effects of human relations training upon parents of emotionally disturbed children. **Journal of Counseling Psychology,** 1970, **17,** 157-161.

Carkhuff, R. R. and Friel, T.
The art of developing a career series. Amherst, Mass.: Human Resource Development Press, 1974.

Carkhuff, R. R., Pierce, R. M., Friel, T. and and Willis, D.
GETAJOB Amherst, Mass.: Human Resource Development Press, 1975.

Dollard, J. and Miller, N.
Personality and psychotherapy. New York: McGraw-Hill, 1950.

Eysenck, H. J.
Behavior therapy and the neuroses. New York: Pergamon Press, 1960.

Franks, C. M. (Ed.) — **Conditioning technique in classical practice and research.** New York: Springer, 1964.

Ivey, A. — **Microcounseling: Innovations in interviewing training.** Springfield, Ill.: C. C. Thomas, 1971.

Krasner, L. and Ullman, L. (Eds.) — **Research in behavior modification.** New York: Holt, Rinehart and Winston, 1965.

Lang, P. and Lazovik, A. — Experimental desensitization of a phobia. **Journal of Abnormal and Social Psychology,** 1963, **66,** 519-525.

Lazarus, A. and Rachman, S. — The use of systematic desensitization on psychotherapy. In H. J. Eysenck (Ed.), **Behavior therapy and the neurosis.** London: Pergamon, 1960.

Mowrer, O. — **Learning theory and personality dynamics.** New York: Roland, 1950.

Murray, E. — A case study in a behavioral analysis of psychotherapy. **Journal of Abnormal and Social Psychology,** 1954, **49,** 305-310.

Pierce, R. and Drasgow, J. — Teaching facilitative interpersonal functioning to psychiatric patients. **Journal of Counseling Psychology,** 1969, **16,** 295-298.

Rotter, J. — **Social learning and clinical psychology.** Englewood Cliffs, N. J.: Prentice-Hall, 1954.

Shoben, E. — Psychotherapy as a problem in learning theory. **Psychological Bulletin,** 1949, **46,** 366-392.

Truax, C. B. and Carkhuff, R. R. — **Toward effective counseling and psychotherapy.** Chicago: Aldine, 1967.

Ullman, L. and Krasner, L. (Eds.) — **Case studies in behavior modification.** New York: Holt, Rinehart and Winston, 1965.

Wolpe, J. — **Psychotherapy by reciprocal inhibition.** Stanford, Calif.: Stanford University Press, 1958.

Chapter Six

PEI:
The Learning Outcomes

P	E	I

When we entered the Black community in Springfield, Massachusetts in the 1960's, we came with what we thought was special expertise in counseling, human relations and education. As we attempted to deliver our products, however, we realized their limitations and, thus, our own limitations.

We enjoyed the middle class luxury of helping concepts that did not necessarily translate to human benefits. Our concepts made the people feel "good" and helped us to become important influences in their lives. And that was good. But to what end?

We addressed the issues of outcome. There were several.

At the most fundamental level, we found, the issue of outcome involves value judgments about what our product should look like. The recipient of the product should be able to see and touch and hear and try it out so that he or she knows whether or not it fits. Nevertheless, the outcome still involves value judgments.

Where the values of the recipient converge, there is a fit and there are no problems. Or, as is so often the case, where the recipient has no well-developed set of values, he or she is relieved to have the opportunity to learn those we offer. Where the value judgments which the recipients have made and those we have made diverge, we have an instance which argues for making the value judgments in the broadest possible way. This requires an accurate assessment of the needs of the people in the community.

81

The second issue flowed from this consideration. We saw that many of the conditions that contributed to the destruction of the poor, the Black and Brown and the needy were interdependent. Certainly the environment, in terms of poor housing, health and employment conditions contributed to human deterioration.

Similarly, within the people there was an interdependency of functioning. The health of many was poor. This precluded the energy levels necessary for emotional and intellectual investments. At another level, the people's emotional attachments were retarding and tended to drag down their physical and intellectual functioning. Finally, the intellectual efforts were unsuccessful and tended to hold back the physical and emotional involvements.

In other words, whether the people were up in one area or down in another, their level of functioning in any one area seemed to have a distinct effect upon their level of functioning in other areas. This conclusion was supported by our research in all areas.

We attempted to define our outcomes, then, in the broadest possible way. We attempted to define our outcomes not in terms of specific symptom reduction but in terms of the physical, emotional and intellectual resource development of the population with which we worked. This presented still another issue concerning how to develop human resources.

The people themselves gave special insights into the issue of development. When we delivered our programs, we were met with very vivid responses:

"Break it down, man!"

"Give me something I can take home."

"Give me something I can use."

It was clear that human resources could not be developed by simply addressing them grossly. It was clear that human resources could only be developed by skills development.

We realized that there were many skills ingredients in the HRD equation. And most of them were missing!

We began with responsive and, then, initiative inter-personal skills. We added problem-solving, decision-making, program development and program implementation skills. We underpinned the programs with physical fitness skills programs which enabled the people to develop their physical and emotional resources.

We realized that living skills were insufficient to help the people to develop their resources. We developed learning skills and, then, working skills programs which enabled these people to develop their intellectual resources.

We discovered that the only way to develop human resources was through skills development. This was the only way that you could observe and measure HRD. Skills development was the only way that you could replicate or repeat the outcomes and, therefore, train people to achieve them. Skills development was the only way you could predict, within limits, the effects on human functioning. Skills development was the only thing that translated to valuable human benefits.

Indeed, skills development **was** HRD.

A Skills Model

What emerged was a skills model for HRD. The dimensions of HRD are physical, emotional and intellectual. The levels of physical, emotional and intellectual development are levels of skills development. In other words, the only way of determining the level of physical, emotional and intellectual development (PEI) is through skills programs leading to that development.

Physical Development

Another way of looking at PEI development is in terms of the major areas incorporated within these dimensions. Thus, for example, within the physical area we may be concerned with the fitness dimensions

83

of cardio-respiratory functioning, endurance, strength and flexibility (see Figure 6-1). Within each of these areas, in turn, we must have some way of determining an individual's level of functioning. And that level of functioning implies a program that leads to the next level of functioning.

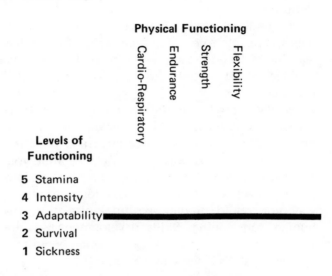

Figure 6-1. Levels of physical development

In Figure 6-1, we have characterized gross levels of functioning, each of which implies a program for the achievement of the next highest level of functioning. Therefore, at the highest levels the individual has the stamina to invest himself or herself intensely in all areas of endeavor requiring cardio-respiratory functioning, endurance, strength and flexibility. At the next level, an individual is functioning so that he or she can invest himself or herself with intensity in some areas of endeavor. At minimally effective levels, the person can adapt to the tasks of daily living. At less than minimal levels, the person merely survives. And at the lowest levels the individual is sick.

Now, people can be diagnosed in terms of their functioning on each of these dimensions (Carkhuff, 1974;

84

Collingwood, 1976). For example, they can obtain an index of their cardio-vascular functioning from their total pulse rates for two minutes after doing the "step test." They can obtain an index of their endurance from the amount of distance run/walked within 12 minutes. They can obtain an index of their strength from the number of sit-ups which they can do in one minute. They can obtain an index of their flexibility from their ability to do the toe-touch exercise (Collingwood, 1976).

The diagnosis of their levels of functioning in each of these areas implies a skills program leading to the next highest level of functioning. Lacking such a program, they cannot improve, they cannot grow, except in random ways.

The following illustrates how a helper-teacher may respond to a male accountant in his late 30's, who is in need of a physical program.

Helpee: I'm all ... well ... OK for something ... well ... for a while then I don't know ... I sort of get off track.

Helper-Teacher: You're lost because you don't know what your goals are.

Helpee: It's like being lost, I guess ... something ... well when I should, I don't care about getting going...

Helper-Teacher: Like you feel sort of down because nothing seems really worth the effort.

Helpee: A lot of things are worth the effort I think ... I don't or can't care enough to do anything about it ... can't get up for much ... and then things pile up ... the family doesn't get much from me ...

Helper-Teacher: Sometimes you feel guilty because you don't do what needs to be done.

Helpee: I don't do enough ... but I try ... I really do

	but I can't ... well ... stay with it ... stay in there ...
Helper-Teacher:	You're scared because things are getting out of hand and you can't do much about it.
Helpee:	I end up giving up or not caring ... sleep a lot ... watch TV, anything but what needs to be done ... sometimes ... well often ... I have to concentrate to move ...
Helper-Teacher:	You feel helpless a good deal of the time because you just don't have any energy.
Helpee:	I have good ideas ... and I guess I do care but I'm beginning not to care about myself ... just look at me! I'm a mess ... and I don't do anything about it.
Helper-Teacher:	You're fed up with yourself because you can't pull yourself together but you need to do something about your low level of energy.
Helpee:	It's like ... well needing to feel what it feels like to be alive ... and useful ... active ...
Helper-Teacher:	You're disgusted with yourself because you experience yourself as lazy and you don't do anything about it. But well ... now you better do something or it's all over. Your first effort will be to do something about your energy. The first thing you can do is get a checkup by your family physician, then we can make out a plan to systematically increase your energy with a personalized exercise program, diet and rest.

Emotional Development

In a similar way, we may look at the levels of functioning in the emotional-interpersonal realm. The relevant areas of emotional-interpersonal functioning include human relationships at home, school, work and in the community (Carkhuff, 1972, 1974). (See Figure 6-2.) Within each of these areas, we have developed the levels of functioning which, in turn, dictate skills programs to improve functioning.

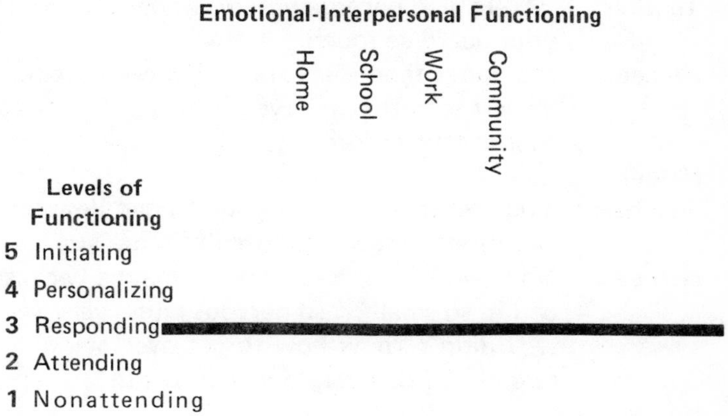

Emotional-Interpersonal Functioning

Home · School · Work · Community

Levels of Functioning

5 Initiating
4 Personalizing
3 Responding ▬▬▬▬▬▬▬▬▬▬▬▬▬▬▬
2 Attending
1 Nonattending

Figure 6-2. Levels of emotional development

In Figure 6-2 we have characterized the levels of emotional-interpersonal functioning. At the lowest level the person is not even giving attentiveness to others, while at the next level he or she exhibits attending behaviors which, while necessary, are nevertheless not sufficient for effective human interactions. At minimally effective levels, the individual enters the other person's frame of reference and responds to that frame of reference. At the next highest level, the individual not only responds but personalizes the other person's experience. And at the highest level, the individual not only personalizes his or her understanding but initiates to help the other person to achieve desired goals. Again, the diagnosis of levels of functioning in each of these areas implies a skills program leading to the next highest level of functioning.

In the following excerpt the helpee, a woman in her early 20's, reports to a helper-teacher how things are going with her emotional program.

Helpee: I'm not scared anymore ... you know ... not worried all the time.

Helper-Teacher: You're glad because you don't need to be on your guard so much.

Helpee: It's better than that! Ha ... I'm even sure of myself sometimes .. even in social situations that got me before.

Helper-Teacher: You feel safer because you can handle some situations that ... that used to scare you.

Helpee: You said it ... I used to be ... maybe because of I'm so small ... so nervous with everyone ... I didn't know how to get over being scared ... I didn't know who to trust.

Helper-Teacher: You feel relieved because you can tell more about what other people feel and think.

Helpee: I was scared because I didn't know what to do ... or what I wanted really ... just to feel less tense all the time with other people.

Helper-Teacher: You were afraid because you could not trust yourself to make the right judgments but now you know how to respond to other people and that helps a lot.

Helpee: It helps because I have some control over things ... it's not just up to the other person ... when I respond they ... well ... sort of tell me more ... more important they seem to trust me! Isn't that something! Trust **me!**

Helper-Teacher: You are stronger because you are in more control of things that used to make you anxious. It's exciting to know you can be more confident.

Helpee: It sure is ... but I want to make it all go somewhere now ...

Helper-
Teacher: Sometimes you feel bothered because you know there is more to a relationship and you can't make it happen. In addition to responding you need to know how to personalize the experience not only for you but for the other person. That's the next goal ... learning how to personalize. The first thing here is to relate the feeling and the meaning of what is being said to the person ... sort of: "You still feel lonely because you haven't made as many friends as you want to."

Intellectual Functioning

The same transfer can be made to the intellectual realm. Again, the relevant areas of intellectual functioning include the home, school, work and the community (Carkhuff, 1974; Carkhuff and Berenson, 1976). (See Figure 6-3)

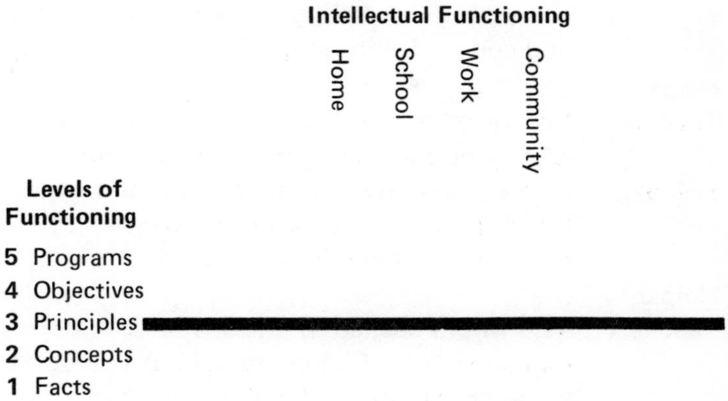

Intellectual Functioning

Home   School   Work   Community

Levels of
Functioning

5 Programs
4 Objectives
3 Principles ▬▬▬▬▬▬▬▬▬▬▬▬▬▬
2 Concepts
1 Facts

Figure 6-3. Levels of intellectual development.

Within each of these areas, we have developed the levels of functioning which, in turn, imply skills programs to improve functioning.

In Figure 6-3, we have characterized the several levels of intellectual functioning. At the lowest level, the individual is only able to grasp the facts of the situation and not to organize the facts into concepts which is the next highest level of functioning. At minimally effective levels, the individual is able to develop the principles involved, while at the next highest level he or she is able to translate the principles into objectives. Finally, at the highest levels, the objectives are translated into programs which enable him or her to achieve the objectives. Again, the diagnosis of levels of functioning in each of these areas implies a skills program leading to the next highest level of functioning.

The following excerpt depicts how a helper-teacher responds to a male college student who is having difficulties studying.

Helpee: It's hard for me to know what is important ... I can't decide and all the stuff gets confused ... I end up reading ... and re-reading everything ... until I get sick of the material and end up feeling stupid.

Helper-Teacher: You're frustrated because you never know where you stand with what you are studying.

Helpee: I don't have the time to go over and over the material ... but I want to do well ... I think everything is important.

Helper-Teacher: You would be glad to know what is important and what is fill-in material but you don't know how to make the discrimination.

Helpee: It would be great ... but I may not be smart enough or something. I sure work hard enough ... most of the time.

Helper-Teacher: You feel dumb because you don't know

where you stand each step of the way ...
you don't even know when you have learned
what you need to learn and you want very
much to make it all worthwhile ... efficient.
The first goal here is to learn how to discriminate between what is relevant and what
is not.

Helpee: Great! What do I do ... though ... I mean
what is the thing I can do in addition to
read, read, read? I've tried to think of things
... then I get worried so I stay with reading
and re-reading.

**Helper-
Teacher:** You feel lost because you can't come up
with something but you must. Your first big
goal is to get oriented to the material. You
can do this by reading the chapter title, the
summary at the end of the chapter, then go
back and read the bold face type, charts
and tables, then read the summary again. It
shouldn't take you more than five or ten
minutes.

In a similar manner, we may develop overall levels of
functioning for physical, emotional and intellectual
functioning (Carkhuff, 1974). (See Figure 6-4.) Thus, a

Overall Functioning

Levels of Functioning	Physical	Emotional	Intellectual
5 Leader	Stamina	Initiating	Programs
4 Contributor	Intensity	Personalizing	Objectives
3 Participant ■■■	Adaptability ■■■	Responding ■■■	Principles
2 Observer	Survival	Attending	Concepts
1 Detractor	Sickness	Inattentiveness	Facts

Figure 6-4. Levels of overall development

person functioning modally at the lowest level can only be a detractor or even a disruptor in relation to the world around him and the people in it. At the next level, he can only passively observe the goings-on because he cannot participate, since participation requires minimal physical, emotional and intellectual resource development. At the next highest level, he or she has the resources not only to participate but to contribute in some specialty areas. Finally, at the highest levels she has the resources to be a leader in all areas.

Now there can clearly be some variation in one or the other areas of physical, emotional and intellectual functioning. However, as one area tends to move up or down it tends to influence the movement of the other areas, provided programs are available. Thus if an individual's physical fitness improves, it will tend to influence the person to be more emotionally facilitative and more intellectually acute. **Vice versa,** if the individual's physical fitness deteriorates, it tends to influence the person to be more emotionally retarding and more intellectually numb. In a similar way, movement in the emotional or intellectual areas tends to have a "pull" upon functioning in the other PEI areas.

Skills Outcomes

What, then, are the outcomes of HRD? There are several different ways that outcomes can be viewed. One is the more traditional way of looking at some index measuring a specific social cost. Typical indices here include the incidence of treatment or recidivism. Usually, these outcomes are obtained by simple frequency tabulations or cost figures. The desirable outcome in these instances is invariably some kind of reduction.

Skills outcomes are another way of talking about outcomes. Usually an improvement in skills leads to an improvement or reduction in the indices of the more traditional outcomes. There is an even greater likelihood of this being the case when specific skills programs are set up for specific outcome reduction: for example, interpersonal skills training for treatment or recidivism reduction.

Another way of looking at skills is in terms of a repertoire of responses. If I have no responses or only one response in my repertoire, I have a very limited repertoire of responses and my effectiveness as a human being is extremely limited.

The effect of a limited response repertoire is no more clearly seen than in the juvenile delinquent whose emotional and intellectual responses are extremely limited. For example, in intellectual terms, he or she is typically three or more years behind grade level and, thus, is ill-equipped to handle the school situation. Our own recent findings comparing delinquent, non-delinquent and outstanding children lead us to conclude that if a child does not have the intellectual skills to stay in school, he or she stands a good chance of being delinquent. And, conversely, if a child has the intellectual skills to stay in school, he or she stands a good chance of not being delinquent, or with high enough level skills, of being an "outstanding" citizen, an "outstanding" contributor, an "outstanding" producer. As a consequence, he or she will contribute to the reduction of many indices of outcome including drop-outs, vandalism, discipline and delinquency.

If I have a large number of responses to a given situation, then I have many more degrees of freedom in approaching that situation and, thus, have · a good chance of being effective in it. In addition, if I have a high enough quality of responses to a given situation, then I stand a good chance of excelling or being outstanding in that situation and, thus, reducing many traditional outcome indices.

One side of the outcome picture is reflected by improvement in functioning or skills improvement while the other side is reflected in frequency tabulations of incidence reduction. The improvement side of the picture directly influences the reduction side of the picture.

In organizing the outcome picture, then, we do so in terms of the living skills that lead to improved physical and emotional functioning and the learning and working skills that lead to improved intellectual functioning.

Living Outcomes

In presenting the living skills outcomes, we are presenting a brief picture of the answer to the questions which we asked many years ago: "What should our products look like?" You may ask the same question now.

Our answer, for which we now have extensive evidence (Carkhuff, 1969, 1971, 1976), is seen in Figure 6-5.

Figure 6-5. Living skills outcomes

Helping Programs	Human Outcome Measures	Results
More than 100 studies on the effects of counselor and therapist functioning on functioning of psychiatric inpatients and out-patients. (Truax & Carkhuff, 1967)	Number of days out of institution MMPI Clinical Scales Rorschach Projective Test Constructive Personality Change Index Ego Strength Social Desirability Anxiety Internalization Self-Adjustment Self-Expert Correlation Self vs. Ideal Self-Correlation Social Self-Correlation Social Self-Consciousness Psychiatric Ratings Authoritarianism	Significant relationships with helper-offered conditions in different studies and in combined outcomes employing standard score procedures.

		High Level Helpers	Low Level Helpers
Effects of counselor functioning on counseling center clients and psychiatric out-patients. (Pagell, Carkhuff & Berenson, 1967)	Expert Ratings Therapist Ratings Tape Ratings Interviewee Ratings Self-Ratings	 100% positive 100% positive	 10% positive 30% positive

Helping Programs	Human Outcome Measures	Results
	Gross Ratings of Patient Behavior (Disturbance, Self-Care, Sociability, Degree of Improvement)	80% positive 43% positive 80% positive 47% positive 30% positive 13% positive
	Expert Ratings Therapist Ratings Interviewee Ratings Self-Ratings	88% positive 16% positive 88% positive 29% positive 56% positive 27% positive 88% positive 46% positive
Effects of counselor level of functioning on client exploration. (Carkhuff & Alexik; Hirschberg, Carkhuff & Berenson, 1967; Holder, Carkhuff & Berenson, 1966; Piaget, Carkhuff & Berenson, 1968; Truax & Carkhuff, 1967)	Self-Exploration	Client self-exploration is significantly a function of counselor level of functioning.
The effects of helper level, race and social class on helpees. (Banks, Berenson & Carkhuff, 1967; Carkhuff & Pierce, 1967)	Self-Exploration	Below minimally effective helper levels, helpee self-exploration is related to helper race; above minimally effective helper levels, helper self-exploration is not related to helper race and social class.

Helping Programs	Human Outcome Measures	Results
Effects of helper level and verbal conditioning program on helpees. (Vitalo, 1971)	Student Personal Expression	Verbal expression significantly greater for highs.
Effects of helper level and vocational information-seeking conditioning on helpees. (Michelson & Stevic, 1971)	Vocational Information-Seeking Behavior	Vocational information-seeking significantly greater for highs.
Effects of trained hospital attendants on inpatients	Ward Behavior Ratings Discharge from Hospital	**Treatment Group** **Control Group** 58% improved 27% improved 1% deteriorated 17% deteriorated 16% discharged 9% discharged
Effects of trained community helpers on students. (Carkhuff, 1971; Carkhuff & Griffin, 1970)	Student Interpersonal Functioning Parent Interpersonal Functioning School Staff Interpersonal Functioning Teacher Interpersonal Functioning Officers' Interpersonal Functioning	Significant Improvement Significant Improvement Significant Improvement Significant Improvement Significant Improvement
Effects of trained community helpers on students. (Carkhuff, 1971)	Black Student Classroom Expression	All students significantly increased self-expression.

97

Helping Programs	Human Outcome Measures	Results
Effects of trained officers on inmates. (Hall, 1969, 1970, 1971a, 1971b, 1972, 1973)	Self-Reports	80%—90% positive
Effects of trained helpers and interpersonal skills training on parents and children. (Carkhuff & Bierman, 1970)	Parents' Interpersonal Skills Parents' Relationship to Children Parents' Constructive Personality Change Child Adjustment Changes	Improvement significantly greater than control conditions. No significant differences No significant differences No significant differences
Effects of trained helpers and interpersonal skills training on parents and children. (Carkhuff & Griffin, 1971)	Parents' Interpersonal Skills Children's Interpersonal Skills	Significant Improvement Significant Improvement
Effects of trained helpers and interpersonal and program development skills training on parents and children. (Carkhuff & Pierce, 1974)	Parents' Interpersonal Skills Parents' Constructive Change Children's Interpersonal Skills Children's Adjustment Changes	Significant Improvement Significant Improvement Significant Improvement Significant Improvement
Effects of trained helpers and interpersonal skills training on psychiatric inpatients. (Pierce & Drasgow, 1969)	Patients' Level of Interpersonal Functioning Hospital Discharge	Improvement significantly greater than four treatment control conditions. Significantly greater than four control conditions.

Helping Programs	Human Outcome Measures	Results
Effects of trained helpers and interpersonal skills training on psychiatric inpatients. (Vitalo, 1971)	Patients' Level of Interpersonal Functioning	Significantly greater than two treatment control conditions.
	Taped Client Statements	Significantly greater than two treatment control conditions.
	Live Interaction	Significantly greater than two treatment control conditions.
	Patients' Ward Behavior	Significantly greater than two treatment control conditions.
	Patients' Clinical Pathology	Significantly greater than two treatment control conditions.
	Patients' Anxiety Level	Significantly greater than two treatment control conditions.
Effects of trained officers and interpersonal skills training on inmates. (Carkhuff, Banks, Berenson, Griffin & Hall, 1971)	Inmate Interpersonal Functioning	Significant Improvement
Effects of trained institutional personnel and systematic training programs on delinquents. (Carkhuff, Berenson, Griffin, Devine, Angelone, Clinton, Keeling, Muth, Patch & Steinberg, 1974)	Student Physical Functioning	Improved 50%
	Student Interpersonal Functioning	Improved 100%
	Student Self-Reports	83% positive
	Staff Reports on Students	84% positive
	Student Runaway Rate	Reduced 57%
	Student Recidivism Rate	Reduced 34%
	Student Crime Rate	Reduced 34%

Helping Programs	Human Outcome Measures	Results
Effects of trained helpers and inter-personal skills training on inmates. (Devine & Steinberg, 1974)	Recidivism	19% Recidivism Rate 7% After Training
Effects of trained helpers and inter-personal skills training on inmates. (Montgomery, 1974)	Inmate Interpersonal Functioning	Significant Improvement
Effects of trained helpers and inter-personal skills training on ex-felons. (Griffin, 1973)	Prison Recidivism Drug Usage	7% Recidivism Rate 0% Drug Usage

As can be seen, living skills outcomes reflect improvement in a variety of indices of physical, emotional and intellectual functioning and reduction in a variety of traditional outcome indices: incidence of treatment, institutionalization, runaways, recidivism, crime and drug usage. Again, the improved levels of functioning generalize to reduced incidences of malfunctioning.

The following excerpt shows a female helpee in her 30's looking back and trying to make sense out of her earlier experience.

Helpee: I don't know where it's going ... but ... maybe I'm getting spoiled. Everyday feels like Christmas.

Helper-Teacher: You feel great because everything is falling into place.

Helpee: I know where it's going or I don't even need to know ... I just think I can take care of things ... make things happen. I wasn't sure before ... you know ... if there was a place ... I'll **make** my own.

Helper-Teacher: You're confident because you understand more about who you are, where you want to go and you know something about how to get there.

Helpee: You know, when I learned how to relate better to other people ... they tried to know me better. When I helped them, more people wanted to help me ... especially my family and friends ... I think they know who I am ... I don't always have to be who they want or think I am.

Helper-Teacher: When you learn to love yourself you learn to love others all at the same time.

Helpee: I know who I am, I know who I want to be and I think I can make it happen because I've got some realistic plans.

Most helpees want to know if there is anyone who can tap in on their inner experience and private identity for constructive purposes. Having had the experience the helpee has taken the first step toward being a helper because the helpee is more open to learning new responses. All living, learning and working outcomes, if they are to translate to personal growth must begin and end with the helpee-learner's frame of reference.

Learning Outcomes

The learning skills outcomes may be seen in Figure 6-6. In a similar way, the learning skills outcomes are reflected in improved communication and computation achievement, cognitive processes and other indices of intellectual functioning; and reduced absenteeism, truancy, tardiness, drop-outs, vandalism, discipline problems and other indices of school crises. Remember, the improved levels of functioning generalize to reduced indices of dysfunctioning; and they do so most efficiently and effectively when programs are systematically developed to reduce incidence.

Figure 6-6. Learning skills outcomes

Helping and Teaching Programs	Human Learning Outcome Measures	Results
Effects of teacher level of functioning on students. (Aspy, 1969)	Student Educational Achievement	Significantly greater improvement on 5 of 6 indices for students of high level teachers.
Effects of teacher level of functioning on students. (Aspy & Hadlock, 1967)	Student Educational Achievement	Significantly greater for students of highs.
	Student Truancy	Significantly greater for students of lows.
	Student Attendance	Significantly greater for students of highs.
Effects of parent and teacher level of functioning on students. (Kratochvil, Berenson & Carkhuff, 1969)	Student Physical Functioning	No Differences Significant Intercorrelations
	Student Interpersonal Functioning	No Differences
Effects of teacher level of functioning on students. (Truax & Tatum, 1966)	Student Adjustment	Significantly greater for students of highs.
Effects of teacher level of functioning on students. (Truax & Carkhuff, 1967)	Academic Grades	Significant Relationship
	Academic Progress	Significant Relationship

Helping and Teaching Programs	Human Learning Outcome Measures	Results
Effects of teacher level of function-ing on students. (Stofer, 1970)	Student Achievement	Significant Relationship
Effects of supervisor level of function-ing on supervisee. (Pierce & Schauble, 1970)	Supervisee Level of Interpersonal Functioning	Significantly greater for supervisees of highs.
Effects of teacher level of functioning on students. (Roebuck & Aspy, 1973)	Non-Verbal I.Q.	Generally Significant Relationship
	Vocabulary	Generally Significant Relationship
	Reading	Generally Significant Relationship
	Spelling	Generally Significant Relationship
	Arithmetic	Generally Significant Relationship
	Manifest Anxiety	Generally Significant Relationship
	Dependency Proneness	Generally Significant Relationship
	Social Reaction	Generally Significant Relationship
	Motivation	Generally Significant Relationship
	Self-Perception	Generally Significant Relationship
	Creativity-Fluidity	Generally Significant Relationship
	Creativity-Flexibility	Generally Significant Relationship
	Creativity-Originality	Generally Significant Relationship
Effects of teacher level of functioning on school crises. (Aspy & Roebuck, 1973)	Incidence of School Crises	Significant Relationship

Helping and Teaching Programs	Human Learning Outcome Measures	Results
Effects of trained teachers and inter-personal skills training on trainees. (Pierce, Carkhuff & Berenson, 1967)	Trainee Level of Interpersonal Functioning Termination	Significantly greater for students of highs. Significantly greater for students of lows.
Effects of trained teachers on students. (Aspy, 1972)	Student Educational Achievement Student I.Q.	Significant Improvement Improvement of 9 I.Q. Points
Effects of trained teachers on students. (Aspy & Roebuck, 1973)	Student Cognitive Processes	Significant Improvement
Effects of trained teachers on students. (Berenson, 1971, 1972)	Student Achievement Situation Reaction	Significantly greater for students of highs. Significantly greater for students of highs.
Effects of trained teachers on students. (Griffin, 1971)	Student Interpersonal Skills	Significant Improvement

Helping and Teaching Programs	Human Learning Outcome Measures	Results
Effects of trained teachers and parents and learning to learn skills training on students. (Carkhuff & Pierce, 1974)	Student Achievement	Significant Improvement
Effects of trained teachers and learning to learn skills training on students. (Berenson, 1974)	Student Achievement	Significant Improvement
Effects of trained teachers and community helpers and learning to learn skills training on students. (Berenson, Berenson & Griffin, 1974)	Student Achievement	Average over 100% Improvement

The following dialog depicts a Helper-Teacher working with an attractive 45-year-old male professor who's world is now larger and fuller by learning to learn.

Helpee: I never worked at learning before ... it was new to me ... you know that ... I got by on other things.

Helper-Teacher: In a way you are happy because I caught you.

Helpee: That kind of work was for other people ... I could always handle people ... get what I want because people wanted me ... took me as I am ... they didn't really care what I could do or what I knew. It got to me when I met you.

Helper-Teacher: You feel used because you didn't have the substance. You got by on your good looks and charm.

Helpee: I felt cheated somehow but I could not put it together. I even resisted learning anything that I didn't already know. I was becoming ... I was a manipulator ... I guess that's kind of sick.

Helper-Teacher: You felt empty because nothing was being taken in ... it was all superficial.

Helpee: I was staying in one place. I could predict what would happen ... not much fun ... and I felt superior one minute and cheap the next. It would have stayed that way if you had not tuned in and helped me realize that if I didn't grow I'd, well, die. But more, that ... that I could begin to learn something new when you tied the learning to who I am and some personal goals.

Helper-Teacher: You felt worthwhile when we tapped in on

107

| | your experience, what was there, what was missing ... set goals that reflected your values and got to work. |
| **Helpee:** | It was a long time ... I thought I was too old to learn ... I wasn't motivated to ... no reason. The first thing I had to learn was to work and then I learned that I could produce something. What got me started really was the steps you gave me. They were do-able and I could relate them to feeling more like a real person ... inside ... before it was empty ... like I was a shell. You not only left room for me, you made room for me ... now I can do that for myself and others. |

Working Outcomes

The working skills outcomes may be seen in Figure 6-7. The working skills outcomes are reflected in improvements in career knowledge, information, use of sources, questions, job classificiaton skills, expanding and decision-making skills; in job finding, acquisition and promotion skills; in work productivity, quality and cooperativeness and dependability; and in a number of other indices of career planning and preparation skills. In turn, these improvements are reflected in a reduction of many traditional outcome indices: absenteeism, sick leave, job transfer, work idleness.

Figure 6-7. Working skills outcomes

Planning Programs	Human Planning and Working Outcomes	Results
Effect of ECES I program on students. (Super, Minor, Thompson, Lindeman, Clar, Bohn, Friel, Gillen, Pilatto, 1970)	Specific Occupational Knowledge	Significantly greater for students of ECES vs. non-ECES.
	Amount of Useful Occupational Info.	Significant differences for 12th vs. 9th graders.
	Acceptance of Responsibility for Career Decisions	Significant differences for college vs. non-college.
	Economic Returns as a Work Value	Significant decrease for college vs. non-college.
	Interests	Significantly away from "practical" by 10th graders.
		Significantly toward "practical" by 12th graders.
	Confidence	Significantly more definite about careers.
	Parent Support	Significantly more involved in children's career planning.

		Groups				
		I ECES & HRD Counselor	II ECES Counselor	III HRD Counselor	IV Counselor	V ECES	VI Base Rate Control
Differential effects of ECES and HRD counselor training on students. (Carkhuff, Friel, Berenson, Bebermeyer, Mahrt, Mallory, & Forrest, 1972)	Self-Reports on Impact of Guidance Program	74%	67%	91%	25%	50%	13%
	Self-Reports on Impact of Guidance Counselor	67%	91%	100%	50%	27%	21%
	Self-Reports on Impact on Career Plans	87%	91%	100%	91%	88%	78%
	Self-Reports on Impact on Course Preparation	60%	85%	60%	75%	60%	58%

Planning Programs

Differential effects of decision-making skills (DMS) training and ECES II program on students.

(Myers, Thompson, Lindeman, Super, Patrick, Friel, 1972)

Human Planning and Working Outcomes	Results		
Informed Planning	DMS	ECES	Controls — Significant Differences
Relating Self-Information to Occupational Information	DMS	ECES	Controls — Significant Differences
Concern with Choice	DMS	ECES	Controls — Significant Differences
Specificity of Planning	DMS	ECES	Controls — Significant Differences
Amount of Occupational Information	DMS	ECES	Controls — Significant Differences
Extent of Information Resources Used to Explore Career Opportunities	DMS	ECES	Controls — Significant Differences
Occupational Information	DMS	ECES	Control
Integration of Knowledge & Action	DMS	ECES	Control
Certainty of Vocational Choice	DMS, 283% increase; ECES, 66% increase; Control, 12% increase		
Absenteeism	DMS, 38% reduction; ECES, 49% reduction		
Educational Planning	Significant Improvement in DMS & ECES/DMS & Counselor		
Occupational Planning	Significant Improvement in DMS & ECES/DMS & Counselor		
Developing Courses of Action	Significant Improvement in DMS & ECES/DMS & Counselor		
Self-Awareness re: Educational Goals	Significant Improvement in DMS & ECES/DMS & Counselor		
Self-Awareness re: Occupational Goals	Significant Improvement in DMS & ECES/DMS & Counselor		
Finding New Information About Careers	Significant Improvement in DMS & ECES/DMS & Counselor		
Expand Educational Alternatives	Significant Improvement in DMS & ECES/DMS & Counselor		
Identify Important Factors in Educational Decision-Making	Significant Improvement In DMS & ECES/DMS & Counselor		
Identify Important Factors in Occupational Decision-Making	Significant Improvement in DMS & ECES/DMS & Counselor		
Making Better Educational Decisions	Significant Improvement in DMS & ECES/DMS & Counselor		
Making Better Occupational Decisions	Significant Improvement in DMS & ECES/DMS & Counselor		

Planning Programs

The differential effects of decision-making skills (DMS) training and ECES II program on students.

(Friel, Carkhuff, Mallory, Drake & Tyler, 1974)

Human Planning and Working Outcomes

Quantity of Occupational Activities

Quality of Occupational Activities

Quantity of Occupational Information

Quantity of Career Information Sources

Quantity of Career Information-Seeking Questions

Quality of Occupational Classification Skills

Quantity of Occupational Alternatives Generated

Quantity of Occupational Decision-Making Skills

Quality of Occupational Decision-Making Skills

Increase in Career Planning Readiness

Choosing high school programs

Relating courses to occupations

Choosing post-high school training

Choosing post-high school institution

Choosing an occupation

Making career plans

Selecting career information

Relating personal requirements to occupations

Results

DMS ECES Controls; 10th gr. DMS 14th gr. Controls; Significant differences.

111

Planning Programs	Human Planning and Working Outcomes	Results
	Expanding occupational alternatives	
	Identifying occupational choice values	
	Identifying educational choice values	
	Making logical career decisions	
	Making logical personal decisions	
	Student Ratings of Career Planning Readiness	
	Counselor Ratings of Student Career Planning readiness	Significant Improvements
Effects of ECES & HRD counselor training on community college students (Tyler, 1972)	Attitudes Towards Career Planning	Significant Improvements
	Attitudes Towards Working with a Counselor	Significant Improvements
	Self-Awareness & Self-Questioning	Significant Improvements
	Levels of Self-Evaluation	Significant Improvements
	Career Evaluation	Significant Improvements
	Career Information Collecting Skills	Significant Improvements
	Career Information Evaluating Skills	Significant Improvements
	Career Fact Finding Skills	Significant Improvements
	Career Source Finding Skills	Significant Improvements
	Responsive Interviewing Skills	Significant Improvements
	Initiative Interviewing Skills	Significant Improvements
	Career Resource Utilization Skills	Significant Improvements
	Career & Personal Objectives	Significant Improvements

Planning Programs	Human Planning and Working Outcomes	Results
	Acquisition Skills	Significant Improvements
	Quantitative Assessment Skills	Significant Improvements
	Career Plan Development Skills	Significant Improvements
	Career Reevaluation Skills	Significant Improvements
	Reduction of Expressed Feelings of Inadequacy	Significant Improvements
	Reduction of Career Planning Confusion	Significant Improvements
Effects of HRD teacher training and career achievement skills training on students. (Friel, Berenson, Pierce, Carkhuff, Battenschlag & Rochow, 1974)	Career Expanding Skills	Significant Improvements
	Quantity of interest areas	Significant Improvements
	Quality of interest areas	Significant Improvements
	Quantity of educational levels	Significant Improvements
	Quality of educational goals	Significant Improvements
	Quality of occupational classification strategies	Significant Improvements
	Quantity of information sources	Significant Improvements
	Personalization of information sources	Significant Improvements
	Quantity of information seeking strategies	Significant Improvements
	Personalizing information seeking strategies	Significant Improvements
	Quantity of career information	Significant Improvements
	Quantity of personalized career information	Significant Improvements

113

Planning Programs	Human Planning and Working Outcomes	Results
	Quality of personalized career information	Significant Improvements
	Career Narrowing Skills	Significant Improvements
	Quantity of self-relationships	Significant Improvements
	Quality of self-relationships	Significant Improvements
	Quantity of personal values	Significant Improvements
	Quality of personal values	Significant Improvements
	Quantity of decision-making skills	Significant Improvements
	Quality of decision-making skills	Significant Improvements
	Quantity of career ladder evaluation skills	Significant Improvements
	Quality of career ladder evaluation skills	Significant Improvements
	Quality of occupational readiness skills	Significant Improvements
	Quantity of occupational readiness skills	Significant Improvements
	Career Preparation Skills	Significant Improvements
	Quantity of career route decision-making skills	Significant Improvements
	Quality of career route decision-making skills	Significant Improvements
	Quantity of job requirement skills	Significant Improvements
	Quality of job requirement skills	Significant Improvements

Planning Programs	Human Planning and Working Outcomes	Results
	Quantity of skill acquisition steps	Significant Improvements
	Quality of skill acquisition steps	Significant Improvements
	Personalizing skills acquisition steps	Significant Improvements
	Quantity of program development skills	Significant Improvements
	Personalizing program development skills	Significant Improvements
	Quantity of placement preparation skills	Significant Improvements
	Quality of placement preparation skills	Significant Improvements
	Personalizing placement preparation skills	Significant Improvements
	Quantity of placement interview skills	Significant Improvements
	Quality of placement interview skills	Significant Improvements
	Personalizing of placement interview skills	Significant Improvements
	Quantity of career reevaluation skills	Significant Improvements
	Quality of career reevaluation skills	Significant Improvements
	Personalizing career reevaluation skills	Significant Improvements

Planning Programs	Human Planning and Working Outcomes	Results
	Career Maturity	Significant Improvements
	Educational aspiration level	Significant Improvements
	Parent Involvement	Significant Improvements
	Number of discussions	Significant Improvements
	Number of parents involved	Significant Improvements
	Number of students viewed by parents as improving	Significant Improvements
	New occupational possibilities	Significant Improvements
	Getting Useful information about occupations	Significant Improvements
	Making systematic occupational choices	Significant Improvements
	Relating systematic occupational choices	Significant Improvements
	Relating values to occupations	Significant Improvements
	Relating school experiences to future plans	Significant Improvements
	Developing step-by-step programs to reach their goals	Significant Improvements
Effects of teacher level of functioning on student vocational adjustment. (Truax & Carkhuff, 1967)	Work Productivity	No significant difference
	Work Quality	Significant relationship with teacher functioning
	Work Attitude	Significant relationship with teacher functioning
	Dependability	Significant relationship with teacher functioning
	Cooperativeness	Significant relationship with teacher functioning

Planning Programs	Human Planning and Working Outcomes	Results
Effects of trained community helpers on unemployed. (Carkhuff & Griffin, 1972)	Employment	88% of graduates gainfully employed one year later.
Effects of interpersonal skills training on patients. (Vitalo, 1971)	Work Productivity	No differences
Effects of interpersonal skills training on ex-felons. (Griffin, 1973)	Gainful Employment or Education	98% gainfully employed
Effects of trained correctional officers on inmates. (Day & Methany, 1972; Day, Graddick & Methany, 1972; Hall, 1970a, 1970b, 1970c, 1974a, 1974b; McGathlin & Day, 1970, 1972)	Work Idleness Work Accidents Sick Leave Job Transfers	Reduced Significantly Reduced Significantly Reduced Significantly Reduced Significantly

117

The following illustrates how a Helper-Trainer might help a 45-year-old woman resolve an identity crisis resulting from a major family change.

Helpee: I've had a lot of experiences over the past twenty years—getting the family through those years. Well, they're on their own now ... now it's my turn and I don't know how to take advantage of it.

Helper-Teacher: You feel trapped because you only thought of others for so long.

Helpee: It's like I'm not sure of who I am ... I mean me ... myself ... not as a mother or wife ... me the person, the woman.

Helper-Teacher: It's a bit scary because you're not sure who you have become or what you can do without your family.

Helpee: I'm certain there is something more there ... but I'm not sure what I can do that's useful ... unique and, well, that reflects who I am. I had the same problem when I got married ... in a way I could not give myself fully to the family or marriage until I was sure my husband was certain about what and where he was going.

Helper-Teacher: You feel alone because this time you must get your goals from inside and you're a bit anxious about what, if anything, you are going to find.

Helpee: I have plenty left to give but I'm not sure what except that I can't go back to doing what I did before I got married. I was a nurse. I guess I should start there ... but I'm so out of it I'd be afraid to go back to work ... besides I'd like something different.

Helper-Teacher: It's sort of exciting to start all over again but it also makes you nervous because you don't know where to go from here. We need to expand your alternatives in terms of what is important to you, then we can work at narrowing the choices and developing strategies to prepare for a new career.

Helpee: I think I know what interests me but I don't know what it adds up to ... except I enjoyed my kids.

**Helper-
Teacher:** Our first objective then will involve expanding possible alternatives ... let's start with careers that involve people ....

All of these outcomes—the living, learning and working outcomes that define physical, emotional and intellectual resource development—converge to define our goals for our helpee-learners in the learning process. We know what we want our learner products to look like.

We have made and achieved our value judgments. We have defined and developed the PEI programs. We have operationalized these skill programs in ways that facilitate HRD. It remains for us to operationalize the process by which our learners learn to achieve these outcomes.

References

Aspy, D. N. The effect of teacher-offered conditions of empathy, congruence, and positive regard upon student achievement. **Florida Journal of Educational Research**, 1969, **11**, 39-48.

Aspy, D. N. and Hadlock, W. The effects of high and low functioning teachers upon student performance. In R. R. Carkhuff, **Beyond Counseling and Therapy.** New York: Holt, Rinehart and Winston, 1967.

Aspy, D. N. and Roebuck, F. N. An investigation of the relationship between levels of cognitive functioning and the teacher's classroom behavior. **Journal of Educational Research.** May, 1972.

Aspy, D. N. and Roebuck, F. N. **Humanizing education.** Summary Report, Monroe, Louisiana, 1973.

Banks, G., Berenson, B. G. and Carkhuff, R. R. The effects of counselor race and training upon counseling process with Negro clients in initial interviews. **Journal of Clinical Psychology,** 1967, **23**, 70-72.

Berenson, D. H. The effects of systematic human relations training upon the classroom performance of elementary school teachers. **Journal of Research and Development in Education,** 1971, **4**, 70-85.

Berenson, D. H. A follow-up study of the effects of interpersonal training upon student achievement. Mimeographed manuscript, Western Connecticut University, 1972.

Berenson, D. H. Effects of trained Urban League teachers on learning to learn skills training on students. Progress Report, Springfield, Massachusetts, 1974.

Berenson, D. H.,
Berenson, S. R.
and
Griffin, A. H.
Effects of trained teachers, community helpers and learning to learn skills training on students. Progress Report, Springfield, Massachusetts, 1974.

Carkhuff, R. R.
Helping and human relations. New York: Holt, Rinehart and Winston, 1969.

Carkhuff, R. R.
The development of human resources. New York: Holt, Rinehart and Winston, 1971.

Carkhuff, R. R.
The art of helping. Amherst, Mass.: Human Resource Development Press, 1972.

Carkhuff, R. R.
How to help yourself. Amherst, Mass.: Human Resource Development Press, 1974.

Carkhuff, R. R.
Everything is education. Amherst, Mass.: Human Resource Development Press, 1976.

Carkhuff, R. R.,
(Ed.);
Berenson, B. G.,
Griffin, A. H.,
Devine, J.,
Angelone, R.,
Clinton, W.,
Keeling, T.,
Muth, E.,
Patch, W.,
Steinberg, H.
Cry Twice! From Custody to Treatment: The Story of Institutional Change. Amherst, Mass.: Human Resource Development Press, 1974.

Carkhuff, R. R.
and Alexik, M.
The effects of the manipulation of client depth of self-exploration upon high and low functioning counselors. **Journal of Clinical Psychology,** 1967, **23,** 210-212.

Carkhuff, R. R.,
Banks, G.,
Berenson, B. G.,
Griffin, A. H. and
Hall, R.
The selection and training of correctional counselors on physical, emotional and intellectual indexes. **Journal of Counseling Psychology,** 1971, **18.**

Carkhuff, R. R. and Berenson, D. H. **The art of teaching series.** Amherst, Mass.: Human Resource Development Press, 1976.

Carkhuff, R. R. and Bierman, R. Training as a preferred mode of treatment of parents of emotionally disturbed children. **Journal of Counseling Psychology.** 1970, **17,** 157-161.

Carkhuff, R. R., Friel, T., Berenson, B. G., Bebermeyer, J., Mahrt, J. and Forrest, D. The differential effects of systematic computer and human relations training. **People, Programs, and Organizations.** Amherst, Mass: Human Resource Development Press, 1972,

Carkhuff, R. R. and Griffin, A. H. The selection and training of human relations specialists. **Journal of Counseling Psychology,** 1970, **17,** 443-445.

Carkhuff, R. R. and Griffin, A. H. The selection and training of functional professionals for Concentrated Employment Programs. **Journal of Clinical Psychology,** 1971, **27,** 163-165.

Carkhuff, R. R. and Pierce, R. Differential effects of therapist race and social class upon patient depth of self-exploration in the initial client interview. **Journal of Counseling Psychology,** 1967, **31,** 632-634.

Carkhuff, R. R. and Pierce, R. Training teachers and parents to support student learning. Progress Report, Springfield, Massachusetts, 1974.

Collingwood, T. **Get fit for living.** Amherst, Mass.: Human Resource Development Press, 1976.

Day, S. R., Graddick, R. R., and Matheny, K. B. Inmate change as a result of human relations training for non-professional correctional personnel. **Canadian Journal of Corrections,** 1972.

122

Day, S. R. and Matheny, K. B.   Human relations program for non-professional personnel in correctional setting. **Journal of Corrections,** 1972.

Devine, J. P. and Steinberg, H.   **Kalamazoo County Jail Rehabilitation Program,** Progress Report, Kalamazoo, Michigan, 1974.

Friel, T. W., Drake, J. W., Mallory, A. E., Jr., Tyler, N.   Four articles on the delivery of career decision-making skills to students. **Michigan Personnal and Guidance Journal.** Vol. IV, No. 1, Fall, 1972 and Vol. V, No. 1, Fall, 1973.

Friel, T., et al.   The differential effects of decision-making skills training and ECES II program on students. **Michigan Personnel and Guidance Journal.** Fall, 1974.

Griffin, A. H., in Mosher, R. L. and Sprinthall, N. A.   Psychological education: A means to promote personal development during adolescence. **The Counseling Psychologist,** 1971, 2(4), 3-84.

Griffin, J.   **Home-Based programs.** Final Report, Springfield, Massachusetts, 1973.

Hall, R. H.   **Atlanta Correctional and Industrial Counseling: First Annual Report.** Washington, D. C.: Federal Bureau of Prisons, 1970a.

Hall, R. H.   **Institute in Correctional Counseling: Brief Report.** Washington, D. C.: Federal Bureau of Prisons, 1970b.

Hall, R. H.   **Ninety-day follow-up on institutes in correctional counseling.** Washington, D. C.: Federal Bureau of Prisons, 1970c.

Hall, R. H.   **Superintendent's Budget Statement.** North Dakota Senate Appropriations Committee Hearing, 1974a.

Hall, R. H.   New "skills" system at SIS. **Care and Counsel.** North Dakota Social Service Report, pp. 8-13, August, 1974b.

Hershberg, F., Carkhuff, R. R. and Berenson, B.G. The differential effectiveness of counselors and therapists with inpatient schizophrenics and counseling center clients, in **Beyond Counseling and Therapy.** New York: Holt, Rinehart & Winston, 1967.

Holder, T., Carkhuff, R. R. and Berenson, B. G. The differential effects of the manipulation of therapeutic conditions upon high and low functioning clients. **Journal of Counseling Psychology.** 1967, **14,** 63-66.

Kratochvil, D. W., Carkhuff, R. R. and Berenson, B. G. Cumulative effects of parent and teacher offered levels of facilitative conditions upon indices of student physical, emotional and intellectual functioning. **Journal of Educational Research,** 1969, **63,** 161-164.

McGathlin, W. and Day, S. The effects of systematic training for correctional counselors. **American Journal of Corrections,** 1970.

McGathlin, W. and Porter, T. **The effects of facilitative training provided correctional officers stationed at the Atlanta Federal Penitentiary.** Washington, D. C.: U. S. Justice Department, 1969.

McGathlin, W. and Day, S. R. Facilitation training: An experiment with adult correctional officers. **American Journal of Corrections,** 1972.

Mickelson, D. J. and Stevic, R. R. Differential effects of facilitative and non-facilitative behavioral counselors. **Journal of Counseling Psychology,** 1971, **18,** 314-319.

Montgomery, C. Federal Bureau of Prisons Training Program. Manuscript, Seagoville, Texas, 1974.

Myers, R. A., Thompson, A. S., Lindeman, R. H., Super, D. E., Patrick, T. A. and Friel, T. W. **The education and career exploration system: Report of a 2-year field trial.** Teachers College, Columbia University, New York, New York, 1972.

Pagell, W., Carkhuff, R. R. and Berenson, B. G. The predicted differential effects of the level of counselor functioning upon the level of functioning of outpatients. **Journal of Clinical Psychology,** 1967, **23,** 510-512.

Piaget, G., Carkhuff, R. R. and Berenson, B. G. The development of skills in interpersonal functioning. **Counselor Education and Supervision,** 1968, **2,** 102-106.

Pierce, R. M., Carkhuff, R. R. and Berenson, B. G. The differential effects of high and low functioning counselors upon counselors-in-training. **Journal of Clinical Psychology,** 1967, **23,** 212-215.

Pierce, R. M. and Drasgow, J. Teaching facilitative interpersonal functioning to psychiatric inpatients. **Journal of Counseling Psychology,** 1969, **16,** 295-298.

Pierce, R. M. and Schauble, P. Graduate training of facilitative counselors: The effects of individual supervision. **Journal of Counseling Psychology,** 1970, **17,** 210-215.

Roebuck, F. N. and Aspy, D. N. **Humanizing education.** Progress Report, Monroe, Louisiana, 1973.

Stofer, D. L. Investigation of positive behavioral change as a function of genuineness, non-possessive warmth and empathic understanding. **Journal of Educational Research,** 1970, **63.**

Super, D., et al **Columbia University report on field trial of ECES I program.** Columbia University, New York, 1970.

Truax, C. B. and Carkhuff, R. R.	**Toward effective counseling and psychotherapy.** Chicago: Aldine, 1967.
Truax, C. B. and Tatum, C. R.	An extension from the effective psychotherapeutic model to constructive personality change in preschool children. **Childhood Education,** 1966, **42,** 456-462.
Tyler, N.	Effects of ECES and HRD counselor training on community college students. **Michigan Personnel and Guidance Journal,** Fall, 1972.
Vitalo, R.	Teaching improved interpersonal functioning as a preferred mode of treatment. **Journal of Clinical Psychology,** 1971, **27,** 166-171.

Chapter Seven

EUA:
The Learning Process

	P	E	I
E			
U			
A			

In implementing the program of group training as a preferred mode of treatment, we realized that the helpee-learners went through the same phases of learning that the child goes through in the classroom—indeed, the same phases that the human goes through in life. There is a phase where they need to explore their personal experience of their worlds and the people in them. They do this so that they can understand their experience; their understanding in turn, enables them to act upon their experience.

In exploring their experience of where they are in their worlds, the helpee-learners want the assurance that someone is with them, that someone can really hear them. The following excerpt illustrates an early phase of exploration from group training of parents as a preferred mode of treating emotionally disturbed children. In other words, we were teaching parents how to rear their own children (Carkhuff, 1969).

Bill: You take two ... no ten people trying to understand what is going on in their kids' heads and you'll get ten things that don't reflect what is in the kids' heads. We could talk all night and we won't know what the kids are thinking ... we could only guess. If you knew what they were thinking then you'd know how to cope.... You'd know what to do about it ... but we don't.

Helper-
Teacher: You're at a loss because you can't tune in.

Bill: Ya, well ... sometimes they go their way ... I go mine ... we argue about pros and cons but ... they don't listen.

Helper-
Teacher: You feel bad because you can't get the kids to listen ... like you're not important to them anymore.

Bill: It makes me wonder sometimes ... it gets you down ... you can't do your job as a father if they don't listen. I get pretty mad sometimes. I remember what it was like to be a kid ... but it don't help me get through ... I know this, that no kid of mine is going to write me off.

Helper-
Teacher: You're determined to make a difference but you don't know how so you're left with your frustration and anger.

Bill: You wonder what to really say to them ... it really gets to you ... gets you down ... I can get really low ... and you wonder.

Helper-
Teacher: You wonder if you can ever get up again and if anyone ... or if I can ever really understand how low a black man can feel.

Bill: That's it ... you make up things to tell your children ... I can't say what you can say to your kids. Your child can dream. Can mine dream?

Helper-
Teacher: It makes you furious because you want to make sure they have an even break but you can't give them that.

One of the members of the group explores a concern with the parent of the parents' group, the helper-teacher. The helpee-learner poses the question in terms of whether any parent could ever understand a child. In

128

terms of immediacy, the helper-teacher answers the question by understanding the helpee-learner. The teacher helps the learner to know that the learner as parent may come to understand his child by helping the learner to know that the teacher can understand the learner. The teacher would be unable to do this if he did not assume the reins as parent of the parents' group and thus provide a model for the learners to assume the reins as parents of their family groups. The teacher would also be unable to understand the learner if he did not accept, at the deepest level, that he could never be black and see the world as a black man. In turn, the parent can understand the child only if he accepts, at the deepest level, that he cannot be a child and see the world as a child.

In group training, the helpee-learners have an opportunity not just to explore where they are but also to understand where they are in relation to where they want to be. Group training provides an opportunity for this in the role-playing practice and feedback. The following excerpt offers an illustration of the understanding phase within the parental group training experience.

Stan: I try to get along with him ... but sometimes ... most often he acts like he never even heard of me ... I think ... well I don't like to sit on him too hard but, well, he needs a heavy hand sometimes ... I just won't take any back talk from him. I tell him what to do ... something simple and he never hears me.... As soon as I think I know where he is at he changes....

Irene: You feel hurt because you can't seem to help him....

Stan: Ya, but ... more like....

Irene: More like angry with yourself because you don't know what to do.

Stan: I've just about lost my head ... he does the opposite of what I expected him ... and it really burns me that a kid of eight defies me ... dares to defy me....

Irene: You're bewildered because you don't understand it and he is your son.

Stan: I can't quite reach him. Like a radio. You know he hears you ... you can tell by the expression on his face that he's listening, but then you say it the second time and he'll say "What?" as though he never heard the expression before. Boy, that sends me right up a....

Irene: You get furious because he shuts you out.

Stan: Yes.

Irene: And then he does it all the more and you get more angry with him and yourself.

Stan: Yes, well, I don't know whether he really enjoys it. He usually has sort of a chagrin attitude afterwards. It's like he did something wrong ... not enjoying it ... but he did do something wrong. Just putting it in perspective ... like we even said tonight ... that's negative attention. But I never looked at it that way before. All I know is I can't quite reach him.

Irene: You feel helpless ... because you can't even get help to understand him.

Stan: Yeah, but what I don't understand is that he seems to enjoy it so much when he's "normal," in other words you might say, "Going on an even keel or having a good time." Why he goes the other route and then has that real sad attitude about him ... even while he's doing it, even while he's being defiant ... this I don't get. But if you never experience going off and having a good time I could see the sadness here ... his more or less deliberate agitation ... and yet there are times when the only identity he does have are good, happy feelings and happy attitudes about ... I just can't....

Helper-Teacher:	O.K. Tom? Let's have your rating.
Tom:	I say a 3.
Mary:	I say 2.5.
Ann:	I'd say 3 plus.
Karen:	2.5.
Joe:	3.
Bill:	I said 3, too.
Jane:	I said 3.
Helper-Teacher:	There were some real good things ... Stan?
Stan:	She had part of it, a lot of it.
Helper-Teacher:	It's almost like, "If we continue this way we'll never really get to anything." One of the ... go ahead.
Stan:	That's it. I was just going to say that about wraps it up ... start down a path and it looks pretty good then all of a sudden you're on a detour again or you still don't know what to do.
Helper-Teacher:	It's still frustrating because you still don't know or understand.
Stan:	You come along with the encouraging sign and then when it's cut out from under you, you're still up in the air.
Bill:	I think we've got to the point ... we've reached the point where we can hear the big guns going off. It's actually reality and we have to realize it is reality. In order to do something about it you got to get down to the nitty gritty. That's where we are now, and that's why each one's got their own thoughts and they're thinking about just what path am I going to take and what would be the best solution for me. I know we're all working in a group, but at the same time ... but I think even with us working in

a group and each taking a little part of others' hardship and all we still, within ourselves, we feel that our own little problem should get settled and which is the best way to settle it.

Helper-Teacher: You feel certain about where you are and the others in the group but you are not sure about where you need to be.

Stan: Yes ... we need ... each of us ... goals for each of our situations. I need to learn how to listen to what my boy is saying ... and ... well, Bill needs to be more honest about being Black and what it means to his kid.

Helper-Teacher: Great ... Stan your goal is listening and in order to do that you need to learn how to attend to and observe your son. Bill, your goal is helping your children to personalize their experiences.

Understanding the children, the parents also learn to understand themselves. Their own direction is based upon this understanding. In the same way, the helper-teacher's direction is based upon her or his understanding of individual group members. Too often the children's problems are a function of rigid behavioral patterns on the part of the parents, whether these patterns are authoritarian or permissive. When the parents search desperately to understand the source of their children's difficulties, they often abdicate many of their responsibilities as adults with meaningful direction in their lives. Under the trainer's guidance, they return again to find themselves and their own direction and, in so doing, find their relationships with their children.

Finally, in group training as in all learning, the helpee-learners have an opportunity to act upon their understanding. They prepare to act to get from where they are to where they want to be. The following excerpt offers an illustration of the action phase within the parental group training experience:

Tom: Talking about what I'm going to do ... you know ... trying something. Really getting my thoughts together and really ... you know ... setting up a program, getting guidelines to follow and go through with it and once and for all make up my mind....

Mary: ... make up your mind as a man what direction your life is going to take ... yours and ours.

Tom: ... the family's, let me stand on my own two feet and if I fall, I fall. Let me get up by myself, if I can get up.

Mary: Let you do it alone. You are determined to make it because it means you can do what you need to do ... help your family.

Tom: Yeah. To make a lot of decisions on my own and if at times you think I'm going way out ... that this is another one of my flings ... this is where you'll probably maybe have to help me ... you know ... try to tell me or remind me or what.

Mary: You want to stand on your own, but in a sense you want to know that I'm there to help you when you fall or if you should fall.

Tom: If I'm that blind that I'm going to be making the same mistakes and you think that I'm so blind I can't see I'm making the same mistakes ... to maybe ... you know, just talk things over, but the main thing is that I want to succeed in something.

Mary: You feel insecure because what you try may not come off.

Tom: Well, I'm trying to think of what I actually could do and do fairly well.

Mary: And you want to be certain that it's all your's....

Tom: That is my own, my own ideas. It's going to be a lot of work, but this is the type of work that I like, and once I get involved in something like this that's when I ... I'm afraid I'll be so involved in my work ... or involved in this ... that I'll be passing the buck off to you as far as the kids are concerned or something like that. In other words, I'll be gone, come home, be gone. I'll have to try to work something out so that I'll be home sometimes.

Mary: It is something you do enjoy and you want to try it, but can you take it?

Tom: Yeah, because I've been passing the buck on to you as far as almost every other thing goes ... see like as far as disciplining the kids now ... unless I can work it out until I can be home more often, be a father to them, give them the discipline if they need it, plus go whole-hearted ... put my best self forward ... in this particular project....

Mary: You do want very much to try it, but at the same time you're afraid of what it's going to do to us at home because you can foresee what can happen and the time that it will involve, and this scares you because, "Can I take it?" and, "Can the kids take it?" And where do you stand then in the picture?

Tom: If the same things are going to arise, I don't see where ... whether I succeed in this, as something I want to do ... the real purpose is succeeding in solving our problems at home, making our own home happier.

Mary: You feel determined to resolve this within yourself, and we'll come along. Like you say, "Give me a chance."

Tom: I'm giving myself the chance, but what chance am I giving you?

Mary: Well, give me a chance to see what I can do, and I think we can both work together.

Tom: That's it ... if we can both work together and still keep harmony in the home ... that any progress we made with Tim or any of them keeps progressing instead or all of a sudden stops because Daddy's being selfish again or self-centered. The first thing we must do is listen and really respond before acting.

Mary: And I told you that I wanted you to take your chance and use it. At the same time, it does scare me. There is some uncertainty in not knowing what the future holds or what will come of it but like you say if we respond to each other ... understand ... like we are doing now!

Tom: I guess nobody really knows what the future holds. I guess that's what makes up keep going. If we knew, maybe we wouldn't want to go but we can control it more if we plan our actions.

Mary: That's true, but what I meant was from a woman's viewpoint. A man kind of looks at it with the uncertainty of his job and where it will lead to, where a woman ... I look at it ... well, I want you to take it ... that it is uncertain for me. I know there will be a lot of times where I'll come across problems, but I feel that I can handle them if I know that you have really found your way in life ... that as long as you're happy, I can be happy. I can find my way.

Tom: You feel certain this is really what would make you happy because....

Mary: ... many times I might ... I want what you want. Certainly I'm thinking of the welfare of the children, but I feel that it all rests ... not all ... but that it will all work out if you find some area where you have found yourself.

Tom: I don't know if I can even accomplish this one feat ... but I think that it'll give me more

135

confidence in myself. I'd be solving some problems of my own that you're not there to help me with as far as ... you know ... the dimensions of a room or something like that. I'll be on my own.

Mary: It'll be something that would be just yours and you can be proud.

Tom: Yeah. And if I really have it or not in this field here ... I mean if I have the potential ... the basis to go on and learn more, do better. With the understanding that Beth and Ted have I'm sure that if I botched up the whole job I don't even know if they would really say so, but I would know if I did or not ... you know ... if I did botch it up and didn't say anything to them, I still think they would say it was lovely or beautiful.

Mary: In other words, no matter what you did, they wouldn't really hold you accountable, but you would hold yourself accountable.

Tom: Because I would know.

Mary: And you feel better because this is a good starting place.

Tom: ... maybe it's a crutch or whatever you want to call it ... maybe on second thought it wouldn't be too good because I'd be giving myself a false confidence, but I think, though, that I would really know if this was something ... you know ... when I got finished with it if I had really put forth my best efforts and even if they weren't really pleased with it at least I could say I did my best....

Mary: You'd feel strong because you did it.

Tom: ... and I know that this is out and from there we can maybe go on to something else. Even so, I think it has a way of letting me be out in front.

Mary: All alone, in a sense.

Tom: Yeah.

Mary: And at the same time, like I said, I know there will probably be many times when I feel I could use you at home, and these are perhaps the times when I may be tired, but you know me ... you should know me ... that I don't always mean what I say ... sometimes I strike out in anger, and when I stop to think about it I want what's right and what's good.

Tom: Right. But at the same time, while you're doing this you're trying to tell me something. You know, "Hey, I'm here too!" Right?

Mary: At the moment, Tom ... at the moment, maybe. Yeah.

Tom: Even though, even at the moment ... even at that moment sometimes I don't even recognize that you're calling for help ... not help but recognition.

Mary: But if the moments that you have perhaps to give me ... if they're fruitful ... I can get through the rest. Do you hear what I'm telling you? If when you are home and with us and you give us what you're capable of ... and me ... perhaps I'm not putting that....

Tom: In other words, when I am there if I do do my duties, so to speak, as a father and as a husband ... that I do recognize these symptoms. If I can, no matter how short or how long they may be that this would take a ... you know ... not a burden, but it would help your ego too? Or....

Mary: Well, no, not my ego, but help take some of the load off my shoulders, perhaps, because even last night, now, when I had so much to do yesterday and had to take the boys out last night ... even just your offering to do up the dishes with Cindy ... hey, that was a big thing! It was a small thing maybe to you, and you felt maybe you didn't complete it because you didn't know where all the dishes

	went, but this was a big thing to me.
Tom:	You really appreciated it!!!
Mary:	I really appreciated it. These are the small things that I'm talking about that when you are at home and are rested and the children are there ... there's not only one parent in the house, they don't always have to go to Mommy. Hey, I wish that they'd come to you more, and if you took an active part in it, I feel that they would.
Tom:	In other words you really don't feel I ... lately, anyway ... have been taking enough active part in the family?
Mary:	Well, sometimes you tend to let me handle it, but maybe there again I start to take it away from you or something when you do. I mean I've been trying to let you handle some of it, but when they holler or do something, even if they yell, "Mommy," if you went and....
Tom:	...found out what they're yelling, "Mommy" for?
Mary:	...asserted yourself. Right. I'm not saying all the time, because I know there are many times when you come home and you'll be tired, but a lot of times I guess a woman just hates to say to her husband, "I will never make it in 45 minutes if you don't do the dishes. Will you do dishes?" And I guess she just kind of expects him to....
Tom:	...to say, "I volunteer, I'll do them."

The husband and wife are no longer role-playing. They are dealing with very real problems which they have flipped over to become goals. And they are doing so with fine and sensitive communication. They are able to share their fullest experiences. They are able to take directionful action based upon all they have shared and understood. They have practiced the things that will make a constructive difference in their lives so that they, in turn, can make a constructive difference in the lives of those they love.

There are two basic ways that people learn (Carkhuff, 1971). Each way involves developing new behavior.

The first way may be called the insight-action approach. The second may be called the action-insight approach. In the former the behavior follows understanding, while in the latter, the understanding serves to consolidate behavior.

Insight-Action

Within the insight-action approach, there are several sources of learning that are familiar to us. Among these are the expectations that the helper or teacher has for the growth of the learner. Expectations on the part of the people who are important to us lead to learner behavior that is congruent with the expectancies: high expectations promote high functioning and low expectations promote low functioning.

We all know the story of the rats, drawn from the same litter, who performed differentially according to the expectancies of the experimenters who were informed that one group of rats was bright and the other group was dull. Children and adults perform in a similar fashion according to the expectancies that people who are important to them have for their performances.

Obviously, there is a sometimes subtle, sometimes not so subtle influencing process going on where the important people set up the conditions for one group to succeed and for another to fail. Few know the story of the city rats who did not run the maze but, instead, ate through the walls to get to the cheese. In addition to upsetting generations of experimental psychologists, these city rats make the contrasting point: where expectancies have not been transferred or where expectancies as we know them do not exist, the subjects do not necessarily perform in accordance with the expectancies.

Another source of learning within the insight-action

approach is participation. Participation in the learning or decision-making process by the learner tends to increase learner motivation and personal satisfaction with learning, although it does not necessarily improve performance. Thus, over time, the learner will tend to approach rather than avoid the learning situation.

The failure of many social action programs has been their inability to involve the recipient populations from the beginning in assessing their own needs and establishing their own goals. Part way through the program, we wonder where all the people went when they were never there psychologically in the first place.

But the heart of the insight-action approach is the development of insight as a discriminative stimulus which increases the probability that related behaviors will occur. However, the learner's ability to commit himself or herself to act is contingent upon the development of systematic action programs that flow from the insight.

While the insight-action approach has been questioned in terms of its therapeutic utility, it has never really been tested because the insights are not systematically developed, with each new understanding built carefully upon all previous understanding, thus increasing the probability of producing an insight that the learner can act upon.

Action-Insight

Within the action-insight approach, there are also several sources of learning. Perhaps the most critical source of learning is modeling and imitation.

People learn by imitating or emulating the important role models in their environment. Again, the more systematically the helper or teacher "shows" or models the behavior to be learned or imitated, the more efficiently and effectively the learner learns.

Most of a child's behavior is imitative of the adults and older children in his or her environment. The problem is that the behavior which is imitated is not necessarily that which most directly promotes human resource development.

The heart of the action-insight approach involves the use of reinforcements to shape and support the learning of new behaviors. Reinforcements simply emphasize a system of rewards and punishments in which constructive or goal-directed behaviors are rewarded, destructive or goal-avoidance behaviors are punished and apparently neutral behaviors are observed vigilantly in order to determine whether the behaviors are constructive or destructive. In regard to the function of vigilance, all behavior ultimately moves the learner toward or away from the learning goal.

Again, the use of reinforcements is seen most vividly in child-rearing procedures. Whether consciously or unconsciously, the parents reinforce the children's behavior by a system of rewards and punishments. The problem is that they do not always necessarily reinforce constructive behavior.

Unfortunately, just as the insight-action approach tends to develop neither the insights nor the action programs systematically, so the action-insight approach does not always tend to systematically consolidate the learning of the action behavior with the necessary insights. Thus the discriminative stumulus necessary for the production of future behavior is not available to the learner.

The Phases of Learning

In practice, these two approaches, the insight-action and the action-insight approaches, are part of the same on-going learning process. In a very real sense, it does not matter whether we begin with one—insight or action —so long as we continue with the other. In a larger respect, each leads to the other—insight to action and action to insight—in a never-ending cycle of learning (Carkhuff, 1976). In this context, let us take a more detailed look at the phases of learning.

Learning is reflected in some kind of observable and measurable behavior (see Figure 7-1). This means that the learner acts in some way to demonstrate a significant change or gain in his or her behavior. In other words, outcome = action = behavior.

CONSTRUCTIVE ACTION OR BEHAVIOR
(Outcome)

LEARNER

Outcome means that the learner has acted to demonstrate a significant change or gain in her behavior.

Figure 7-1

Whether we begin with the "shaping" of this behavior or with the insight or understanding which leads to the behavior is not critical. What is critical is that the learner learns to make the discriminations necessary to act effectively in the future (see Figure 7-2). In this case, we have portrayed an accurate understanding of his or her world as the mediating process necessary for the learner to act predictably.

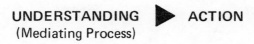

UNDERSTANDING ▶ **ACTION**
(Mediating Process)

LEARNER

In order to act predictably the learner must have an accurate understanding of her world.

Figure 7-2

Finally, whether it follows the action behavior or precedes the understanding, the learner must at some point explore his or her experience of the world (see Figure 7-3). If the learner is being introduced to learning, then she must initiate the process with an exploration of the experience. If the learner has acted to demonstrate behavior, then she must explore the learnings from that action.

EXPERIENTIAL EXPLORATION　▶　UNDERSTANDING　▶　　ACTION
(Initiating Process)

In order to understand her world the learner must have explored her experience of the world.

Figure 7-3

In this regard, the phases of learning are recycled (see Figure 7-4). The feedback from action behavior stimulates further exploration which facilitates more accurate understanding and, ultimately, more effective action or improved outcome.

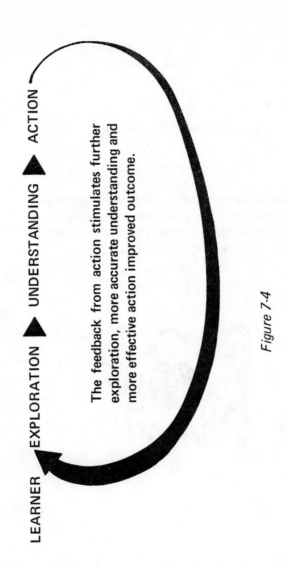

LEARNER ► EXPLORATION ▲ UNDERSTANDING ▲ ACTION

The feedback from action stimulates further exploration, more accurate understanding and more effective action improved outcome.

Figure 7-4

Viewed from the beginning, then, (see Figure 7-5), in order to demonstrate constructive outcome, the learner must first explore **where she is** in relation to herself, her world and significant others in it, including the teacher, as well as any learning materials or experiences with which she is presented.

I

LEARNER EXPLORING

where she is

In order to demonstrate constructive outcome the learner must first explore where she is in relation to herself, her world and significant others in it, and learning materials.

Figure 7-5

The purpose of exploration is understanding (see Figure 7-6). The learner explores where she is in order to understand **where she is in relation to where she wants or needs to be** in her world.

II

▶UNDERSTANDING

where she is in relation
to where she wants to be

**In order to demonstrate constructive outcome
the learner must use her exploration to understand where she is in relation to where she
wants or needs to be.**

Figure 7-6

Finally, the purpose of understanding is action (see
Figure 7-7). The learner understands herself in relation
to her world so that she can **act to get from where she is
to where she wants to be.** This action behavior is the
outcome of learning.

III

ACTION

**to get from where she is
to where she wants to be**

**In order to demonstrate constructive outcome
the learner must use her understanding to act
to get from where she is to where she wants
or needs to be.**

Figure 7-7

It is important to understand that there are many
learning activities that are subsumed within these phases
of learning (see Figure 7-8). Within the exploration
phase are included the physical attending, observing,
listening and analysis skills in which a learner must
engage in order to explore where he or she is. The
understanding phase involves the learner activities of
association, comparison, contrasting, classification and
generalization in order for the learner to understand
where he or she is in relation to where he or she wants
or needs to be. The action phase incorporates the
learner activities of problem-solving and decision-making,
convergent thinking, program development and implementation and evaluation.

Phases of Learning

Learner	I **Exploring**	II **Understanding**	III Acting
	Analysis	Generalization	Evaluation
	Listening	Classification	Program Development
	Observing	Comparing & Contrasting	Convergence
	Attending	Association	Decision-Making

Figure 7-8. The phases of learning incorporate many categories of learning activities.

Again, whether we begin with exploration, understanding or action, the cycle of learning continues (see Figure 7-9). The action outcomes stimulate a more exacting exploration of where the learner is now as a consequence of having acted; the exploration facilitates new and/or more accurate understanding of where the learner is in relation to where the learner now wants or needs to be; the understanding sets the stage for new and/or more effective action to get from where he or she is to where he or she wants or needs to be, and so on.

In summary, the phases of exploration, understanding and action constitute the process by which we achieve our living, learning and working outcomes for our learner product. In other words, learners who are learning skills that conclude in living, learning and working outcomes are constantly recycling through the phases of learning, learning more and more refined and higher and higher levels of skills.

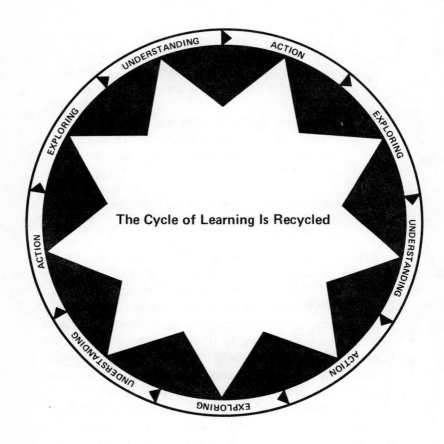

The Cycle of Learning Is Recycled

Figure 7-9

Exploration, understanding and action constitute the phases of learning. Recycled, they constitute the phases of growing or for the growing individual, the phases of life.

150

References

Carkhuff, R. R.   **Helping and human relations. Vol. I.
                   Selection and training.** New York:
                   Holt, Rinehart & Winston, 1969.
Carkhuff, R. R.   **The development of human resources.**
                   New York: Holt, Rinehart & Winston,
                   1971.
Carkhuff, R. R.   **Toward   excellence   in   education.**
(Ed.)   Amherst, Mass.: Human Resource De-
                   velopment Press, in press, 1976.

Chapter Eight

LLW:
The Teaching Skills

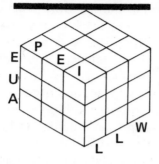

Man's cardinal rule is that no one can have more than he himself can have. The therapist who has not chosen life himself cannot enable another to choose life. He cannot recognize the life and death urgency of the choices confronting his clients, his students and, indeed, his own children.

When we conducted a series of studies to understand the effect of the helper's level of functioning upon the helpee's level of development both inside and outside of the helping process, we came to some very important conclusions about the helper's skills. We found that the helpee moved as the helper moved: higher with high-functioning helpers; lower with low-functioning helpers.

The low-functioning counselors function in counseling as they do in their lives; they emphasize the irrelevant roles and impersonal aspects of human functioning; **they ignore the fabric of life, woven from the threads of human crises.**

Below is a composite description of helpers functioning at different levels compiled by one of the helpee-subjects in one of our studies (Carkhuff and Berenson, 1976). The first is a description of the type of low-functioning behavior which is to be avoided at all costs.

A composite of the low-rated therapist shows an unimaginative, uncreative, boring and pedestrian person. He performed his

152

function in a mechanical, perfunctory manner, never expressing any emotion, and he didn't respond to the feelings I expressed. The tenacity of these therapists **not** to get involved with anything human was frightening. He seemed to be comfortable only in a safe, neutral range. This often was evidenced by the questions asked—detailed information communicating surface values such as societal status, financial means and other unimportant details. His questions didn't communicate respect. One showed a complete lack of concern for me until his questions revealed my financial status. Then his voice showed life for the first time as if then I was worth paying attention to. I was really disgusted.

With more frequency than I found tolerable, there was a lot of sick kind of giggling and I didn't think my problem was all that funny, (and I know that he did not understand the experimental purposes of my session). I struggled desperately to get something out of him and couldn't. I could handle him on his level but I couldn't bring him up to mine. My lack of respect for him showed in my responses to his questions. During the middle section I found it not only easy but sadistically pleasurable to manipulate him, for within the first five minutes I found myself unable to feel any respect for him. I felt most comfortable talking chit-chat with these people as opposed to the internal struggle experienced with the more facilitative therapists.

His "blah" voice and lack of reaction dragged me down. I couldn't reach out and grab anything because it's just a mask with words coming out. He made me feel as if I, as a client, was some kind of animal, and he couldn't go down to the client's feelings or he'd just get soiled. What he was really saying to me was "I am worthless, empty, sterile, nothing, only I have learned to keep this from the world and you. In intimacy with you, you bring me back to who I really am and you get me dirty again."

I knew this ineffectual didn't know and couldn't ever know me. I would have erased him from my memory except for purposes of this study, as an interesting example of destructive therapy. I invariably left depressed from sessions with these people.

Even the helper who is functioning at so-called moderate levels is not helpful. He can only help another to continue as he does, benignly and innocuously, slowly weaving his way through the maze of conformity, always neutralizing the efforts of others as well as his own.

Below is a composite description of the moderate-functioning helper. Many of you will find yourselves here.

A composite picture of the therapist who was neither facilitator nor retarder gives no vitality or life. He accepts weakness where I keep trying to show my strength. He is so depressed in manner and voice that I need to cheer him up. His technique is to let you know he's weak and can't help. He's very polite and so sorry but he has his own needs, so that you end up feeling compassion and start working around his needs. The dominant feeling the client goes away with is that this guy must be left unhurt and unharmed so you have to be very careful and not get into anything that might disturb his equilibrium. He tunes in on your strength and asks you for it.

There are lots of quips and smiles to show what a great guy or gal the therapist is. He asks many factual questions, shallow, bright but often leading to obtuse answers. He laughs too much. I say I'm practically psychotic over this picture and he laughs. He is happy during the middle section when he can talk superficially about himself. It's the middle part when I'm tapping in on who the therapist really is. He can be active now. He thinks I'm bringing the focus on him and he thinks I deserve something from him. I stirred up a reservoir of guilt for not acting before. As soon as he spills some shallow emotion, he is able to maintaih his former equilibrium, the only place where he feels safe.

The middle range people can listen with a bare minimum of respect and make some effort to treat you as a kind of human, but they are unable to carry you for any length of time and usually find a way to get you to carry them. Often these people can sympathize and give you the feeling that we're just two frail people huddled together in this cruel, cold world and I'll comfort you and you comfort me and somehow we'll survive. But they cannot show you how to stand up and fight or try to go beyond this point, and probably don't want to see anyone able to go beyond the point at which they themselves are stuck. These therapists never recoup after the middle section.

The helper handles the crises or not as he is a whole helper or not. The helper handles the crises or not as he is a whole human or not.

The whole helper is a whole human being.

Below is the composite description of the high-functioning helper.

The composite high-rated therapist is an exciting, stimulating, intelligent, creative, exploring, adventurous person. He offers life. It's like the air he breathes. He is really only being what he has to be. He is living himself.

He gives me new concepts rather than merely parroting mine. He helps me to see places to go. He gave me the impression of a genuine commitment to an interpersonal encounter. He seemed to be experiencing it rather than intellectually following. He is with you and will fight for your life with you. That's the comfort of him. He is siding with the constructive forces in you. He will add his 100% to your 20% that's constructive. His analogies and concreteness are such that you don't have to ponder about what he means —you immediately understand intellectually and simultaneously feel it as never before.

During the middle section I had a real internal struggle to pull myself away from reality and involvement so that I could complete the experiment. With these people, it hurt me to try to manipulate them, as if they deserved more respect from me. During the experimental period, manipulation, the high-rated therapist starts grabbing to keep you from falling away. He plunges in and becomes more intense.

I never needed to take notes afterwards on my impressions of high-rated therapists because I knew that I could never forget the encounter. His intensity made me feel like throwing myself into his arms, and that I could trust his holding. I could feel him peeling away the layers. He wanted my deepest feelings and I felt he respected them. He always left me feeling more hopeful and more courageous. I knew that he knew a lot about me and that he could really someday come to know me.

But the really high level helpers do more than help. They teach—by model—by action—by content.

Teaching Skills

If exploration, understanding and action is the process by which learners learn, then we must develop the skills by which teachers teach. Put another way, the teachers must learn the skills which they need in order to facilitate the learner's movement through exploration, understanding and action.

The background for this conclusion is the now-extensive evidence which indicates that the learner moves—over time and with intensive and extensive contact—toward the teacher's level of functioning in particular skill areas. The learners of high-level functioning teachers improve in their development as reflected on a variety of indices while the learners of low-functioning teachers may be retarded or even deteriorate in their development. This means that the learning process is, in large part, influenced or even controlled by the teacher (Carkhuff and Berenson, 1976; Carkhuff and Pierce, 1976).

The learners learn what they are helped to learn. In turn, the teachers teach what they are helped to teach.

At another level, the same skills that the helper or teacher needs to involve the helpee or learner in the learning process are the skills which the teacher delivers to the learner. Thus the helper uses helping or living skills to deliver living skills to the learner; teaching or learning skills to deliver learning skills to the learner; planning or working skills to deliver working skills to the learner.

The difference between the skills used by the teacher and those delivered to the learner is that the teacher applies the skills to someone else while the learner applies the skills to himself or herself.

In this way the teaching and learning process is put together. The same skills that are used to involve the learner are delivered to the learner.

In addition, all sources of learning are employed, both the insight-action and the action-insight approaches. In particular, the most critical course of learning, modeling and imitation, is integrated with the content of the teaching delivery. The teacher uses what he or she delivers to the learner.

Living Skills

With regard to the phases of learning, then, the teachers must learn the skills that will facilitate learning. The first set of these skills which the teacher must learn in order to help his or her learners may be conceived of as helping or living skills.

These helping or living skills revolve around the first basic principle of learning: **all learning begins with the learner's frame of reference.** This principle is the cornerstone of the learning process.

If the program is not hooked up with the learner's frame of reference, whether before or after the action behavior, **there is no learning.** The learner simply will not have available to him or her the skills to recycle the phases of learning: more detailed exploration of where he or she is; more accurate understanding of where he or she is in relation to where he or she wants to be; more effective action to get from where he or she is to where he or she wants to be.

In other words, **if the learning process is not related to the learner's frame of reference, then learning is not recycled.** Again, while behavior may be shaped through reinforcement and supported through the re-institution of the original stimulus complex and the continuation of the reinforcement schedules, it will not be under the control of the learner until the learner's frame of reference has been related to the behavior. The learner may not acquire the behavior without learning the learning skills involved. Thus he or she will be unable to recycle and transfer learning from one situation to another.

The first of these helping or interpersonal skills revolving around the learner's frame of reference is attending (see Figure 8-1). Attending simply means that the helper or teacher is giving physical attention to the learner. Attending includes squaring, leaning toward and making eye contact with the learner. Attending is a pre-learning skill that the teacher uses to involve the learner in learning.

Phases of Learning

TEACHER   PRE-LEARNING

LEARNER

In order to involve the learner in a process leading to constructive outcome the teacher must attend to the learner.

Figure 8-1

When the learner involves herself in learning, she begins to explore where she is in relation to her world. During this first phase of learning, the teacher is most effective in facilitating exploration when she responds to the learner (see Figure 8-2). Responding involves the feeling and meaning or reason for the feeling of the learner's experience. Responding at the level of the learner's behavioral or verbal expression serves both to stimulate and reinforce the learner's exploratory efforts.

159

I

RESPONDING

EXPLORING

In order to facilitate learner exploration the teacher must respond to the learner.

Figure 8-2

Learner exploration leads to learner understanding. The teacher is most effective in facilitating this process when he or she **personalizes the learner's learning experience** (see Figure 8-3). By personalizing the meaning, feeling, problems and goals, we make the learner responsible for his function in the learning equation. It helps the learner to understand his role in determining where he is in relation to where he wants to be with the learning experience or program.

II

PERSONALIZING

UNDERSTANDING

In order to facilitate learner understanding the teacher must personalize the learner's understanding.

Figure 8-3

Finally, learner understanding leads to learner action. It does so most efficiently and effectively when the teacher initiates in relation to the learner (see Figure 8-4). By initiating, we mean defining and operationalizing the goals and developing the program steps to achieve the goals. Initiating makes the teacher both model and agent for the action steps which the learner must take to get from where she is to where she wants to be.

Together, the helping or interpersonal skills of attending, responding, personalizing and initiating constitute the living skills which the teacher must employ to facilitate learner movement through the phases of learning.

III

INITIATING

ACTION

**In order to facilitate learner action the teacher
must initiate in relation to the learner**

Figure 8-4

These living skills are the skills which the teacher needs
in order to put the learner into the learning equation—
the human into the human equation. These living skills
are what enable the teacher to enter and relate the
learner's frame of reference to the learning programs.

By themselves, the living skills are insufficient. They
enable the learner to involve himself in the learning process and develop the action steps to get there. The
teacher, through his or her contribution of living skills,
helps the learner to develop her contribution to the
learning process—herself and her skills. Now the teacher
must develop and deliver his or her second contribution
—the content of the learning programs. While the teacher

helps the learner to make his or her contribution, her helping skills, he or she also makes his or her own distinct contribution through his or her teaching or learning skills.

Learning Skills

Just as the helping or living skills are built around the first principle of learning, that all learning begins with the learner's frame of reference, so are the teaching or learning skills built around the second basic principle of learning: **all learning culminates in a skills objective.** The facts, concepts and principles which we learn are useful only insofar as they translate to skills. Skills that are achievable and repeatable are the only things that we carry away from the learning experience that we can use in later life. Indeed, skills are the only observable and measurable indices which we have for reflecting human growth and development.

Teaching or learning skills are related to the same phases of learning. Like the helping skills, they operate to facilitate learner involvement through exploration, understanding and action.

In the pre-learning phase, the teacher prepared the content which she is to deliver to the learner (see Figure 8-5). The content is the organization of the facts, concepts and principles necessary to achieve a skills objective. The content offers the skills which learners and teachers have determined are worthwhile learning objectives to achieve. Put another way, the content offers the skills which the learner needs to achieve worthwhile objectives in his life.

Just as the teacher uses his helping or living skills to respond internally from the learner's frame of reference in the first phase of learning, so does he simultaneously diagnose externally from his own frame of reference (see Figure 8-5). Diagnosis means a determination of the level of functioning that the learner has achieved in terms of the content which the teacher has developed.

Together, responding and diagnosis serve to facilitate·
the learner's exploration of where she is in relation to
the learning program.

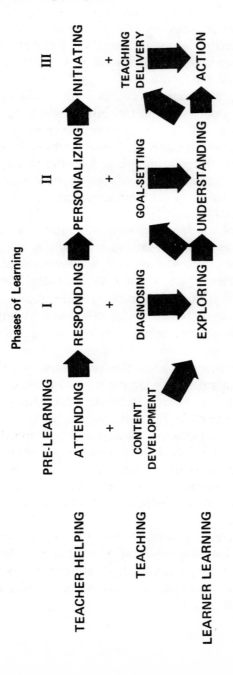

Figure 8-5. Living and learning skills

Similarly, just as the teacher personalizes the learner's experience in the second phase of learning, so does she simultaneously set goals for and with the learner (see Figure 8-5). The goals are based upon the diagnosis of the learner's level of functioning in the content area. Together, personalizing and goal-setting facilitate the learner's understanding of where he is in relation to where he wants or needs to be.

Finally, while the teacher initiates in the third phase of learning, so does he simultaneously deliver to the learner the skills which the learner needs to act to achieve his goals (see Figure 8-5). These teaching delivery skills include the teaching methods, learning strategies, and classroom management procedures necessary to help the learner to act to get from where she is to where she wants or needs to be.

These teaching or learning skills, including content development, diagnosis, goal-setting and teaching delivery skills constitute the educational achievement skills which the teacher must employ to facilitate learner movement through the phases of learning. Again, the essential difference between teaching and learning skills is that the teacher applies them to someone else while the learner applies them to himself or herself.

Together, the living and learning skills serve to relate the learning program to the learner's frame of reference and to deliver to the learner the skills which he or she needs to act effectively in his or her world.

However, even together, the living and learning skills cannot transfer the learning to real-life contexts. In order to transfer student learning to the world of life and work, the teacher requires planning or working skills in addition to her helping or living and teaching or learning skills.

Living skills are built around the first basic principle of learning: **all learning begins with the learner's frame of reference.** Learning skills are built around the second basic principle of learning: **all learning culminates in a skills objective.**

Working Skills

The third set of skills, planning or working skills, are built around the third basic principle of learning: **all learning transfers to real life.** The only learning that is useful is the learning that can be transferred to real-life living, learning and working situations. All other learning is limited to the learning context and is therefore dysfunctional. Learning has utility in life or it does not promote growth and productivity. And human resource development and human productivity are, after all, the goals of education.

The planning or working skills are related to the same phases of learning. Like the helping and teaching skills, they operate to facilitate learner movement through exploration, understanding and action.

In the pre-learning phase, the teacher integrates his curriculum with the real world (see Figure 8-6). This career curriculum integration involves a transfer from the classroom to the world of living, learning and working. In this regard, "career" is defined as the way you live your life, whether or not you ever hold a job. The career curriculum integration involves the manipulation of contexts, components, processes and functions in such a way as to insure the maximum transfer of learning.

In the first phase of learning, exploration, the teacher uses expanding skills in conjunction with his or her responding and diagnostic skills (see Figure 8-6). These expanding skills serve to expand the career alternatives available to a learner through a consideration of career areas and educational levels. Again, expanding facilitates the learner's exploration of where he or she is in relation to his or her world.

In the second phase of learning, understanding, the teacher uses narrowing skills in conjunction with her personalizing and goal-setting skills (see Figure 8-6). The narrowing skills serve to narrow the career alternatives available to the learner through a consideration of the

166

learner's personal value system as well as the occupational requirements. The narrowing facilitates the learner's understanding of where he is in relation to where he wants to be in his world.

Finally, in the third phase of learning, action, the teacher uses career preparation skills in conjunction with his initiating and teaching delivery skills (see Figure 8-6). The preparation skills serve to prepare the learner for the implementation of his or her action course through the development of a career plan and a career route. The preparation skills facilitate the learner's acting to get from where she is to where she wants to be in her world.

These planning skills, including career curriculum integration, expanding and narrowing, and preparation skills, constitute the career achievement skills which the teacher must employ to facilitate learner movement through the phases of learning. Together, the living, learning and working skills serve to relate the learning program to the learner's frame of reference and to deliver to the learner the transferable skills which he or she needs to act to achieve worthwhile goals in his or her life.

In summary, the living, learning and working skills give the teacher all of the skills which he or she needs to teach learners how to learn. In order to achieve a level of excellence in his or her functioning in living, learning and working, the teacher must first be taught or trained in the basic skills.

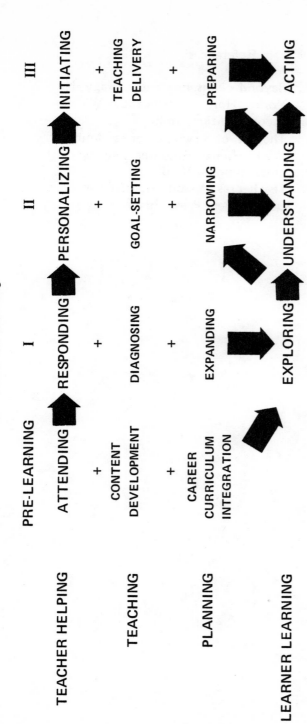

In order to facilitate the demonstration of constructive working outcome the teacher must employ planning skills

Figure 8-6. Living, learning and working skills

References

Carkhuff, R. R. and Berenson, B. G. **Beyond counseling and therapy.** New York: Holt, Rinehart & Winston, Second Edition, 1976.

Carkhuff, R. R. and Berenson, D. H. **The art of teaching series.** Amherst, Mass.: Human Resource Development Press, in press, 1976.

Carkhuff, R. R. and Pierce, R. M. **Teacher as Person.** Human Resource Development Press, 1976.

Chapter Nine

HEC:
The Training Program

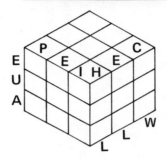

One of the HRD projects most relevant to the helping professions was the development and testing of the Education and Career Exploration System (ECES), a computer-based career guidance program which provided us with some rich insights into the counseling profession of the 1970's. Based upon the career development models of Super (1957) and developed by IBM (Friel and Minor, 1970), the ECES system was first given a field trial in Montclair, New Jersey. After several months' investment in attempting to develop support for the program, the net result was that one guidance counselor learned to use the system effectively.

As a consequence of these discouraging results, the ECES program was redesigned by Friel (1972) incorporating the systematic problem-solving models of Carkhuff (1969, 1972) and a comprehensive training program was designed for a second field trial in the Genessee Intermediate School District, in and around Flint, Michigan. We set up an interesting design involving training and evaluation for both computer and human resource development skills (see Figure 9-1).

Group I received systematic training in the computer-based career guidance program and in human resource development (HRD) skills including interpersonal and

Counselor Groups

I	II	III	IV
Systematic Training in ECES and HRD Skills	Systematic Training in ECES Skills	Systematic Training in HRD Skills	Traditionally Trained (No systematic training control group)

Figure 9-1. Training and Control Groups for ECES and HRD Training Programs.

problem-solving skills. Group II received systematic computer-based career guidance skills training only. Group III received systematic HRD skills only. Group IV, a traditionally trained group of counselors, was left alone.

During the evaluation phase, a sample of 75 student counselees was assigned randomly to one of five different groups. A sample of fifty counselors participated under the first four conditions. In groups I and II, the students visited in order 1) the counselor, 2) the computer terminal and 3) the counselor again. In Groups III and IV, the students visited only the counselors. For Group III, problem-solving programs were assigned to the students as an intervening experience analogous to visiting the computer in Groups I and II. Group V, in which the students visited only the computer terminal, was added for evaluative purposes.

What we found was most interesting and revealing! We found that the base success rate of guidance programs according to the self-reports of students entering the project was 13%. That is to say that *13% of the students involved reported themselves as having experienced their high school guidance programs as successful in helping them "to work out any important problems" in their lives.* A very distressing number—13%! Far lower than we might have expected from the data of Eysenck, Levitt and Lewis!

No counselor may be better than the average counselor!

While these figures expose some of counseling's undergarments or lack thereof, what we discovered with training was much more significant (see Figure 9-2). We found that *this base rate of success was doubled with traditionally trained counselors by simply insisting that they see their counselees for a full fifty-minute hour.* As part of the design, the students visited the counselors in Group IV for two complete sessions. In 75% of the cases, the counselors reported themselves as having completed the session within 5 to 10 minutes. When we insisted that they see the student for fifty minutes, we found

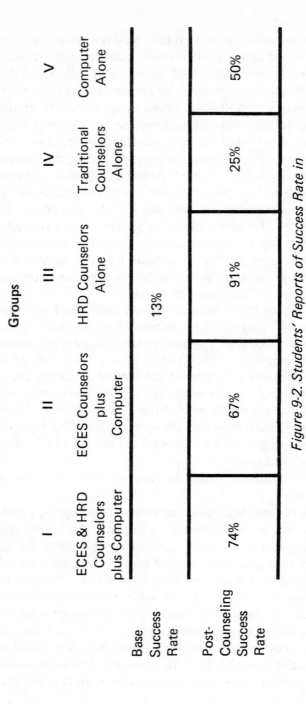

Figure 9-2. Students' Reports of Success Rate in Helping Students with Important Life Problems.

that 25% of the students reported the sessions as having been successful in helping them work out important life problems. The implications are important. *With no additional investment of time and energy in training, we can double our base success rate by simply insisting that the counselors discharge the responsibilities for which they are paid.*

A working counselor is better than the average counselor!

But, alas, even 25% is an extraordinarily low rate for paid professionals. We found that we could do something about this low success rate—without the help of counselors. *When the students visited the computer terminal alone, we found that they indicated a success rate double that of traditionally trained counselors.* Without interacting with counselors, the students reported a 50% success rate for the computer alone (Group V) compared to the 25% rate of the traditionally trained counselors (Group IV) who did what they were paid to do (see Figure 9-2).

An effective program is better than the average working counselor!

But a good program is not better than a good program plus a counselor trained to utilize that program. When the students visited both the computer terminal and counselors trained in computer skills, they reported a success rate one-third greater than those visiting the computer alone. Counselors in Group II received training in computer and terminal functions and data interpretation and oriented the students before they visited the terminal. The students visiting both the terminal and computer-trained counselors indicated a success rate of 67% (see Figure 9-2).

An effective program plus a working counselor trained in the program's skills is better than an effective program alone!

From this point on the data get even more interesting. *When students interact with counselors trained in the kinds of skills they should have been trained in during graduate study, the students indicate success rates higher than those of counselors trained in computer program skills alone.* The counselors in Groups I and III received systematic HRD training in both interpersonal skills and problem-solving skills, the kinds of skills which counselors should have received in graduate training. In Group I, the students visited both the computer terminal and counselors trained in both HRD and computer skills and reported a success rate of 74% (see Figure 9-2). In Group III, the students visited counselors trained in HRD skills alone and reported a success rate of 91% (see Figure 9-2).

Effective counselors and effective programs are effective complements!

The Ingredients of Helping Effectiveness

Perhaps this is a tenuous conclusion to draw from the data, although the HRD skills trained groups fared better than the computer skills trained groups. Perhaps the strongest conclusions that we can derive from the introduction of systematic training is that the groups that received systematic training in skills that would make them more effective and would allow them to complement their efforts with relevant programs were most effective.

Effective counselors plus effective programs constitute the significant sources of effect in counseling.

Most important, from a base success rate of 13% for unmotivated counselors or, if you will, 25% from working counselors, we are able to produce counselors with success rates ranging from 67% to 91%. We are able to do this with systematic training programs culminating in tangible and usable skills. If we do not incorporate such systematic programs, our counselees are at least twice as well off with a good computer program. Indeed, our counselees may be as well or better off without any professional counseling at all.

175 *Systematic training programs are the source of personal and program effectiveness.*

The manner in which the project points up the differential or complementary ingredients of counseling effectiveness is critical. *The equation of counseling effectiveness involves both people and programs: effective people plus effective programs.* Indeed, these dimensions are the effective ingredients of any operation, whether it is administrative or educational. To be sure, the equation is not complete until we also develop a way of relating the people to the programs. In other words, we need a way of organizing the people and the programs involved. The equation for effectiveness may be summarized as follows:

$$Effectiveness = \begin{array}{l} Effective\ People\ + \\ Effective\ Programs\ + \\ Effective\ Organizations \end{array}$$

Effective helping in any role, then, is primarily a function of two factors: the skills with which the helper relates to other people and the skills which he or she has in his or her specialty program area. Whether we are speaking of the high school counselor in the study which we just reported or a second grade reading teacher or an administrator in school or in industry, these factors hold. The effective counselor has both the ability to relate to the counselee and the ability to offer the counselee some skills in resolving his or her problem. The effective second grade reading teacher has the ability to relate to the children and the ability to devise reading methodologies to meet the students' unique needs. The effective administrator has the ability to relate to his or her employees and superiors and the ability to put his technical skills into operation.

Effectiveness is a function of interpersonal skills and specialty area program skills.

Effective People

A person's effectiveness, then, is largely a function of his or her interpersonal skills. Effective interpersonal skills accomplish several things for both the helper (counselor, teacher, administrator, parent) and the helpee (counselee, student, employee, child). First, they enable the helper to establish an experiential base for the learning or relearning process that follows. Effective interpersonal skills enable the helpee to have the experience of being understood: "The helper knows where I am coming from." In addition, such skills provide the helper with the opportunity to check himself out: "Am I really in tune with the helpee?" The experiential base services to prepare both helper and helpee for later stages of helping.

The helper's interpersonal skills enable him to establish the experiential base for learning.

Effective interpersonal skills also enable the helper to serve as a model for the helpee. The helper not only relates to where the helpee is "coming from" but he also establishes himself as having something that the helpee wants. The helper can function effectively in interpersonal areas where the helpee cannot. Given that the helper has related to the helpee's frame of reference, this desirable quality constitutes the *basis for the helpee's motivation: the helpee knows that he is understood at the level that he is functioning and he sees before him a person whom he wants to emulate and imitate.* What theories of motivation have never comprehended fully is that people motivate people: it is the helper and the level of skills that she has and the helpee needs and wants that motivates the helpee to learn. Motivation is reinforced when the helper understands the helpee and the level of skills that he has and when the helper is committed to helping the helpee bridge the gap between them.

The helper's interpersonal skills enable her to establish the modeling base for learning.

Perhaps most important, effective interpersonal skills enable the helper to teach didactically or shape the helpee's interpersonal and other skills. Having established herself as an important influence or potent reinforcer of the helpee's behavior through the experiential and modeling sources of learning, *the helper can now teach the helpee those skills necessary for the helpee's functioning, interpersonal and otherwise.* The helper uses herself, particularly in terms of her ability to develop a program for the helpee in the interpersonal area, to develop and reinforce improved skills for the helpee.

The helper's interpersonal skills enable her to establish the didactic base for learning.

Another way to summarize interpersonal effectiveness is in terms of the helper's repertoire of responses. Effective people have a large repertoire of high-level responses. Indeed, *the central occurrence in any helping relationship is the transformation of a person with a limited repertoire of responses (a helpee) into a person with an extensive repertoire of responses (a helper).* It is his limited repertoire of responses that dictates the helpee's low probability of functioning effectively in a given situation. It is his extensive repertoire of responses that dictates the helper's high probability of functioning effectively in a variety of situations.

Effective people are a function of the quantity and quality of responses which they have in their interpersonal skills repertoire.

The most efficient and effective means for improving the quantity and quality of responses in the helpee's repertoire is training. While the investigation of the effects of interpersonal skills began from an experiential frame of reference, primarily the client-centered approach under Rogers' influence (Rogers, et al, 1967; Truax and Carkhuff, 1967), the effectiveness of these skills in counseling has been found to be a function of their extension to the systematic operationalization and training of initiative as well as responsive dimensions (Carkhuff, 1969). *The counselor will be effective to the degree that the counselor is systematically trained in interpersonal skills. The counselee will be effective to the degree that the counselee is systematically trained in interpersonal skills.* The counselor's task then, is not simply to conquer the skills and offer them in counseling. Nor is it enough to teach the counselee how to utilize the counseling process most effectively, although this is a step in the right direction. The counselor must conquer the interpersonal skills and the training skills to transmit those skills to others. The counselor will be most helpful when he trains the helpee directly in the interpersonal skills which will enable the counselee to function effectively in the helpee's world (Carkhuff, 1971).

Effective people train ineffective people to become effective.

Effective Programs

It is not enough, then, to be interpersonally effective. Effective people also have effective programs in their specialty areas. Whether the program grows out of the helpee's needs, as happens in many counseling situations, or the program is part of the helper's offering in many teaching and management situations, *effective helpers have effective programs.* Indeed, in those few assessments of educational programs which have been conducted on a national level, it usually develops that there is one teacher in every setting who beats all combinations of teachers and programs. And this teacher is one who develops his or her own programs tailored to the student's needs!

Effective people develop effective programs.

Perhaps most important, systematic programs give the helpee the steps which he needs to bridge the gap from where he is to where he wants to go. That is, the basis of motivation, as we have already suggested, involves establishing the discrepancy between the helper and the helpee's levels of functioning or the discrepancy between the repertoire of responses or skills of helper and helpee. *The essential task of helping is to bridge that gap between the helpee's skills level and the helper's skills level.* Programs are the most effective means for accomplishing this because *programs demonstrate to the helpee that if she takes the steps involved she can get to where she*

179

wants to go (see Figure 9-3). The figure represents the simplest organization of learning in which people are related to programs. Helper and helpee are related through the program that makes it possible for the helpee to move in the helper's direction. The more systematic the program, the higher the probability that the helpee can achieve his or her goals.

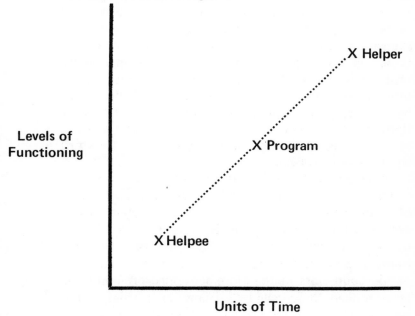

Figure 9-3. Illustration of learning organization relating helpee to helper through step-by-step program

Effective programs achieve goals.

There are many different programs in the different specialty areas of helping. We will not concentrate in this piece upon the teaching programs of education or the technical programs of administration. With regard to counseling, there are the programs given us by the trait-and-factor (Super, 1957; Tyler, 1953) and behavior modification approaches (Krasner and Ullman, 1965; Krumboltz and Thoreson, 1969). These systematic approaches are effective not only in the distinctive contributions which they make but also in the methodologies which they enable us to employ creatively. *They offer us systematic methodologies for operationalizing goals and for developing step-by-step programs for attaining these goals.* They objectify goals in behavioral terms and develop behavioral sequences in progressive approximations of movement toward the goals. It is noteworthy that the systematic computer and HRD skills-training programs reported earlier are based upon these methodologies. Thus the interpersonal skills, problem-solving skills, program development skills and other skills programs are made possible and operational by these approaches. There are no other major orientations that have demonstrated such unique programmatic contributions (Berenson and Carkhuff, 1967; Carkhuff and Berenson, 1967).

Some approaches offer effective programs.

There are also a number of developing approaches that offer the promise of effective helping programs. However, most of these provide a structure within which training can take place rather than the substance of the training itself. In this regard, it is significant that many of the counselors in the aforementioned programs had been trained in so-called "systems approaches." It is simply not enough to label a box "Empathy" or even to suggest to the counselor that he enter the counselee's frame of reference. The prospective counselor must be taught systematically the necessary discrimination and communication skills involved in operationalizing "Empathy." It is not enough to ask or tell a counselor to develop and implement a course of action for or with her counselee. The counselor must be systematically taught to operationalize problems and goals and to consider alternative courses of action in terms of the counselee's value hierarchy.

Nor is it sufficient to develop a framework for employing existing training programs when the basic skills have not been conquered. The attempt of Mosher and

Sprinthall (1971) to develop a curriculum for "psychological education" focusing upon personal development is laudatory. However, in order to implement the model, different skills areas like interpersonal skills must be conquered so that legitimate conclusions with potentially far-reaching implications may be drawn. For example, the ratings of interpersonal functioning of middle class children when rated by untrained middle class raters would appear to be enormously inflated (rated near level 3.0 on 5-point scales). This would provide an erroneous comparison with the ratings of interpersonal functioning of ghetto children when rated by trained raters (rated slightly above level 1.0 on 5-point scales).

All this is not to recommend, as the psychoanalysts do, a closed system in which you must be indoctrinated before you can employ specific skills. It is simply to say that the skills cannot be employed effectively or creatively if they are not in the working response repertoire of the "systems" builders. In that case the framework in which the "skills" are employed is an abstraction that does not translate to specific behaviors. On the other hand, the audio-visual feedback methods (Kagan, et al, 1965) offer promising approaches for shaping effective counselor behaviors. However, variations of these methods often do not entail the detailed frameworks necessary to culminate in constructive helping behaviors. Obviously, for example, it is not enough to record and offer feedback for gross behaviors that make very little difference. In our experience, the feedback methods run the danger of becoming superficial gimmicks if their promulgators have not developed the necessary basic responses in their helping repertoires that lead systematically to more effective helping behaviors. In this regard, the teaching and learning of molecular "attending" behavior is an important development (Ivey, et al, 1968). However, attending behavior *per se* does not culminate in helpee benefits because attending behavior is unrelated to counseling outcomes. Attending behavior is, at best, pre-helping behavior or, more appropriately, pre-training behavior. We often find ourselves more concerned with the "psychological education" of the model-builders than we do with the psychological substance of their models. A model is only as good as the constructs and methods it incorporates. After the counselor has learned to sit forward in her chair and maintain eye contact, then she looks at her trainer and asks: "Now, how do I help?" In any event, as these feedback methods attempt to become more specific and systematic, they must incorporate empirically-based, substantive models and methods. Accordingly, while these attempts are certainly steps in the right direction, they are not adequate in and of themselves. While they employ methodologies that will likely prove to be effective shaping devices, they do not have the skills necessary to translate the methodologies to substantive contributions. *The methodologies are only as good as their promulgators are effective in discriminating and developing the substance of the skills to be learned in the shaping program.*

Some approaches offer the promise of effective programs.

Other approaches, whatever their labels, do not even qualify as programs. The best illustration is the currently popular vogue of so-called "sensitivity training" and all of the gross perversions of this expulsive theme. The term "training" is a misnomer, for the procedure bears not even the slightest resemblance to a systematic program. Furthermore, there is little evidence documenting its translation to human benefits and a bit more evidence to indict it as a contributor to human detriment. This is worth mentioning in passing, since a "training program" that is not programmatic may be more harmful than helpful because of the implications of learning complex behaviors in a random or non-systematic fashion (Carkhuff, 1971). As learning theorists have long known, skipping steps in attempting to learn more difficult behavior before simple behavior may have potentially harmful effects upon the learner. In any event, *when the*

*sensitivity training approaches come around to objecti-
fying their behavioral goals, we can find significantly
more efficient and effective programmatic ways of
achieving these goals.*

Some approaches do not offer effective programs.

Perhaps the best way to conceptualize skills in the
specialty program area is also in terms of response repertoires. *Just as we analyzed personal effectiveness as
quantity and quality of interpersonal responses in one's
repertoire, so we can now analyze program effectiveness
in terms of the quantity and quality of specialty
responses in one's repertoire.* Just as an effective counselor draws from his repertoire of interpersonal responses
to understand the counselee's need and motivate him
for learning, he draws from his repertoire of specialty
responses, such as the problem-solving or computer-
based career guidance program mentioned earlier, to
match and individualize the program to the counselee's
unique needs. Just as our effective teacher draws from
his or her repertoire of interpersonal responses to understand the student's needs and motivate him for learning,
he or she draws from his or her repertoire of teaching
methodology responses, such as reading, to match and
individualize the program to the student's unique needs.
Similarly, in administration, just as the effective administrator draws from his repertoire of interpersonal
responses to understand the employee's needs and motivate him for learning, he draws from his repertoire of
specialty responses, such as his technical specialty area,
to match and individualize the program to the employee's
unique needs.

*The greater the repertoire of interpersonal and spe-
cialty program responses, the higher the probability that
the helper can meet the helpee's unique needs.*

Again, it is most efficient and effective to train
helpees in the responses which the helper has. Just as
the effective counselor trains her counselees in interpersonal skills in order to facilitate their functioning in
their worlds, so does she train them in problem-solving

skills that will enable them to function with autonomy. Just as the effective teacher trains his students in interpersonal skills in order to facilitate their functioning in the classroom, so does he train them in the different teaching methodology skills that will enable them to function with autonomy. Just as the effective administrator trains her employees in interpersonal skills in order to facilitate their functioning in her operation, so does she train them in the different technical skills that will enable them to function with autonomy. In this regard, effective helpers do not only train helpees in specialty program areas. *Effective helpers also train their helpees in the program development skills that will enable them to create their own effective programs.*

Effective people utilize effective programs to train effective people to utilize effective programs.

Effective Organizations

Effective organizations are simply ways of relating effective people to effective programs or, more specifically, effective people to effective people, effective people to effective programs and effective programs to effective programs. While many consultancies begin and end with organizational schemata, independent of people and program effectiveness, it is fraudulent to do so. People and programs are the essence of organization. Functional organizations cannot be defined independent of the caliber of the people and the programs in them. The caliber of the people and the programs can be defined in terms of the quantity and quality of responses in the relevant repertoires. Simply stated, *the function of organizations, then, is to develop a hierarchy of effectiveness.* Based upon the criteria of functionality, the most effective people must oversee the activities of those less effective; the most effective programs must subordinate and/or incorporate the systems of the less effective programs. The function of effective organizations, then, is to appoint the most effective persons to the leadership roles and equip them with programs that will not only service the functions of the operation but also develop additional effective leadership within the operation.

Effective organizations relate people to programs in a hierarchy of effectiveness.

The Ingredients of Training Effectiveness

With increasing concerns for the "rights and interests of society" (Clark, et al, 1964), the different associations of the helping professions have involved themselves with the preparation of helpers, credentialed as well as functional professionals (Carkhuff, 1969). With specific regard to counseling, there have been a number of efforts made by the American Personnel and Guidance Association and the American Psychological Association to develop standards of preparation for counselors (Patterson, 1966). Prominent among these efforts was the 1964 Greyston Conference conducted by the Division of Counseling Psychology of the APA. Including reports by Berdie, Darley, Myers, Samler and Tyler, *the conference endorsed "the historic statements of the Division of Counseling Psychology on the roles and preparation of counseling psychologists."* The millennium had been reached!

Training conferences have not generated new training models.

Further, the conference recommended that counselors should "be prepared to understand and to work with persons at all age levels in all stages of ability or disability, and in all types of settings" and in doing so "the practice of counseling should embrace far more than the traditional function of individual appraisal and counseling in individual interviews." Unfortunately, this recommendation *does not get down to the "nitty-gritty."* As Patterson suggests, it fails to specify these "other important ways to facilitating personal and social development."

Training conferences have failed to detail the specifics of training.

Instead, these training conferences have focused upon the now-traditional identity concerns of counselors rather than upon their preparation. It is difficult indeed for counselors to facilitate the resolution of the identity problems of their clients when they have not resolved these problems for themselves. Directionful and goal-directed professionals have no such concerns. They will do "anything that works" to make themselves more effective with the populations whom they are paid to help. *They are dominated by criteria of functionality, particularly in times when the privileged growth of some is dependent upon the neglected survival of others.* Identity concerns are a luxury of prosperous professionals.

Training conferences have been of limited training value.

Perhaps the major function of these conferences has been to bring together old-thinking people with older ideas. *So long as any organization continues to extend policy-making invitations to persons 20 or more years after their essential contributions, if any were made, and then only with assurance that the person is no longer in fermentation, it is doomed.* The supportive evidence for this statement comes from the fact that, in spite of the alleged "diversity" of training programs, there have been no basic changes in the training programs in the past 25 years. Most important, there have been no basic changes in the "millennium" years since the Greyston conference —and this independent of the effectiveness of our efforts. There will be no changes in the years that follow this proposal so long as considerations of influence dominate considerations of delivery. Counseling is not in an identity crisis.

Counseling is in a delivery crisis!

When organizations become so professional that they are more concerned with spheres of influence than with the acquisition of skills necessary to make deliveries, they have lost their essential functionality. Accountability and its relationship with the voted funding of school budgets reinforce the concern for what a counselor can deliver. *Counselors can deliver only what they have skills to deliver.* And counselors, as we have seen, by-and-large have not learned or been taught the skills which they need to make observable and tangible deliveries to those whom they serve.

Counseling is in a skills crisis!

Yet in spite of the lethargy of their mentors, those who are on the firing line—the counselors— are increasingly aware of their lack of skills. When they are asked to develop criteria of accountability, they are often unable to do so. It is not always clear to them what changes they are being asked to affect. It is only clear to them that they lack the skills necessary to affect any changes with predictable results. Most important, *it is clear to their counselees that the counselors do not have the skills necessary to make a difference in their lives.* Witness the study reported earlier. There are many other studies which support those results. Accordingly, while many resist the recognition that they really have nothing substantive to offer, there is some high degree of receptivity if the skills are offered by experts who ally themselves with the counselors' welfare and who offer systematic skills acquisition programs. The increasing demands upon counselors intensify this motivation.

Counselors are motivated to learn skills.

In our own personal and professional development, we have become increasingly oriented toward a skills acquisition theme. Each stage of our development, we have found, has been a function of realizing the inadequacy of our skills in attempting to make a full delivery to our clientele. Eclectic in orientation, *we have constantly sought to fill in the missing ingredients in the equation for human resource development.* Initially, we were part of a larger effort to operationalize in practice and research some of the responsive interpersonal dimensions of the helping relationship (Rogers, Gendlin, Kiesler and Truax, 1967; Truax and Carkhuff, 1967). Recognizing the absence of the initiative programs necessary to bring the helping process to culmination, we attempted to develop models that incorporated

188

initiative interpersonal dimensions (Carkhuff, 1969) and complementary and systematic programs for change (Berenson and Carkhuff, 1967; Carkhuff and Berenson, 1967). Further, we operationalized and modified these programs by studying the effects of training with credentialed professionals, functional professionals and personnel indigenous to the community being serviced (Carkhuff, 1971). With regard to helpee populations, we have developed and tested the concept of "training as a preferred mode of treatment." In this context, our current efforts have been dedicated to the development of a technology of human resource development in which specific levels of functioning and specific skills are defined.

Our own efforts have led us to emphasize skills acquisition.

A Skills Model

By skills, we do not mean most of the diagnostic tests and notions which we, as counselors, have learned. If our diagnoses do not dictate real differential treatment that in turn translates to tangible human benefits, they do not make a difference. Nor do we mean the many insights which we, as professional helpers, are prone to offer. If insights are not followed by systematic action programs, then they do not make a difference. Nor do we even mean the attitudes which we are disposed to adopt. *If warm responsiveness does not incorporate accurate empathic skills, then it does not make a difference.*

Most counselor behaviors do not make a difference!

By skills, we mean behaviors that are operational, repeatable, trainable and predictable within a delimited range of effects. We might further qualify this definition by a concern for the demonstration of constructive human effects. Put more personally, *a skill is anything that you can teach me a piece of in a minute and tell me where we will be at the end of an hour, a day, 100 hours*

189

or a year. Under this criterion, most counselor behaviors do not qualify as skills. Only those interpersonal behaviors and specialty programs for which we have empirical support qualify as skills.

A skill is something which you can teach others systematically.

It is those counselor behaviors that do make a difference that counselor training must be about. Simply stated, by equipping counselors with skills that have a high probability of translating to human benefits, we increase the probability of translating counselors' efforts to human benefits. Our task in counselor training, then, is to operationalize those skills that do or promise to translate to human benefits and develop our programs to transmit these skills systematically to our counselors. Only when the counselor has available to her all of the skills which she needs to sustain her autonomous functioning in her world has the trainer discharged his or her responsibilities.

The only legitimate theme for counselor training is a skills acquisition theme.

The same skills which made helping effectiveness possible make training effectiveness possible. The level of interpersonal and specialty program skills of trainers translate predictably to the level of interpersonal and specialty program skills of helpees. Only when the helpee has available to him all of the skills which he needs to sustain his autonomous functioning in his world has the helper discharged her responsibilities. *Helping is indeed a process of transforming helpees into helpers.*

The only legitimate theme for counseling is a skills acquisition theme.

Any set of skills, then, that contributes to the probability of a person functioning more fully in his world is the legitimate concern of helper training. As we have seen, a person's functionality in his world, whether he or she is a counselor or counselor trainer, a teacher, an administrator in education or industry or even a parent, is dependent upon the interpersonal and specialty program skills which she has available to her. *These skills are a function of training.* We are a product of the skills in which we have been trained. There are good training programs that maximize an individual's chances to actualize his or her resources.

The only legitimate theme for counseling is the development of good skills training programs.

A Training Model

At the level that counselors—and, indeed, professional helpers of most sorts—are currently functioning, directly dispensing services, we can replace them. We can replace them with persons indigenous to the community being serviced. To be sure, we can if we wish, replace them with nothing. We prefer the former course, although not without standards. We have heard ourselves misquoted many times as recommending that lay people can do the job that professionals can. This is like saying that professionals cannot do the job and lay people can. There is a tendency among counselors—indeed among men—to attempt to imitate potent thrusts in a given area, particularly when they threaten one's economic security—*without becoming potent themselves in the area.* Many programs are duplicated only to neutralize them. Lay training is one of these programs when it is run by people without skills. *Only with the selection and training based upon criteria of functionality imposed by effective professionals can lay people make deliveries of significant human benefit* (Carkhuff, 1969, 1971)! Lay training programs are only as good as their promulgators.

Persons indigenous to the community being serviced can be selected and trained as helpers.

If lay people can be selected and trained to discharge professional responsibilities, then there are important implications for professional helpers. *The alternative to impotence is work!* If the counselor accepts his responsibilities as a contributor to mankind, he must acquire the skills necessary to train others in the skills which they need to dispense helping services. Now, all professional helpers are not going to acquire all of the skills necessary for the development of a human being. Some will. Most will not. Some of those who will not can still contribute by developing one specialty training area within the living, learning or working skills areas: for example, interpersonal skills which translate to constructive gains in helpers and which may, in turn, translate to constructive gains in the helpees with whom the helpers work. It must be emphasized that, just as with helpers, criteria of functionality must be employed in the selection and training of those persons whose resources promise to translate to training skills areas.

Helpers can be selected and trained to train other helpers.

At higher levels, responsible trainers who are committed to their work may conquer several skills areas within a given sphere of functioning. That is, they have acquired the necessary facility in each of several skills areas not only to offer the services that are a function of these skills but also to transmit these skills systematically to others who can offer the services. To cite an obvious example, the trainers may conquer any one set of skills in the living, learning or working skills areas. At the training level, we may refer to the living, learning and working skills (LLW) as human, educational and career achievement skills (HEC) in order to differentiate them from the helping level. But they remain the same skills, distinguished only by the fact that the training skills (HEC) refer to teaching someone else while the helping skills (LLW) refer to oneself. Thus, for example, a trainer may have a specialty in physical fitness or interpersonal or teaching delivery skills or career preparation skills. We may consider such a trainer accomplished in the particular skills area involved. As such, he or she would qualify for selection and training as a master trainer in any one of the living, learning and working skills areas. Of course, such a master trainer must also develop the training skills necessary to train trainers from the ranks of helpers in the different specialty skills areas.

Trainers can be selected and trained as master trainers.

We must provide for the possibility that there are other skill areas relevant to human resource development (HRD). In addition to the human, educational and career achievement skills, there are undoubtedly many other skills that contribute to the physical, emotional and intellectual development of people. In addition, no helpee or helper can fully employ one set of skills if he is not functioning fully in another. If he does not have the physical energy level, speed, power, coordination and endurance necessary to implement his living, learning or working programs, he places a limit upon his development. If she does not have the necessary interpersonal skills, she limits her learning and working as well as her living functionality. If he does not have the necessary content development skills, he limits his living and working effectiveness as well as his learning effectiveness. If she does not have the necessary career preparation skills, she limits her development in living and learning as well as working areas.

Consultants must also acquire all other specialty skills relevant to the consultation on human resource development. Among others, they must acquire skills in organizing and assigning personnel and programs. In addition, they must keep abreast of developments in human resource development. In this regard, we are reminded of an anecdote. When behavior modification approaches were first making significant impact several years ago, we decided that they were appropriate for one of our clients. We sought several professionals who espoused these approaches. None, however, had ever employed these approaches with clients. Possibly none have since. Needless to say, we did so then and have done so a number of times since, in each instance successfully. It is the responsibility of the consultant not only to keep abreast of skill developments but also to practice them.

Master trainers can be selected and trained as consultants.

Perhaps at the highest level there is a place also for the person who has conquered the skills of consultants in different areas of human functioning. *Defined as human environmental planners, these master consultants might relate and integrate the different areas of human functioning in an effective social system.* In addition, they might guide the moral development and employment of functions within the system. This may seem unreal to those of us who have not conquered our first set of basic skills. But certainly such a position is necessary in a social system that shows the same signs of decadence and lack of functionality that the helping professions show. However, unlike the current set of politicians who guide policy-making and yet have few if any demonstrable skills relevant to human functioning, the master consultants will have paid the price of hard work in conquering the skills necessary for human and community resource development. There are no lasting moral standards without lasting skill standards! Or, put another way, a person without skills cannot be trusted, for he or she must secure a living by means other than what he or she has to offer.

Consultants may be selected and trained as master consultants.

Master consultants may utilize the academic community as well as the community-at-large in developing internship programs for helpers, trainers and consultants. These would be two-way programs in which the master consultants first set up programs in the internship agencies that would enable these agencies to offer something worthwhile to the interns. Because an internship possibility exists in a dormitory of the Y.M.C.A. or a Concentrated Employment Program does not mean that it has something to offer its interns. The agencies must be trained in the skills necessary to expand and sharpen their essential contributions. Indeed, the agencies may be seen, just as people are, in terms of the quantity and quality of their people and programs. The interns, in turn, can learn skills in different specialty

194

areas from agency personnel and programs with demonstrated expertise in these areas. For example, dormitory interns could conduct training programs in heterosexual skills, racial relations skills, leadership or autonomy skills, study skills, career development skills and a whole variety of other specialty skills areas relevant to college students; the interns could do this under the direction of persons trained to a master trainer's level of functioning in these areas. In the same manner, similar personnel and programs may be developed in specialty areas relevant to functioning in agencies in the community-at-large.

The training model has implications for internships.

These levels of functioning may be summarized in the living, learning and working spheres (see Figure 9-4). As can be seen, at the most basic levels helpees without the skills necessary to function effectively in their worlds are serviced by helpers with the skills necessary to function effectively in the helpees' worlds as well as their own. These helpers directly dispense services in the delimited areas in which they are proficient. For example, helpers, whether credentialed professionals or functional professionals, may function in the living sphere by establishing a helping relationship and relating interpersonally to the helpee on a one-to-one or a one-to-group basis, making referrals as specialty skills learning becomes necessary. Or helpers possessing both the interpersonal and the specialty teaching skills may function in the learning sphere as tutors in some specialty learning area. Or helpers possessing both the interpersonal and specialty program skills may function in the working sphere as employment coaches in some specialty working area. In each instance, *the helping relationship is defined by the greater quantity and quality of responses which the helper has in his or her response repertoire as compared to the helpee.*

Helpers with skills dispense services to helpees without skills.

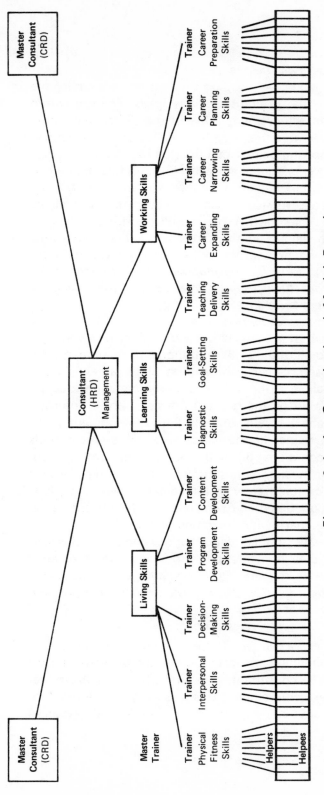

Figure 9-4. An Organizational Model Based Upon Levels of Functioning in Living, Learning and Working Skills Areas.

Helpers service helpees.

At the next level, we can see that trainers service the helpers in the different specialty areas. Trainers within the human achievement skills (living skills) realm may train helpers in either the physical fitness, interpersonal, problem-solving or program development skills. Trainers within the educational achievement skills (learning skills) area can train helpers in content development, diagnostic, goal-setting or teaching delivery skills. Trainers within the career achievement skills (working skills) area may train helpers in the career expanding, narrowing, planning and preparation skills. Thus *trainers will train helpers in both the development and supervision of skills within the specialty area through their personal development programs.*

Trainers service helpers.

At the master trainer level, we find persons who have conquered all of the skills within one of the human, educational and career achievement skills areas. Thus a master trainer in the human achievement skills area has conquered all of the relevant physical fitness, interpersonal, problem-solving and program development skills. A master trainer in the educational achievement skills area has conquered all of the relevant content development, diagnostic, goal-setting and teaching delivery skills. A master trainer in the career achievement skills area has conquered all of the relevant skills in the career expanding, narrowing, planning and preparation skills. These master trainers serve to develop the skills and supervise their implementation by the trainers. Accordingly, *master trainers define and sharpen the construction of the individual skills areas through their program development activities.*

Master trainers service trainers.

Again, as we can see, the consultants serve to coordinate and supervise the activities of the different master trainers. The consultants have all the human, educational and career achievement skills necessary to the development of physical, emotional and intellectual resources

(HRD). In addition, *consultants extend the activities of the master trainers by organizing the activities through the assignments of people and programs.*

Consultants service master trainers.

Finally, as we can see, there are master consultants who, having conquered all relevant human resource development (HRD) skills, extend their concern to the development of the community-at-large. They serve to conduct needs assessments which determine the needs of the community. In this context, *master consultants develop the new technologies necessary to develop the human resources.*

Master consultants service consultants.

The training organizational model is based upon functionality. It defines roles and responsibilities in terms of the quantity and quality of responses in the specialty areas. All other definitions are redundant! The model relates people at every level in terms of their functionality. All other relationships are superfluous! The model organizes people and programs according to their contributions. All other organizations are ridiculous! *Such a hierarchy of effectiveness is the only basis for sane helper training.* Not power! Not position! If sanity cannot occur in helper training, it certainly cannot occur in the social system we would help.

Functional organizations service people.

Toward a Technology of Helper Training

Most of the subject matter currently studied in professional helper training does not translate in any way to any tangible and usable skills. And yet it is our task as helper trainers to assure ourselves that what we are teaching and training can be translated to such skills. In our own efforts, we have devoted ourselves to the development of a technology for helping. One approach which we might employ is to assign our professional trainers a limited period of time in order to force them to operationalize their subject material into systematic programs. Another approach might be to determine what kinds of skills are needed by people in the world out there and what kinds of skills we have. Then we could invest our energies in sharpening skills programs where we have them and developing programs where we have none. Helping programs must translate to technologies that are empirically based and testable in everyday human experience. In our own personal experience, we have found each individual theoretical approach wanting. Accordingly, we have devoted our own efforts to developing *a systematic eclectic approach to helping.*

Responding to an individual does not conflict with engaging in systematic problem-solving efforts with him. Being initially unconditional in order to involve a helpee in the helping process does not exclude being conditional in implementing behavior modification approaches with her. With an eclectic stance, we have found ourselves doing anything with and for the helpee that we would want done for ourselves or our loved ones who found themselves in similar circumstances. When we are forced to defend a position, we are defending nothing! When we cannot be open to the world as it exists, we cannot make our full contribution. The world cannot be incorporated in a closed system.

Helping must translate to a technology.

The technology, as has already been indicated, must offer skills to persons at all levels of development. In our own efforts, we have attempted to develop skills programs for the helpee, helper, trainer and consultant levels. The programs must take two forms: one for the person being serviced, the other for the person offering the service. For example, when you determine to train a helpee to be a helper, you must also plan to train a helper to train the helpee. Thus you must be concerned not only with the immediate services being offered but also with how you are training the person who is offering the services. In this way, *a technology adds skills and responsibilities* at each level of development. In this manner, skills may be multiplied many times over with an effective helping and learning organization.

The technology must develop skills for persons at all levels of development.

Levels of Functioning

At the level of the helpee-learner, programs have been developed to facilitate involvement in helping. The helpee can learn the skills of being a good helpee. In other words, *he can be trained in the "art of learning."* Among the skills the helpee can learn are those involved with the different phases of learning: exploration, understanding, action. Later, the helpee can learn the other things that she can do to get herself "together."

Helpees learn the skills necessary to be helped.

At the level of the helper, programs have been developed to facilitate his service to the helpee to whom he is responsible. The helper must be trained in the interpersonal skills that make the helping or learning process possible. In addition, she must be equipped with the skills of her specialty program area. That is, he must be able to offer the skills in which he specializes, whether his skills fall within the living, the learning or the working spheres of functioning. *He can learn the technology of helping.* Further, he or she must be able not only to offer the services but also, where appropriate, to train the helpee in interpersonal or specialty area skills, thus implementing the concept of "training as a preferred mode of treatment."

Helpers learn helping skills.

The trainer, in turn, must be accomplished not only in her human, educational and career achievement specialty skill area but also in the specialty skill area involved in the training and teaching of skills in both interpersonal and specialty areas. *Thus trainers must learn the technology of training.* In this regard the trainer is responsible to both the helper she trains and to the helpee who is serviced or trained by the helper. Trainers learn to systematize and utilize different teaching and training methodologies in their specialty areas. Flowing from these methodologies the trainer learns the procedures of classroom or learning management. The movement from trainer to master trainer simply involves the conquering of training skills within one of the areas of living, learning or working skills.

Trainers learn training skills.

In addition to all of the other human, educational and career achievement skills which the consultant must incorporate in becoming expert in the physical, emotional and intellectual functions of human resource development, he must also become accomplished in special management or administrative skills. *He must learn the technology of consultancy.* In particular, the consultant must become accomplished in organizational skills that enable him to relate and supervise the activities of the master trainers, trainers, helpers and helpees and their programs. Because he must attend to the community from which the trainers and helpers as well as the helpees come, the consultant must learn the skills necessary to develop an effective environment, both personal and physical. The master consultant extends these directions in emphasizing the skills necessary to develop the community-at-large, for she has responsibility for changing the system that produces the victims with whom she and her subordinates work. Master consultants must learn, then, all of the skills necessary to plan and effect changes on a community-wide basis, all of which brings them into the socio-political realm in their constant search for developing the most effective ways of benefiting humans.

Consultants learn consultancy skills.

At each level, the people and programs become responsible for the people and programs at previous levels; they do so with higher levels of intensity and expertise and with the perspective of other learnings. Helpees are responsible initially only to themselves; they move progressively toward responsibility for their loved ones and those around them. Helpers are responsible for helpees; trainers for helpers and helpees; master trainers for trainers, helpers and helpees, consultants for master trainers, trainers, helpers and helpees. *At each level a technology can be designed to guide the development of the skills which an individual requires to discharge his or her responsibilities as well as those he or she requires to guide his or her movement to the next level.* It must be emphasized that, at each level of development, the leaders must continue to use their best interpersonal skills in sizing up and filling in the needs of their trainees or helpees. Indeed, leaders functioning at the highest levels must respond as much to what is missing as to what is present in behavior; sometimes they may find needs which they cannot fill immediately and they must work with the trainees or helpees or call upon persons with special expertise to develop the necessary technology.

Each level incorporates the previous levels.

Skills

The skills involved may be broken down according to three basic levels: 1) the learner level skills programs involving helpee development; 2) the human, educational and career achievement skills necessary to develop human resources; and 3) the higher-level skills necessary to manage HRD.

Learner-Level Skills

At the most basic skills level the helpee-learner may learn how to do the things that make helping possible. Programs have been developed to teach the helpee-learner how to explore himself, understand himself and act upon his understanding. The helpee learns first to explore herself in relation to her problem and her world and most basically in relation to herself. Behaviorally, the helpee first learns to express personally relevant material with increasingly higher levels of autonomy and emotional proximity. He then learns to understand himself

202

in relation to himself and his problems. Behaviorally, the helpee learns to formulate responses that are interchangeable with the feeling and the meaning of her own explorations. In addition, she learns to employ the base of interchangeable responses to go beyond her own expressions in formulating understanding responses that answer the question "What am I really saying about myself?" Finally, the helpee learns to act upon his understanding. Behaviorally, he learns to develop action programs that flow systematically from his understanding. *In each of these phases the helpee-learner may be taught systematically the learning behaviors involved.*

Skills in being helped emphasize exploring, understanding and action.

Human Achievement Skills

At the levels of both helpers and trainers, the skills are the same, with experience, expertise and training skills differentiating who provides the direct service to the helpee and who develops the helper personnel. Thus within the living skills or human achievement area, both helper and trainer may become expert in the physical fitness skills which lead to improvement on indices of cardio-respiratory functioning, along with rest and nutrition, endurance, strength and flexibility (Collingwood, 1976). Together, these help to define the development of the physical energy level necessary for the development of human resources.

Physical fitness programs emphasize the development of physical energy level.

Another set of skills within the human achievement area involves interpersonal skills. The interpersonal skills emphasize the attending, responding, personalizing and initiating skills necessary to involve the helpee-learner in the learning process of exploration, understanding and action (Carkhuff, 1972).

Interpersonal skills emphasize responsive and initiative dimensions.

Another set of human achievement skills is the problem-solving or decision-making skills. These emphasize the problem definition, goal definition, and value hierarchy development necessary to select preferred courses of action (Carkhuff, 1973).

Decision-making skills emphasize selecting courses of action.

Finally, within the human achievement skills area are the program development skills necessary to implement preferred courses of action to get the helpee-learner from where he or she is to where he or she wants or needs to be. These program development skills emphasize operationalizing the goals in terms of the steps needed to achieve them (Carkhuff, 1974).

Program development skills emphasize steps to goals.

Educational Achievement Skills

With the learning skills or educational achievement skills area, the helpers or trainers learn the skills which they need in order to develop their content or curriculum to a skills objective. Included are the interpersonal and program development skills as well as the facts, concepts and principles which support the achievement of a skills objective (Carkhuff and Berenson, 1976).

Content development skills emphasize achieving a skills objective.

Also, within the educational achievement skills area are the diagnostic skills which enable the helper to diagnose the helpee-learner's level of functioning in terms of the skills objective. This diagnosis is based upon the number of steps that the helpee-learner is able to achieve toward the skill objective (Carkhuff and Berenson, 1976).

Educational and diagnostic skills emphasize assessments of the helpee-learner's level of functioning.

Another set of educational achievement skills are the goal-setting skills which are based upon the diagnosis of the helpee-learner's level of functioning. The goals are

204

set and sequenced according to the diagnosis of the number of steps that the helpee-learner is able to achieve and the learning style preferences which he or she has (Carkhuff and Berenson, 1976).

Educational goal-setting skills emphasize setting achievable goals.

Finally, within the educational achievement skills area are the teaching delivery skills. These emphasize the teaching methods, learning strategies and classroom management procedures utilized in order to make the delivery of the skills involved (Carkhuff and Berenson, 1976).

Career Achievement Skills

Within the working skills or career achievement skills area, the helpers or trainers learn the skills which the helpee-learners need in order to expand their awareness of career alternatives. These career expanding skills emphasize the occupational areas and educational levels that generate new career alternatives (Carkhuff and Friel, 1974).

Career expanding skills emphasize the awareness of career alternatives.

Also within the career achievement skills area are the career narrowing skills which the helpee-learners need in order to choose their career alternatives. These career narrowing skills emphasize the development of value hierarchies and job requirements necessary to narrow career alternatives (Carkhuff and Friel, 1974).

Career narrowing skills emphasize choosing career alternatives.

Another set of skills within the career achievement skills area are the career planning skills which the helpee-learners need in order to achieve their career alternatives. These career planning skills emphasize the development of career routes and career action programs (Carkhuff and Friel, 1974).

Career planning skills emphasize developing a career program.

Finally, there is the set of career achievement skills that involve preparing for the career. In addition to the vocational-technical skills preparation, these preparation skills involve finding, acquiring, holding and being promoted in a job (Carkhuff and Friel, 1974; Carkhuff, Pierce, Friel and Willis, 1975).

Career preparation skills emphasize achieving a career.

Higher-Level Achievement Skills

At the levels of master trainer, consultant and master consultant there are a variety of other skills that must be developed. At the master trainer level we find the training necessary to supervise trainers and the program development skills necessary to develop programs in human, educational and career achievement skills (Carkhuff, Berenson, Friel and Pierce, 1977). At the consulting level we find the organizational development and management skills needed to make the personnel and program assignments necessary to develop human resources (Carkhuff, Friel and Pierce, 1977). Finally, at the master consultant level we find the skills necessary to conduct needs assessments and to develop the technologies to meet these needs (Berenson, 1977).

At all of these levels we find the research and evaluation skills necessary to assess program effectiveness. The teaching-as-treatment process is incomplete until it is evaluated. Evaluation skills include, of course, design and research skills. However, the real-life purpose of evaluation, often forgotten, is not to prove or to disprove hypotheses but to improve promising people and programs in order to increase their effectiveness in a continuous search for the most effective ways of helping people.

Summary and Implications

The real advantage of a technology is that it provides

an individual with the direct opportunity to test it out in his or her own experience. Not abstract or theoretical, hopefully empirically-based and modified, the technology nevertheless does not rest upon its research but upon its usefulness in everyday experience. Thus a technology puts itself to the test of functionality: *either it is useful or it is not.* A technology is the only honest way for a profession to proceed to attempt to make delivery to its clientele.

The technology is testable in experience.

The development of a technology for helper training is not really a new direction. It is as old as science itself. Certainly as old as the study of behavior! Surely as old as trait-and-factor approaches in counseling! Only no one carried their constructs and methodologies far enough to account for human and community resource development. We can do this now—drawing upon those constructs and methodologies. We must do this now!

A technology can account for human and community resource development.

Developing a technology has many implications. Perhaps the most important of these is the implication for the evaluation of professional standards. Professionals must develop skills beyond the direct dispensing of services in the helping role because they can find others to do that job as well as they can. *Professionals must be developed and compete on the basis of functionality.* This assumption of functions provides a unique opportunity for the development of professional resources, for productivity and creativity at unprecedented levels.

A technology contributes to the elevation of professional standards.

Resistance is to be anticipated. There are many who have been attracted to the helping area simply because there are no criteria—simply to avoid the "crunch" of the outside world. There are many who would argue that a technology takes the spontaneity and creativity out of helping—indeed out of life. *There is no spontaneity and creativity without the basic responses in one's repertoire!* Besides, those who choose the "free" course need not be paid for it.

A technology elicits resistance.

Most important, a technology delivers results. Because the skills are defined; because the goals are operationalized in behavioral terms; because the steps to achieve the goals move systematically from the least to the most difficult; because a technology is both means and ends: for all these reasons, a technology delivers the results which it sets out to achieve. It is ironical for the helping professions in general and for counseling specifically, but *with the development of a technology these specialties, which are currently not accountable for any outcomes, may be the only ones offering people—students and counselees, parents and teachers—tangible skills which they can use in their everyday lives.*

A technology delivers results.

Our basic principle in life is this: *the only reason to live is to grow; therefore growth is worth any price.* Our growth as individuals and our contributions to the growth of our profession or our community are predicated upon this principle. A technology allows us to pay the price of growth for it defines the skills and the work to be accomplished to achieve the skills. We might restate the principle: *growth is worth any price—even work!*

A technology allows us to grow.

The choice is ours. We can continue to live like fools producing unmotivated counselors with 13% success rates or motivated counselors with 25% success rates or even 50% or 67% success rates. Or we can demand of ourselves and the counselors we train a level of skill acquisition necessary for success rates closer to 100%. And in those instances where we fall shy of our goal, we can choose to determine the reason why. We can choose, like our helpees, between resisting growth and growing. When we choose for ourselves, we choose for all mankind. If we cannot choose to grow, then there is no future for us, our profession or our world.

A technology allows us to choose life or death.

References

Berenson, B. G.   **Introduction to human technology.** Amherst, Mass.: Human Resource Development Press, in press, 1977.

Berenson, B. G. and Carkhuff, R. R.   **Sources of gain in counseling and psychotherapy.** New York: Holt, Rinehart and Winston, 1967.

Carkhuff, R. R.   **Helping and human relations. Volumes I and II.** New York: Holt, Rinehart and Winston, 1969.

Carkhuff, R. R.   **The development of human resources.** New York: Holt, Rinehart and Winston, 1971.

Carkhuff, R. R.   **The art of helping.** Amherst, Mass.: Human Resource Development Press, 1972.

Carkhuff, R. R.   **The art of problem-solving.** Amherst, Mass.: Human Resource Development Press, 1973.

Carkhuff, R. R.   **How to help yourself: The art of program development.** Amherst, Mass.: Human Resource Development Press, 1974.

Carkhuff, R. R. and Berenson, B. G.   **Beyond counseling and therapy.** New York: Holt, Rinehart and Winston, 1967.

Carkhuff, R. R. and Berenson, D. H.   **The art of teaching series.** Amherst, Mass.: Human Resource Development Press, 1976.

Carkhuff, R. R., Berenson, D. H., Friel, T. W. and Pierce, R. M.   **The art of training.** Amherst, Mass.: Human Resource Development Press, in preparation, 1977.

Carkhuff, R. R., Friel, T. W. and Pierce, R. M.   **The art of consulting.** Amherst, Mass. Human Resource Development Press, in preparation, 1977.

Carkhuff, R. R. and Friel, T. W. **The career skills series.** Amherst, Mass.: Human Resource Development Press, 1974.

Carkhuff, R. R., Pierce, R. M., Friel, T. W. and Willis, D. **GETAJOB.** The art of placing yourself on a job. Amherst, Mass.: Human Resource Development Press, 1975.

Carkhuff, R. R. and Pierce, R. M. **Helping begins at home.** Amherst, Mass.: Human Resource Development Press, 1976.

Clark, K. E., et al. Committee on the scientific and professional aims of psychology, Report to Board of Directors and Council of Representatives of APA. **American Psychologist,** 1964, **20,** 95-100.

Collingwood, T. **Get fit for living.** Amherst, Mass.: Human Resource Development Press, 1976.

Friel, T. and Minor, F. An experimental, educational and career exploration system. **Personnel and Guidance Journal,** 1970, **49,** 193-194.

Friel, T. Educational and career exploration system: The development of a systematic, computer-based, career guidance program. New York: International Business Machines Corporation, 1972.

Ivey, A. E., Normington, C. Miller, C. D. Morril, W. H. and Haase, R. F. Microcounseling and attending behavior: An approach to prepracticum counselor training. **Journal of Counseling Psychology, Monograph Supplement,** 1968, **15,** 1-12.

Kagan, N., Krathwohl, D. R. and Farquhar, W. W. IPR-Interpersonal process recall: Stimulated recall by videotape. Research Report, No. 24, 1965, Bureau of Educational Research Services, Michigan State University.

Krasner, L. and Ullman, L. **Research in behavior modification.** New York: Holt, Rinehart and Winston, 1965.

Krumboltz, J. D. and Thoreson, C. **Behavioral counseling.** New York: Holt, Rinehart and Winston, 1969.

Mosher, R. L. and Sprinthall, N. A. Psychological education: A means to promote personal development during adolescence. **The Counseling Psychologist,** 1971, **2,** 3-84.

Patterson, C. H. Counseling. In **Annual Review of Psychology,** Palo Alto, California: Annual Reviews, Inc., 1966, 79-110.

Patterson, C. H. What is counseling psychology? **Journal of Counseling Psychology,** 1969, **16,** 23-29.

Rogers, C. R., Gendlin, E. T., Kiesler, D. J. and Truax, C. B. **The therapeutic relationship and its impact.** Madison, Wisconsin: University of Wisconsin Press, 1967.

Super, D. E. **The psychology of careers.** New York: Harper & Row, 1957.

Thompson, A. S. and Super, D. E. (Eds.) **The professional preparation of counseling psychologists: Report of the 1964 Grayston Conference.** New York: Teachers College, Columbia, 1964.

Truax, C. B. and Carkhuff, R. R. **Toward effective counseling and psychotherapy.** Chicago: Aldine, 1967.

Tyler, Leona **The work of the counselor.** New York: Appleton, 1953.

Chapter Ten

TTS:
The Teaching-as-Treatment System

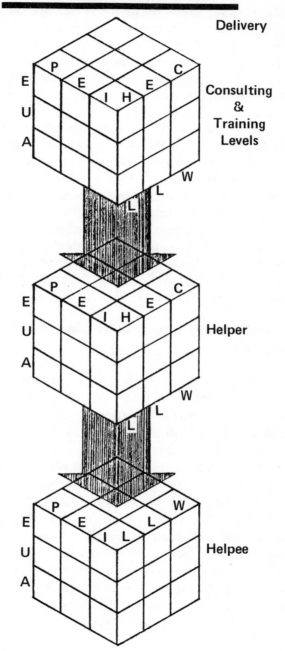

The typical counselor behaves in stereotyped ways (Friel, 1971). In schools, he or she works an average of 32.8 hours a week. He or she is assigned 347 students. He or she sees each student an average of 3.8 times per year for a total of 343 hours per year or 8.6 hours per week. During the week, he or she sees around 50 students for a little over 15 minutes each. Over 50% of these student contacts are related to filling out transcripts.

The typical counselor does many other things (see Table 10-1). He or she goes to two meetings a week for over an hour each time. He or she spends 12 25-minute blocks of time on clerical activities each week, sees teachers 8 times each week for 13 minutes each and parents 9 times each week for 17 minutes each, sees administrators 4 times for 15 minutes each, college representatives 2 times for 14 minutes and heads of departments 2 times for 11 minutes each. There are many more things that he or she does or does not do, depending upon how you look at it.

There is very little time for counseling, let alone for helping.

The typical counselor does not enter the environment of the students with whom he works. He almost never visits their homes except by accident. He often lives outside of the neighborhoods of his counselees. He does not know most of the parents, the people who have the greatest effect upon the kids. And what he does know is sparse and could hardly make a beneficial difference.

The typical counselor does not try to affect the people who affect the student most in school. He or she does little work with teachers because, to tell the truth, they don't respect him or her. They see her as a teaching drop-out or as a quasi-administrator "on the make" at the counselor rung in the career ladder. The counselor, in turn, does little to teach parents to support teachers or to prepare employers to receive students.

213

Table 10-1

Allocations of Time and Contacts of Guidance Counselors

	Administrators	Clerical	College Post High	Graduate	Heads of Dept's.	Job Reference	Meetings	Misc. Others	Misc. Forms	Students	Parents	Special School Services	Group Speaking	Teachers	Testing	Transcripts	Visit Colleges	Visit Employers
% of Total Contacts (with transcripts)	3	10	2	1	2	1	2	2	1	45	8	2	—	7	—	11	—	1
% of Total Time	3	9	2	1	2	1	8	5	1	39	7	2	1	5	—	12	2	1
% of Total Contacts (with transcripts)	4	12	2	1	2	1	2	3	1	51	9	2	—	8	—		—	1
% of Total Time	4	10	3	1	2	1	10	6	1	44	8	2	1	5	—		2	1
Avg. Time/Contact in Minutes	15	25	14	7	11	2	67	30	5	17	17	16	11	13	4	9	26	4
Avg. % of Contacts/Week (28 weeks)	4	12	2	1	2	1	2	3	1	51	9	2	—	8	—	13	—	1

The typical counselor does not enter the frame of reference of the counselees. To be sure, he has little time. But time problems aside, he has few interpersonal skills. His mind is on other things, like transcripts and other clerical tasks. He hardly ever uses feeling words, let alone accurate ones, because to do so would break his concentration. Even those counselors supposedly "trained" in interpersonal skills say "You feel that ..." and proceed to restate the problem that the counselee presented in a much poorer way than the counselee did.

The typical counselor does not bring the session to a course of action, let alone a simple homework assignment. She does not know how to go about systematically helping someone else to solve problems or make decisions systematically because she does not know how to solve problems or make decisions for herself. She does not know how to go about systematically helping someone else to develop programs because she does not develop programs for herself. Witness her growing flabbiness—physical, emotional and intellectual.

The typical counselor does not teach skills because he does not have skills, either to teach or to teach with. He does not know how to live effectively—if you don't believe it, take a look at his family before you seek his help for yours. He does not know how to learn effectively. Try asking him questions in his teaching specialty area and see if he can answer any beyond the junior high school level. See when he really read his last professional book—not the popular version meant for the consumption of his counselees. He does not know how to work effectively. Just take another look at his working schedule.

The typical counselor does not use materials, either for training the counselees or for making homework reading assignments. He wouldn't even know what materials to use if his counselees asked him to provide some—which they do, only he doesn't hear them.

The typical counselor sees the counselees individually and not in groups. At that, he sees very little of the counselees because he can't see over the top of the transcript.

The typical counselor does no training, whether for individuals or for groups. She talks about things rather than doing things, deals with concepts rather than principles or skills.

The typical counselor does no systematic follow-up on the growth and development of the counselees. He has only an anecdotal accounting system based upon random meetings.

The typical counselor does not even use the barest skills necessary for conducting research on the outcomes of her counselees. She does not even use the counting system to categorize her counselees as they move on into the real-life world.

The typical counselor is acutely aware of the burdens which are placed upon him. He verbalizes an eagerness to overthrow all of the irrelevant clerical duties but appears thwarted in his attempts to do anything about them. The system, it appears, does not emphasize the kinds of personal counseling activities that led him into counseling in the first place.

The typical counselor is upset and hurt, yes, maligned, abused, resentful, even angered by this issue of accountability. Here he is exhausting all his energies to complete his 32.8 hours and fill out all of his transcripts by early Friday afternoon in order to have a long weekend to "get it all out of his system" and get "reinvigorated." And these so-called management experts come along and ask questions about the cost benefits of his counseling.

"Why," he comments weepily, "they never even filled out a transcript."

An Effective Delivery

It is no different for other areas within the helping professions. Only the names and faces change. The antecedents and consequences remain the same.

The fault never lies in the system *per se.* The fault lies

216

in people (Carkhuff, 1974).

The system will never ask us to do the things we are committed to doing. Indeed, in its concern with and representation of the apparency of things, it may ask us to pursue activities that are independent of or even opposite to our commitments.

It is up to us whether we are effective or not. We must demonstrate the effectiveness of our programs, either within their schedule or outside of it.

First, the schedule which they appear to assign us is never as bad as we make it out to be. We can carry out most of our assignments more efficiently within the system than we currently do. The system just does not demand that much efficiency in working.

Second, if we cannot carry out our commitments within the allocated time, then we must add time in order to do so. We simply add the necessary hours to the 32.8 we are currently spending on the job. The system never asks for that much time from anyone.

It is not a question of either overthrowing a system or supporting it. Many young people make the mistake of believing that they must "overthrow" the system. They are "wasted" because even if they win, and that is seldom, they are caught up in a lot of activities that are extraneous to their original purposes.

The question is, are we willing to work within the system to achieve our outcomes? Are we willing to reorganize our activities and our schedules in such a way that we achieve the human benefits that we are committed to achieving? The system never asks for human benefits.

What are the benefits we wish to achieve and how do we achieve them?

Growth Benefits

First, we as helper-teachers must be sure that the system affords us an opportunity to grow. There must be something in it for us. Our behavior must be instrumental for some purposes. There must be an opportunity to grow personally and professionally.

If we behave in ways that do not reward us personally and professionally, we decline rapidly in our functioning. And even if we do behave in ways that reward us, we must exercise care that the ways are personalized and the goals individualized for our purposes.

This means that, like helpee-learners, we must explore where we are and understand where we want to be both personally and professionally. Then we must set up systematic action programs to get there.

We must have personal development and career development programs. The personal development programs include our own physical, emotional and intellectual development as well as the development of our loved ones around us. The career development must include the same career routes and action programs that enable us to develop and climb well-defined career ladders within the system.

We must do all of these things for ourselves or we cannot hope to do them for someone else. We must organize ourselves within the system for our own growth benefits or we will not be able to do this for someone else. We will not even be able to empathize with the growth process of the people with whom we work.

When we choose to grow, we choose for all of our helpees.

When we choose to deteriorate, we choose for all of our helpees.

Helping begins by helping ourselves.

Learning begins by learning ourselves.

All growth activities flow from these fundamental assumptions.

Growth Process

There are at least a dozen activities which will allow us to fulfill our commitment to the growth of our helpee-learners. In an organized helping program, these activities will enable us to be accountable as helpers and as human beings.

These activities are related to the phases of learning, with a special emphasis upon the action phase. They begin by entering the helpee's frame of reference and conclude by assessing whether or not the intended outcomes were achieved.

1. **We must enter the frame of reference of our helpees.** This principle reflects the basic principle of learning. All learning begins with the learner's frame of reference. This means that in every helping situation, whether we have five minutes or an hour, we take part of the time to facilitate the helpee's exploration of where he or she is in relation to the world. It is important to remember that this is no more than the beginning point in the growth process.

Here an energetic, bright 40-year-old man in conflict about some of his relationships with people at home and work begins:

Helpee: It used to be difficult for me to know when to draw the line with people ... get angry or come down on them ... I was always told that I had a bad temper ... but I try to do what is fair ... as a matter of fact my world is made up of people. Well now ... I give them three strikes ... then they're out ... I write them off ... or try to ... but it really doesn't work for me ... I want to be sure I've done everything I can.

Helper-Teacher: You feel conflicted because you want to do the right thing but you're not sure when to show your anger.

Helpee: Yes ... but it's more than that ... I really don't want to write anyone off ... it would be like writing myself off. So I tolerate a great deal ... more than I should sometimes.

Helper-Teacher: You often get very angry with yourself because you let some people go too far and

Helpee: I feel bad when I get tough ... or come down on people ... especially my family ... I don't know ... I guess I'm right as often as I miss ... that's really terrible because I really love them.

Helper-Teacher: You often feel guilty because you save it up and then hurt those you care about when you do let go.

Helpee: Hurt them and yes ... hurt myself ... and I'm not in control of it.

Helper-Teacher: You're afraid because you want to be helpful ... be really ... a good person but you don't know when to be tolerant and when to show your wrath.

2. **We must enter the environment of our helpees.** This is an extension of the first activity. It is not enough to see the world as the helpee sees it. We must also continue to see it through our own eyes. This means entering the home, school and work environment of our helpees. This activity provides us not only with a richer picture but also with a "reality check" on our helpee's experience. It is also the first stage of involving the people in the environment in the helping process. We involve them by helping them to explore where they are in relation to their world, especially to our helpee within it.

The helper-teacher visited the helpee's home to learn that the helpee's report of how he responds to his family was largely true. The helper-teacher also learned that the helpee's wife often felt that she was left out of major decisions. In addition she expressed feelings of insecurity about the future. The helper-teacher learns that the helpee has no defined goals.

Wife: My husband really works hard ... does all he

220

	can do ... perhaps ... tries too much because he thinks he can't make mistakes like others ... yet when I make a mistake he leaves room for it. With himself though ... he is never really consistent.
Helper-Teacher:	Sometimes you resent being treated differently than he treats himself.
Helpee's Wife:	Yes ... but more like I'm not sure what he really wants ... so I do what I think needs to be done ... sometimes it works out ... but it's confusing ... he is busy but well ... I don't know where it's going ... what it's leading to.
Helper-Teacher:	You feel lost because you don't know what the goals are ... perhaps because your husband does not know and/or does not share them with you.
Helpee's Wife:	It's more like he doesn't know really ... what his goals are.

3. **We must relate our helpee's frame of reference to goals in his or her environment.** The purpose of facilitating our helpee's exploration is to contribute to his understanding of where he is in relation to where he wants to be. Where he wants to be is a goal which exists in relation to his living, learning and working situations in his home, school, work and community settings. In other words, his goals, personal or otherwise, occur in his real-life environment.

After the home visit the helper-teacher and the helpee interact again:

Helpee:	It's not that they don't respect me ... I know they do ... but there are times when ... they

have feelings like well they wish I was more like ... different ... more forceful.

Helper-Teacher: It hurts because the family acts like you let them down ... even when you try your best.

Helpee: I do what I have to but I don't always know what that is ... so I lay back ... and tell them to grow by trying things out on their own. They reuse it ... that I don't know what to do.

Helper-Teacher: You're fed up with yourself because you haven't given the family direction ... leadership and you know that is what they want and need.

Helpee: Yes ... they ... need to ah ... know that I'm going ... I'm about something ... in addition to good intentions ... if I'm about being a good person than I'd know what I expect from people and I'd tell them.

4. **We must relate the environment's goals to the helpee's functioning within the environment.** Just as an individual has goals that relate to her environment, so the environment has goals that relate to the individual. The home, school, work and community environments have expectations concerning the helpee's living, learning and working performance within these environments. Just as the individual focuses upon where she wants to be, so the environment focuses upon where she needs to be in order to get to where she wants to be.

During a second home visit the helper-trainer teaches the helpee's wife basic responding skills. The helpee's wife readily agrees to use those skills to help her husband think through decisions he must make in the near future. She understands that her immediate goal is to help her husband spell out what is important to him.

222

5. **We must bring helping to a course of action related to achieving the goals.** Having set the goals for where the helpee wants and needs to be, it is now critical that we bring helping to an action course. The choice of a course of action to solve a problem or achieve a goal may be accomplished through problem-solving or decision-making activities. The preferred course of action will then be operationalized and implemented through program development activities.

During several subsequent sessions with the helpee the helper-teacher explores what is important to the helpee.

Helpee: I've got to get it straight before I can give other people direction. All I know is I want them to be their best ... do the best they can do and hope they can do better.

Helper-Teacher: You're certain that you want them to grow and continue to grow and whatever you do must reflect that. The first step is to get input from them.... In order to do that you have to learn how to respond to them ... so that whatever goals you and they define ... reflects **who they are** too.

6. **We must use teaching and training procedures to implement the course of action.** Clearly, it is not enough to develop a program to implement a preferred course of action. We must also teach the helpee everything the helpee needs to know in order to achieve the goals of the preferred course of action. This activity involves teaching or training in any of the specialty areas needed to achieve the goal.

Helper-Teacher: This is a copy of **The Art of Helping.** We're going to use it to learn how to respond and later how to initiate at home. If you look

here ... the first goal is to learn to attend
... let's you and I try it ... O.K. I want you
to sit like I am ... right ... square off ... lean
into me.

Helpee: I get it ... I don't always look at who I'm
talking with ... it helps ... I have the feeling
now that you are willing to or you're ready.

Helper-Teacher: You feel comfortable because you have my
individual attention. Now you might share
something with me because I'm attending to
you.... If I attend well enough then I can
observe you **and** listen.

Helpee: Guess I can't really respond to anyone if I
don't listen ... and ... if I don't observe and
attend I can't really hear what they are
saying....

Helper-Teacher: Right, it is comfortable because it makes
sense. Now I'm going to share an experience
I had today ... while I talk I want you to
attend ... right, lean in ... look in the direction of my face ... your right shoulder to my
left.

7. **We must teach transferable skills.** The teaching
always involves skills because all learning culminates in skills objectives. Skills alone are what the
helpees carry away from the helping sessions. In
this context, skills must be taught in ways that
are transferable to real-life activities involving living, learning and working.

During training the teacher-helper encourages exploring how the helpee might use his new skills in other settings with other people.

Helpee: I can see now why it is so important to attend
and observe ... so that you can respond
appropriately ... to the person ... can't say
the same things the same way to two different people.

Helper-

Teacher: I make you more confident about what you
            are doing ... and keep you on track.

Helpee: Yes ... it ... with knowing how people feel
            and why ... will help ... like you and I did
            ... set useful goals. So I attend to observe
            ... observe to listen, respond to personalize
            so we can do something about whatever.

Helper-

Teacher: It feels darn good to have that kind of direc-
            tion for any situation with people. You have
            the input you need to tell where they are
            coming from ... where they need to be and
            we will work on how to develop steps to get
            them there.

Helpee: And get me there ... where I want to be ...
            I guess this is where I want to be, the **steps,**
            the **skills** ... on how to be helpful. Yeah,
            that's where I want to be.

8. **We must teach the skills to groups.** The most efficient and effective way to teach skills is to groups.
   In groups, the helpee-learners learn not only from
   the helpers but, with training, from the other
   helpee-learners who have acquired the skills.
   Group teaching or group training is the preferred
   mode of treatment.

After the helpee mastered the basic helping and program development skills he trained several people in his
work setting. First he trained with the helper-teacher as
his coach then he trained on his own with periodic consultation sessions with the helper-trainer.

Helpee: It's going fairly well ... but as soon as you
            get to responding ... they forget to attend
            and observe.

Helper-

Teacher: It's frustrating because they seem to forget
            what they learn. You must keep the train-
            ing ... learning cumulative. When you rate

225

their attending **and** observing skills.

9. **We must make homework assignments.** We must not only teach the skills but make homework assignments concerning their use. What happens between sessions is far more important than what happens within the sessions. These assignments must involve specific skills material designed to consolidate helpee skills gains.

Helpee: It's hard to stay on track with the training ... I get off sometimes.

Helper-Teacher: You get lost because you're not sure what the next step is. Here is a copy of **The Art of Helping Trainer's Guide.** Study the first two sections for our next meeting ... and before you start jot down the questions you have ... then read to answer the questions you have. Like "How important is it to give trainees a map of where it's all going?"

10. **We must teach the environment how to support the helpees.** We must utilize the home, school, work and community environment to support the growth of the helpee. This means that we must teach the people in these environments the skills that they need to support the living, learning and working skills development of the helpee. In this manner, the environment becomes a facilitator rather than a retarder.

After the helpee-trainer trained several co-workers he developed support programs. That is programs designed to help his trainees support and guide the efforts of other people in their lives. Together the helpee-trainer and his trainees developed physical conditioning programs, programs to facilitate communications during staff meetings and programs to update each other on technical developments in their departments.

226

11. **We must follow-up on our helping-teaching activities.** More important than the teaching itself is the follow-up. Here we help the helpees to make living, learning and working applications in their real-life worlds. Conducting follow-up programs enables our helpees to surmount the crises that may otherwise have defeated their growth and development.

Even after the helpee-trainer learned training skills the helper visited the helpee's training sessions, work setting and home in order to conduct follow-up consultations and bring the helpee up to date on the latest helping and training technology. In addition these follow-up visits provided the helper-teacher with the input he needed to sharpen his training technology.

12. **We must assess the outcomes of our helping-teaching efforts.** Assessing the outcomes of our helping efforts is, in one sense, the final step in our accountability. We simply determine whether we have achieved the effects that we intended to achieve in the living, learning and working skills areas. In a more important respect, this is not the final step because the outcome assessments provide us with the feedback that we need to modify our programs and recycle the helping process through exploration, understanding and action to still higher level outcomes.

Follow-up visits provided the helper-teacher with the opportunities to assess the helping and training effectiveness of the helpee-trainer. The helper-teacher was able to obtain pre-post measures of the helpee-trainer's trainees levels of physical, emotional, interpersonal and intellectual skills functioning.

If we organize our helping activities to enter the frame of reference and the environment of the helpee to explore and understand goals in that environment, then we bring the helping process to an action course through teaching transferable skills in groups and following up with homework assignments and environmental and crisis-support activities, so that we can achieve the outcomes which we set out to achieve. If we engage in growth activities, we will make an effective delivery to our helpees. We will be accountable, as human beings and as helpers.

An Effective Delivery System

Another way of characterizing our human delivery is to say that we are all teachers. And at another level, in order to be teachers we must first be learners.

The beginning of the development of a functional human delivery system is the recognition that we are all both teachers and learners. We have something to give and something to receive. The function of a delivery system is to fill one person's need so that he or she can fill another person's need and so on.

Delivery systems are simply ways of organizing people and programs to deliver (D) and support (S) the delivery of the desired products (P) or outcomes to the primary recipient population (Carkhuff, 1976). P, D & S are the ingredients of an effective delivery system. In this case, the primary product or outcome is living, learning and working skills development and the primary recipient population is the learner (see Figure 10-1). The learner lacks skills. And we wish to deliver skills so that he or she will be equipped to function effectively. The primary objective of the delivery system, then, is to transform the learner from a person without skills to a person with skills. Put in other terms, the primary objective of the delivery system is to transform the learner into a helper or teacher.

In order to deliver skills to learners, we must first deliver skills to our helper-teachers. One of the problems with current organizational systems is that they have no true delivery component. Whether in education or rehabilitation, the helper-teacher is the primary delivery agent in the respect that he or she makes the delivery directly to the primary recipient, the helpee-learner. But there is no one to deliver the needed skills to the helper-teacher. Pre-service programs are inferior and transitory; inservice training programs are inadequate.

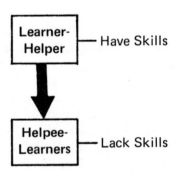

Figure 10-1. A human delivery system delivers skills to learners who lack skills

A typical educational or rehabilitation system is set up to support the helper-teacher (see Figure 10-2). And that is precisely the problem. The clerical personnel collect and process data. The departmental directors or assistant principals administer daily operations. The directors or principals and assistant superintendents manage long-term planning operations. And the executive director or superintendent develops long-term policy and strategies. All support the activities of the helper-teacher. But no one delivers to the helper-teacher the skills which the helper-teacher needs to deliver to the helpee-learner.

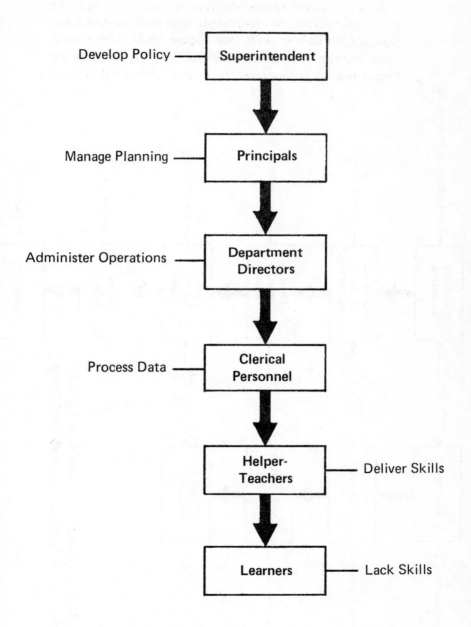

Develop Policy ——— **Superintendent**

Manage Planning ——— **Principals**

Administer Operations ——— **Department Directors**

Process Data ——— **Clerical Personnel**

Helper-Teachers ——— Deliver Skills

Learners ——— Lack Skills

*Figure 10-2. A human delivery system supports the
teacher who delivers the skills to learners who lack skills*   230

In a functional human delivery system, there must be an on-going delivery component with well-defined functions which deliver skills (see Figure 10-3). These functions increase the helper-teacher's skill level so that the helper-teacher can increase the helpee-learner's skill level.

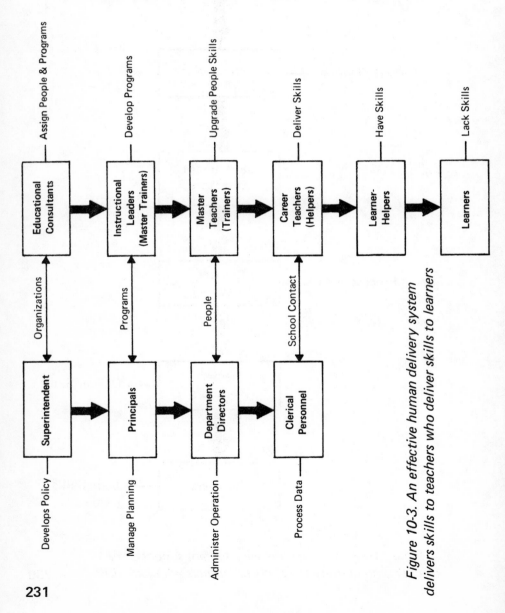

Figure 10-3. An effective human delivery system delivers skills to teachers who deliver skills to learners

At each level, including that of the learner, the personnel function as both teachers and learners. And the support systems operate as a component to support the delivery components.

At the most basic level in a functional human delivery system, the learners who have skills may be used to teach the learners or learnees who do not have skills. This is a classroom management function of the helper-teacher. As such, the procedure is part of the skills which the helper-teacher must learn in order to deliver skills most efficiently and effectively to the learner.

For the learners who have learned the skills, the parents, school teachers and employers may discharge a very critical support function (Carkhuff and Pierce, 1976). They support the practice and application of the skills acquired by helpee-learners. In addition, they serve a monitoring function by providing feedback which the entire delivery system requires in order to make its most effective delivery to the learners.

In order to discharge this critical support function, the parents, school teachers and employers must be equipped at least with the discrimination skills which they require to determine when and what to do and how to report it. In addition, they must learn the necessary interpersonal skills to respond to the helpee-learners' frames of reference; the management skills to stimulate and reinforce learning; and the skills objectives and planning skills to insure the transfer of learning from the helping context to the home, school, work and community context.

Even the helper-teacher level within the system may be developed as a secondary delivery system. Thus helper-teacher candidates may begin at a particular pre-service skill level as helper-teacher interns. With minimum experience and expertise, they may become helper-teachers and, at still higher levels, career helper-teachers.

The content of the teacher's curriculum must include the human achievement skills, in particular interpersonal skills, which enable the teacher to enter the learner's frame of reference; the program development skills that

232

enable the learner to achieve goals developed from his or her frame of reference; the educational achievement skills, including content development and teaching delivery skills, which enable the teacher to develop and deliver skills objectives to the learner; and the career achievement skills, including career awareness and preparation, which enable the learner to transfer his or her experience from the classroom to real-life experiences.

In order to deliver these skills to the teachers, there must be master teachers (trainers) who upgrade the skills of teachers; instructional leaders (master trainers) who develop teaching and teacher-training programs; and educational consultants who organize and assign people and programs. Each of these levels serves a distinct delivery function in a functional human delivery system. In addition, each of these levels is supported by a distinct support function.

Given the support functions at different levels, the main need for the support components is for training in the discrimination skills differentially related to the delivery function. In other words, in order to process data at the school contact level, the clerical personnel must understand the dimensions of the skills delivery made by career helper-teachers. Similarly, the departmental directors must understand the functions of master teachers in training career teachers in order to administer their daily operations in support of the master teachers. Likewise, the principals and other administrators must comprehend the instructional leaders' development of helper-teaching programs in order to effectively manage the long-term planning activities. Finally, the superintendent must understand the consultant's assignment of personnel and programs on functional delivery criteria in order to develop policy and strategies. At every level of the support component, the activities are oriented to the delivery function. The support component does not operate, as is typically the case, with functional autonomy independent of the delivery of teachers and learners. It operates with functional authority to facilitate the delivery of skills through

233

every level of the delivery system.

Perhaps most important to the teacher, while the different levels of the delivery component insure the delivery of skills to the teacher, they also define the steps in the career ladder for teachers who wish to maintain delivery functions rather than taking the traditional route of administration.

A functional human delivery system, then, defines the delivery and support components necessary to deliver skills to the learner. At every level, the personnel have something that they need and something that they give. At the highest level there must be a human technologist or master consultant who develops the information systems to provide the monitoring and feedback support functions as well as the new educational technologies to deliver to the educational consultants (see Figure 10-4).

A functional human delivery system delivers the human technology which develops human resources at every level. Such a system orients the support component to just that function: the support of the activities of the delivery component. And every level of both delivery and support focuses upon its specialty contribution: the direct delivery of skills at the level of human contact; upgrading helper-teacher skills at the people level; assigning personnel and programs to make the system functional at the organizational level; and developing new technologies and the information systems to monitor their delivery at the level of human technologist.

In summary, the teaching-as-treatment system is indeed a teaching system in which every contributor is both teacher and learner. The critical principle is that the helper must become learner before he or she becomes teacher.

Those of us involved in the helping professions have taken a lot for granted. We continue to masturbate by employing practices that have never demonstrated potency. Or we give up and adjust ourselves and become part of the same psychopathic system that produced the victims that produced the helping professions in the first place.

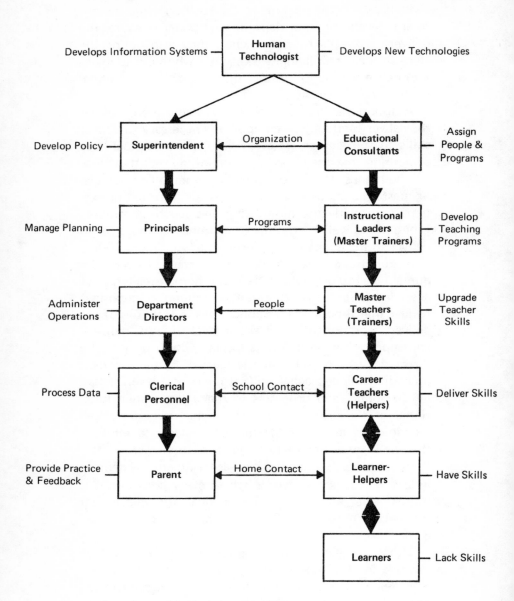

*Figure 10-4. An effective human delivery system
provides the basis for delivery (new technologies)
and support (information systems) components*

The typical counselor lives in a make-believe world. He or she effects the apparency of helpfulness. He or she makes a mutual non-exposure pact with the helpee who effects the apparency of being helped.

The typical counselor chooses this course because he or she has not learned how to live, learn and work effectively because no one ever taught him or her how to do so.

The teaching-as-treatment system offers a choice. To get serious and learn the skills that the counselor needs to become real. Or to give up and continue to be apparent.

References

Carkhuff, R. R.   **Cry Twice!** Amherst, Mass.: Human Resource Development Press, 1974.

Carkhuff, R. R. (Ed.)   **Toward excellence in education.** Amherst, Mass.: Human Resource Development Press, 1977.

Carkhuff, R. R. and Pierce, R. M.   **Helping begins at home.** Amherst, Mass.: Human Resource Development Press, 1976.

Friel, T. W.   Work activities characterizing counselors. New York: International Business Machines Corp., 1971.

Chapter Eleven

Toward Human Values

The choices we think we make in life are only apparent choices. We make many, even most of our choices on the basis of rather superficial concerns or evidence. In reality, the actual choices we make are profound in their common implication: live or die.

The choice is never between one approach to helping or another; that is irrelevant. The choice is never between developing one's own identity or being absorbed into a larger system or larger person; that choice, too, is irrelevant. The only relevant choice and the one we inevitably make, intentionally or not, is to live or to die.

Values and Methods

Individuals cannot choose to live unless they choose to learn: learning that translates to an increased quality of physical, emotional and intellectual responses which, in turn, culminate in living, learning and working productivity.

If you pay the price to learn, then you can grow. If you do not pay the price to learn, then you can only be conditioned.

Those who choose not to pay the price to learn pay with their lives and tragically often with the lives of those with whom they live and work. The reluctant learner is conditioned to rely upon his or her charm and personality; yet he or she knows full well that charm and personality never made a constructive difference to anyone. Charm and personality for the reluctant learner are weapons in the games of seduction and destruction.

There are many variations of the strategies to avoid learning and we have all encountered them. Those employing such strategies range from individuals who assume the role of observer—judges, to those who

238

attempt the role of active critics. In reality, they are the same people: each relying upon image to the exclusion of substance; each leaving learning to others; each asking the teacher to teach in spite of the reluctant learner's best efforts to resist.

The basic value underlying human resource development is growth. All choices can be evaluated positively or negatively depending upon whether anticipated action contributes to growth (life) or not.

Growth is dependent upon learning.

The basic ethic underlying human resource development is a direct translation of the value of growth. The teacher-helper works to: a) give the helpee-learner the skills needed to live, learn and work productively and b) create opportunities for the learner to use these skills.

In the last analysis, the learner may choose to use or not use the skills. If the choice is not to use the skills learned, the teacher-helper can choose to do nothing more for the helpee. The helpee has chosen to remain a victim. The teacher-helper has chosen to continue to grow with or without learners.

If the learner's choice is to learn, then the individual grows to understand:

1. that insights by themselves are impotent;
2. that life demands initiatives, not merely reactions;
3. that at the core of the psychological cripple is the decision to avoid learning at all costs;
4. that logic alone may lead to rigidity, limited input and deterioration;
5. that learning makes it possible to organize life progressively, giving it direction and meaning;
6. that learning makes it possible to view sources of new learning with excitement rather than contempt;
7. that learning equals work and that ignorance breeds cruel cowards;
8. that stupidity is the product of conditioning;
9. that intelligence is the product of learning; and

10. that systematically selected goals and systematic programs to achieve those goals based upon the individual's experience render experience conscious.

Anything less than systematically selected goals and systematically developed programs to achieve goals prepares the individual for conditioning. Conditioning is, in part, the result of limited input that, in turn, limits the organization of experience as well as the meaning of that experience. Under such conditions, the individual comes up empty: without a positive value.

Again, promulgators of rigor and "pure" reason would have us turn logic into debilitating rigidity while the promulgators of meaning would have us turn understanding into impotent concepts. Human resource development will depend upon a human technology that links human values to effective and efficient delivery systems. The human technology will be based upon a comprehensive research—demonstration model complete with formal propositions (Berenson, 1975; Carkhuff and Berenson, 1976). This technology will incorporate rigor within the context of meaning so that description, prediction and partitioning variance will culminate in control and choice because the description will reflect a full exploration, prediction will reflect understanding and partitioning variance will influence action.

Values are not merely reflected in methods.

The methods are the values.

Value "free" systems like behavior modification become victims of their own technology because there are gaps. Technology often organizes only a small portion of human experience because the steps needed to respond fully to human experience are missing. Behavior modification organizes a limited portion of human experience.

In order to be complete, a human technology must create methods that: a) fully respond to what is disorganized in human experience; b) organize what is disorganized; and c) give that organization meaning. The method, if it is this comprehensive, **is** the value.

Because all the traditional approaches to helping are

based upon inadequate responsive methods, they present themselves as value-free systems.

The major ingredients of values in human technology are Learning, Methods and Choices. Learning delivers the responses and skills necessary for the development of comprehensive methods; and comprehensive methods place choices into sharp relief. Learning, Methods and Choices combine to impact the basic physical, emotional and intellectual fabric of life.

When any of the above ingredients are missing, distorted and only apparently constructive human development efforts seek solutions in one extreme or the other of pseudo-dichotomies.

The recent Black movement in this country neutralized its direction when it sought foreign roots.

The politicians seek to control inflation with high unemployment and recession with inflation.

The women's movement has turned to assertive training for its constituents rather than initiative training based upon responsive skills.

Each movement in its own way becomes a victim of the very contempt it has developed for its enemies because the movement lives in a world of pseudo-dichotomies.

Left to systems that do not include learning, comprehensive methods **and** choices, people and their programs become not only apparently value free but immoral as well: there is no ethic because there is no goal related to human growth. Only **some** of the methods can be saved. Only those people willing to learn and use the learnings can be saved.

The ingredients of values in human technology are also the goals and major functions of human technology. Even the learning and the choices collapse into the methods employed so that **responding, organizing** and giving the resulting organization **meaning** is possible.

Together, Learning, Methods and Choices determine goals which, in turn, demand detailed methods (programs) for achieving the goals (see Figure 11-1).

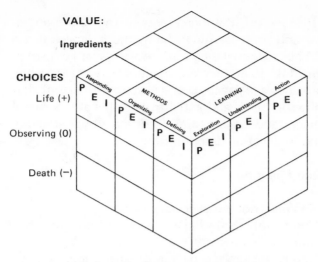

*Figure 11-1. Learning, methods and
choices are the ingredients of values*

All methods, in order to be comprehensive, function by responding to disarray in the human experience, organizing that experience and giving it meaning by operationally defining the experience. The response, organization and meaning are tied to the physical, emotional and intellectual aspects of life just as the exploration, understanding and action necessary for learning are also tied to the physical, emotional and intellectual aspects of the learning task. The choices as they relate to learning and methods have direct implications for the vitality of the physical, emotional and intellectual aspects of life. The basic choice is always one involving life or death. The observer choice, so popular today, is apparent and constitutes a death choice.

The subdivisions of the method—responding to what is in disarray, organizing what is in disarray and giving the organization meaning—are the subgoals in any human resource development program as well as the core method. *The method is the value.*

In a healthy system as in a healthy person, the learning and methods support life choices and life choices are implemented by increased learning and methods.

242

In a sick system, the ingredients of the values are incomplete and limit learning; the methods service death choices. The individual is conditioned to: avoid constructive solutions; tolerate pain; make cruelty reasonable; give his or her allegiance to any system (or person) that helps him or her walk a tightrope; alienate personal experiences; and accept and facilitate physical, emotional and intellectual deterioration.

Values and Learning

Learning does not equal conditioning.

Learning requires entering the learner's frame of reference; conditioning does not.

Learning is not limited by the original stimulus complex and includes transferable strategies. Conditioning is limited and dependent upon the characteristics of the original stimulus complex.

Learning requires systematic goal definition and systematic programs to achieve goals and is therefore conscious. Conditioning is dependent upon externally determined objectives, often random and remote, and is therefore unconscious.

Learning involves the reproduction of behaviors whenever and wherever those behaviors are functional for the achievement of systematically developed, personally relevant goals. Conditioning involves the production of behavior whenever and wherever the original stimulus complex is approximated.

Learning increases input by **requiring** exploration that develops into goals (understanding) and culminates in actions to reach goals. Conditioning does not require exploration or understanding, merely a conditioned or unconditioned response to a conditioned or unconditioned stimulus.

When people limit their input because they have limited their learning (exploration, understanding and action), they limit the organization and meaning they can give their experiences. Conditioned people come up empty and ready for more conditioning.

The understanding of what the ingredients are in a personally relevant learning experience is dependent upon exploration, understanding and the resulting action as well as upon the system **and** the skills, if that action is to be effective (see Figure 11-2).

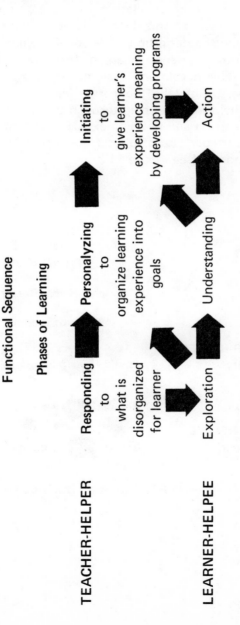

Figure 11-2. The functional sequence of learning

The learning model organizes the basic method (value) of human technology with essential learning behaviors.

The teacher-helper is always responding to the learner's experience of disarray (whether the experience is good or bad) in order to facilitate the learner's exploration of himself or herself in relation to the learning task. The teacher-helper organizes the learner's exploration by facilitating the definition of personalized goals and gives the entire experience meaning (incorporating the new learning) by developing systematic programs to reach the goals. Ultimately, the learner learns to do what the teacher-helper can do: help through teaching by responding, organizing and defining experiences that lead to an expanded repertoire of physical, emotional and intellectual responses (see Figure 11-3).

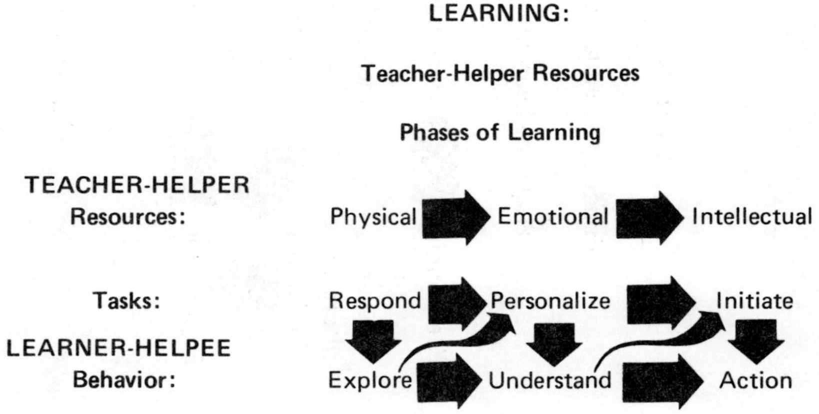

LEARNING:

Teacher-Helper Resources

Phases of Learning

TEACHER-HELPER Resources:	Physical ➡ Emotional ➡ Intellectual
Tasks:	Respond ➡ Personalize ➡ Initiate
LEARNER-HELPEE Behavior:	Explore ➡ Understand ➡ Action

Figure 11-3. The Resources of Learning

The right to learn is earned by exploring, understanding and acting. The right to teach and help is earned by responding, personalizing and initiating. The psychological cripple is someone who cannot or will not learn and, hence, cannot or will not teach. Anything less than a full commitment to learn and use new constructive skills (those that contribute to growth) results in death choices.

The physical resources of the teacher-helper make it possible to respond. The emotional resources **and** the physical resources of the teacher-helper make it possible to personalize goals. The physical, emotional **and** intellectual resources of the teacher-helper make it possible to initiate.

Learning brings together all the critical ingredients of growth or life (see Figure 11-4)—teacher-helper behaviors, learner behaviors, basic life processes—and focuses all of these on methods to organize and give experience meaning so that life choices are more probable. The number of plus choices reflects the learner's level of growth.

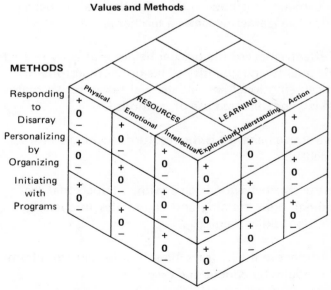

Figure 11-4. The Values and Methods of Learning   **246**

A total learning experience translates to a number of general but important points based upon a set of assumptions about teaching and helping.

Assumptions of a Teaching Approach

Man is intrinsically neither good nor bad.

Man is essentially what he is taught to be or conditioned to be.

The most effective way to help is to teach.

There are an infinite number of teaching programs: as many as there are learners.

If the teaching method is comprehensive, it operationalizes functional intelligence.

Related Points

The learner learns how to do what the teacher-helper can do. The learner becomes a teacher-helper.

The effectiveness of the teacher-helper is directly related to the quality and quantity of his or her repertoire of physical, emotional and intellectual responses so that there is a goal-directed use of methods.

Constructive behavior is the result of teaching constructive behavior.

Constructive behavior begins with interpersonal (responding) skills training and culminates in specialty (definition) skills training.

The learner eventually frees himself or herself from training schedules by conquering them.

The Basic Laws of Teaching-Helping

The more systematic the teaching, the more effective.

The more effective the teaching, the larger the response repertoire learned.

The larger the response repertoire learned, the more creative the learner.

The more creative the learner, the more the learner understands the assumptions and implications of any system.

The more the learner understands the assumptions of any system, the more the learner frees himself of the system.

The more the learner frees himself of any system, the more the learner is likely to conquer and free himself of other systems.

The more the learner conquers and frees himself of other systems, the more the learner is likely to draw from all systems—each as it is appropriate.

The intelligence of the learner is directly related to the number of systems the learner can draw from; and there are an infinite number of systems.

Values and methods lead us to assumptions and the consideration of the implications of our assumptions. The value we assign to growth is implemented by our method; responding to disarray, organizing disarray and giving the organization meaning. The new meaning may cause disarray at another level, hence the method is recycled, opening new systems to draw upon—increasing intelligence—operationalizing intellectual growth.

Such teaching-helping has no need for an unconscious because saving or collecting is not functional or instrumental. Recycling the method is regenerative; the method or technology becomes the simplest and only effective means to implement values once the assumptions of the methods are understood.

Values and Choices

The basic choice is simple: between those systems that increase the individual's capacity to respond and initiate constructively and, on the other hand, those systems that limit the individual's capacity to respond and initiate. An increased repertoire of physical, emotional and intellectual responses translates into the ability to respond in order to enter new systems, conquer them, be free of them and draw upon them when appropriate. The ability to draw upon an increasing number of systems accelerates the acquisition of a still-larger repertoire of responses which, in turn, makes it possible to enter a still-larger number of new systems, conquer them, be free of them and selectively use them. Thus each time the cycle is completed, new disorganization is created and responded to, organized and given meaning. Each time the cycle is completed, the individual is more free. Intelligence equals freedom. There are potentially an infinite number of systems to conquer. There is no limit to intelligence and freedom.

It is ironic that the technology which we fear will limit our freedom actually frees us when its development is determined by human values which, in turn, incorporate comprehensive methodology. Technology used to implement human values, in fact, forces us to raise the most compelling moral issues and answer them.

Those who learn how to increase their physical, emotional and intellectual skills systematically but choose not to use those skills are no longer entitled to be taught more methods and skills, for they have become the enemy. The teacher-helper may then choose to ignore the non-learner, recycle the teaching-learning process from the beginning and/or declare war and destroy the non-learner.

249

When and if the teacher-helper must compete with such enemies, the teacher-helper competes to win and may choose to destroy without humiliating the enemy.

When the teacher-helper competes with friends, as he or she often does, the teacher-helper competes to win.

Such choices are clear, justifiable and possible because the teacher-helper has prepared through training and practice to make such discriminations based upon life and death choices. The teacher-helper begins his or her training by:

Checking and modifying, when appropriate, his or her basic metabolism and sensory/perceptual processes as well as his or her language skills. The teacher-helper must be certain that his or her **basic** bio-physiological and thought functions are optimally operative.

Learning basic discipline skills so that he or she is properly rested, organized and able to define functionally the variety of organized aspects of his or her life. Without a functional level of discipline, the individual can only distort information and act inappropriately upon distorted information.

Doing whatever is necessary to be physically fit. The teacher-helper must have superior cardio-vascular functioning in order to endure and explore, superior physical flexibility in order to manipulate and understand and superior dynamic strength in order to mobilize his or her full initiative when acting upon his or her world.

Doing whatever is necessary to prepare himself or herself as well as potential learners for a constructive experience with the use of decency skills. The teacher-helper greets learners to acknowledge and explore their existence. The teacher-helper is polite to potential learners to establish the bases for mutual decency and understanding. The teacher-helper must also exercise kindness in order to initiate the first constructive action in the relationship with a potential learner.

Learning vigilance skills in order to attend, observe and listen to the learner. Vigilance skills provide the basic information about the learner's energy level, feeling state and relationship with the teacher-helper.

Learning and mastering basic helping skills so that the teacher-helper may respond to the learner, personalize his or her response and initiate appropriately. High levels of these helping skills provide the conditions for the learner's exploration, understanding and action.

Mastering high levels of initiative skills. The teacher-helper systematically solves problems to select appropriate courses of action, develops systematic programs to accomplish the selected courses of action and develops program implementation technology in order to put the program into action (see Table 11-1).

Exploration is facilitated at the widest variety of levels of experience by responding to basic feeling states arising out of some imbalanced metabolic condition.

Understanding is facilitated at the widest variety of levels of experience by organizing what was disorganized; this is accomplished by personalizing goals.

Action is facilitated at the widest variety of levels of experience by giving meaning to what has been organized (goals); this is accomplished with the aid of such teacher-helper initiatives as programs to achieve goals and means to implement programs.

Table 11-1. Teacher-helper behaviors/resources that facilitate exploration, understanding and action

Skills Classification	Specific Skill	Basic Process	Specific Method
Discipline	*E: Resting	Metabolic	Responding
Discipline	U: Neatness	Sensory/Perceptual	Organizing
Discipline	A: Definition	Language/Symbol	Meaning
Physical Fitness	E: Cardio-Vascular	Metabolic	Responding
Physical Fitness	U: Flexibility	Sensory/Perceptual	Organizing
Physical Fitness	A: Dynamic Strength	Language/Symbol	Meaning
Decency	E: Greeting	Metabolic	Responding
Decency	U: Politeness	Sensory/Perceptual	Organizing
Decency	A: Kindness	Language/Symbol	Meaning
Vigilence	E: Attending	Metabolic	Responding
Vigilence	U: Observing	Sensory/Perceptual	Organizing
Vigilence	A: Listening	Language/Symbol	Meaning
Helping	E: Responding	Metabolic	Responding
Helping	U: Personalizing	Sensory/Perceptual	Organizing
Helping	A: Initiating	Language/Symbol	Meaning
Initiative	E: Problem Solving	Metabolic	Responding
Initiative	U: Program Development	Sensory/Perceptual	Organizing
Initiative	A: Program Implementa-tion	Program Implementation	Meaning

*Explore, Understand, Act

The teacher-helper recycles these skills and processes so that the learner may recycle Exploration, Understanding and Action just as the teacher-helper constantly recycles his or her own Exploration, Understanding and Action. The recycling is the essential part of a program to avoid stagnation and to insure continued growth because it:

identifies new areas to conquer;

identifies skill deficits;

determines scope of needed skills;

determines personal responsibility;

delivers effective people;

delivers effective programs;

joins effective people with effective programs;

creates a constructively impactful environment;

nourishes as it delivers skills;

provides the bases for learning and teaching anything;

fully operationalizes the ingredients of teaching and learning as well as the interactions among ingredients; and

enables the learner to do what the teacher-helper can do and is comprehensive.

Because the model is comprehensive, its use optimizes the probability that learning will take place and that life choices will be made.

The choice to live is orderly and systematic. The choice to live has meaning and growth, because it fully integrates learning with methodology.

The choice to die is slow, disordered, often chaotic, because it is a random strategy selected from an infinite variety of random strategies, all leading to deterioration, loneliness, ignorance, cowardice, cruelty, insensitivity and death.

Those who learn to grow master skills and preserve what good learnings good teacher-helpers gave them and continue to learn. Those who no longer learn gave up what the good teacher-helpers gave them and succumbed to conditioning.

References

Berenson, B. G. **Belly-to-belly and back-to-back: The militant humanism of Robert R. Carkhuff.** Amherst, Mass.: Human Resource Development Press, 1975.

Carkhuff, R. R. and Berenson, B. G. **Beyond counseling and therapy. Second Edition.** New York: Holt, Rinehart and Winston, 1976.

Chapter Twelve

Toward a Human Technology

Human technology promises the means to conquer any system. It provides the basic substance, structure, functions and controls tied to human experience in order to systematically increase individual functioning (Berenson, 1975, 1976; Carkhuff, 1976). Increased individual functioning, measurable in terms of the increased quality of physical, emotional and intellectual responses, enables the individual to enter, conquer and free himself or herself from increasing numbers of systems. The greater the number of systems the individual is free of, the greater the number of systems the individual can appropriately draw upon. The greater the number of systems the individual can appropriately draw upon, the more creative and free the individual.

Human Technology promises a synthesis of technique and basic life processes.

Human Technology promises to carry the expression of technology far beyond sterile postulates to give the "breath of life" to organization, direction, means and meaning.

Human Technology promises to respond to the coherent order of nature that emerges after less comprehensive efforts fail by dealing only with the apparently contradictory currents of human history.

Human Technology promises a revolution of human realization.

Human Technology promises a place to grow for every learner.

Human Technology promises wisdom in human matters

because it is more than technique and/or a set of practical results. It is or will be an integral part of a dynamic culture which will express our best aspirations rationally with confidence as well as change. Human technology can do all this because it blends human values with technology so that subjective experience may blend with objective reality to nourish a higher-order reality.

Human Technology breaks free of nonfunctional dichotomies such as responsiveness vs. initiativeness, humanism vs. science, male vs. female, old vs. young and freedom vs. discipline.

Human Technology culminates in a functional system of skills, goals, programs and propositions that make a difference in the rate and quality of human resource development. In addition, human technology raises many fundamental questions about such critical issues as:

> gaining and maintaining human control of all technologies;

> the wisdom of trusting human systems and/or technical systems;

> fully understanding technology as a product as well as a means to produce other products; and

> the dependence of human systems, internal and external, upon mechanical technology.

The Promise and the Roots

In the beginning, the survival needs of early man stimulated the invention of mechanical devices. Sometime later, these same motives stimulated the formulation of mechanical principles. Technology was born. Today there is no doubt that technology has grown to dominate our experience. In many ways, technology determines our future and man no longer determines the future of technology. It seems that only in early history did technology serve the conscious needs of the human community. Today we determine our goals by responding to where we are technologically: by extrapolating the future of technology. We anticipate the future by anticipating advances in technology rather than by determining goals influenced by other criteria.

It may still be possible for man to control and shape his future if he can somehow control the development of all his technologies. First, however, many must come to understand fully the interdependence of mechanical and human technologies. Somehow, over the centuries, man has developed a fascination with non-functional dichotomies. This, more than any other factor, has retarded human development.

Human systems and mechanical technology have never functioned separately, whether in the areas of biological adaptation, politics, economics, industry or agriculture. Our task today is to bring human **and** mechanical technologies into the full service of mature value judgments—value judgments based upon learning, comprehensive methods and life choices.

The separation of human technology and mechanical technology is a myth in experience as well as in nature. There is no real choice between the two, only whether or not we choose truth.

The earliest efforts to organize and systematize information about nature and mathematics (about 2,000 B.C.) set off a chain of useful discoveries and inventions that not only enabled man to exploit his physical environment but also enabled him to learn more about the living world. Mechanical technology made it possible to describe anatomy, create physiology, develop microbiology, interpret genetics and evolution. Pasteur was able to study fermentation directly with the application of optics and confirm the germ-carrying capacity of air with the use of laboratory equipment. Earlier, Kepler even tried to unite morality with the physical universe by applying mechanical relationships.

258

These developments and many more came to serve the demands of new technologies. Yet these technologies came to serve politicians unable to make value judgments that would someday translate to human benefit rather than human exploitation. Thus the essential difference between mechanical technology and human technology is that human technology requires explicit value judgments and subsequent action upon these judgments. Once mechanical systems are set in motion by persons who abdicate to the machine and once initial ingredients are selected, judgments are no longer required or available. Without explicit values, there can be no self-regulation for human benefit: only considerations of friction, power, vectors, heat and energy.

The irony is that technology enables man to develop his worst traits while also providing man with the opportunity to develop his best traits. If technology is used so that the individual can avoid value judgments, he merely goes on to generate a history of crimes. If technology is employed to expand human resources, it provides man with the skills he needs to be responsible for his technologies.

The ethic, indeed the morality in human resource development may even begin with a human technology because technology creates the programs to make and evaluate delivery systems. The criterion is basically simple: delivery systems can put man back into history as a constructive initiator rather than a tragic victim of his own stupidity and cruelty. Humankind must move toward trusting its own motives more than it trusts "objective" technology. In order to develop such trust, humankind must be supplied with a growing series of programs that are aimed toward achieving individually-defined growth goals.

We have traced the growth of effective human resource development models as well as their efficient translations to research, demonstrations and helper-helpee skill acquisition programs (Carkhuff, 1976; Carkhuff and Berenson, 1976). These programs based upon Carkhuff's human technology are the culmination of numerous projects based upon naturalistic, experimental and predictive studies. They include generalization studies to education, training programs, development and program implementation beyond helper-offered skills. This literature moves on to refinements and extension of responsive **and** initiative dimensions of human learning. The applications of Carkhuff's technology include the study of its effects upon the functioning of credentialed professionals, functional professionals and persons indigenous to community development projects. Most important, we now have the details of a technology of program development and implementation which applies to individuals, groups, entire communities, indeed to large segments of society such as education and corrections.

Human technology has good and firm roots in the history of technology, humanism **and** scientific thought. From the first verbal utterances of primitive beings to the application of mechanics to biology, the roots were nurtured and pruned by industrious, disciplined, energetic and empathic minds. These roots broke ground around the time of the transformation of the wheel into a gear. The young and tender sprouts of human technology blossomed sometime between the use of steam to make gears turn and the blending of biology and electronics. The blossoms bore flowers and fruit between the operationalization of responding and initiating skills and their culmination into the highest order of responding.

From the time of the manufacture of a functional microscope to the impact of Darwin's theory of evolution, the mechanics of biology laid the foundation for immunization, genetics, embryology, physiological synthesis, the full appreciation of the supremacy of the nervous system, the maintenance of species, explanations of uncommon biological unions and the rarity of intermediate forms of species. At the same time the base was laid for our present realization that independent creativity and moral judgment are grounded in our ability to use the core of our experience to enter other human and material systems fully.

We owe debts to many sources: the eternally-cited efforts to systematize knowledge, the formation of complete language, the forging of metals, the mechanization of biology and the printing press. Our greatest debt is due to humanity's potential to continue to learn by drawing upon smaller and larger systems.

These events and many more made great strides toward organizing experience. It remains for a human technology to give it all meaning by providing constructive initiatives that translate to the mastery of the teaching-learning process with all of its implied energy and discipline.

Some Substance and Propositions

The challenge in the development of human technology is that it must be comprehensive yet selective enough to be efficient and cohesive. The substance of human technology, then, culminates in the interaction of **basic processes, basic skills, basic objectives, the basic human experience** and **the basic dimensions of learning** (see Figure 12-1).

The basic processes upon which all experience depends are metabolic, sensory, perceptual and linguistic (symbolic). The rehabilitation and preparation for learning may well involve the alteration of the metabolic processes to speed up, slow down and/or balance them. In addition the sensory/perceptual processes, if input is to be useful for the individual, must function to organize input. Linguistic systems and symbolic representations of experience need to reflect perceptual organization. In the cases of the learning disabled, all these basic processes need examination and frequently alteration through the use of training, medication and/or surgery.

All the basic skills of human technology can be classified as being responsive, personalizing, or initiative.

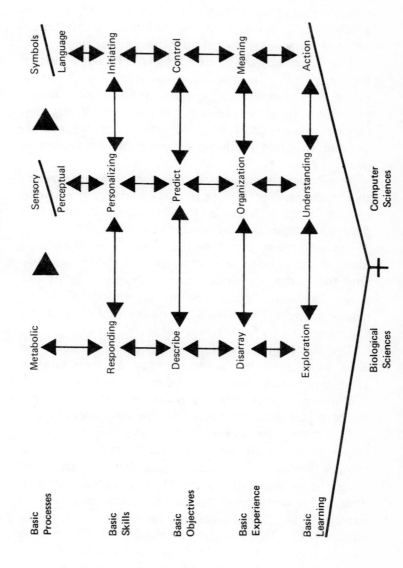

Figure 12-1. The Basic Substance and Processes of Human Technology

262

These include the living, learning and working skills that culminate in the individual's living, learning and working productivity. Perhaps more basically, the individual's physical resources enable him or her to respond. The individual's emotional resources enable him or her to personalize experience. And the individual's intellectual resources enable him or her to initiate effectively.

The basic objectives of human technology emerge from responding, personalizing and initiating. Responding makes description possible. Personalizing makes prediction possible because personalizing yields personally relevant goals. Initiating makes control possible because initiating yields systematic programs to achieve goals.

The basic human experience—the experience which the teacher-helper is continuously expanding and narrowing—is the individual's struggle to organize what is in disarray and give the organization meaning.

Responding in detail to the learner's experience of disarray facilitates the exploratory phase of learning. Organizing the individual learner's experience of disarray facilitates the learner's understanding. Giving meaning through systematic strategies that expand and continue learning facilitates the learner's action.

The underlying substantive dimensions of all the basic aspects of human technology as they interact yield two factors: biological and computational. Human Technology teacher-helpers will need to master the basics of biological sciences and computer sciences.

At a more molecular level of observation, the teacher-helper responds to the individual learner's experience comprehensively. The teaching-helping process must leave the learner with the skills the learner needs to develop his or her own transferable strategies as these strategies facilitate human, educational and career achievement. The process must put the life of the learner together at the level the learner must live his or her life. The focus must be on skills rather than insights, concepts or even a philosophy (see Figure 12-2).

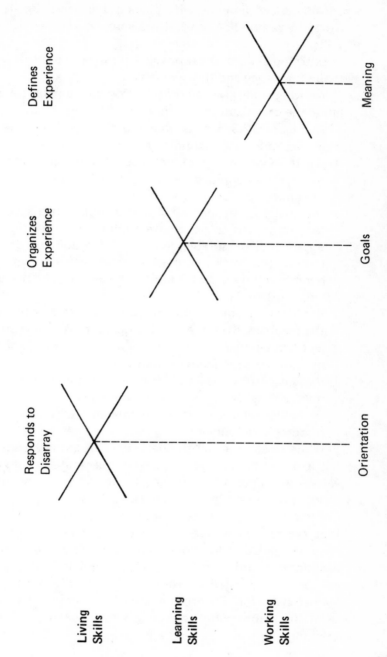

Figure 12-2. *The Experience and Skills of Human Technology*

Individuals can cope with placing themselves in their world by responding to what is disorganized—with living skills.

Learning skills make it possible for people to organize their experience and define goals.

Working skills give the organization meaning by translating the organization of experience into productivity.

In Figure 12-3, we see that the goals, substance and strategies of human technology must:

1. partition variance to pinpoint sources of gain related to effective people, effective programs and their interaction;

2. the goals, substance and strategies must yield systematic means to generalize findings for specific observable, measurable, repeatable and trainable criteria so that students, teachers, administrators and parents will have transferable strategies readily available;

3. the goals, substance and strategies must be shaped by the feedback from the latest program or research project—rather than by the results of testing the same hypotheses over and over; and

4. the goals, substance and strategies of human technology must be guided by a comprehensive model that inter-relates the basic ingredients of human resource development.

While research in all the helping professions was preoccupied with testing hypotheses generated from a variety of "schools" of thought, the field was perennially caught up in questions of rigor vs. meaning.

First, most hypotheses were based upon assumptions that created techniques which either made no difference or had a deleterious impact. In any event, the assumptions **and** techniques (often unrelated) accounted for a very small percent of the total variance of learner behavior. Theorists as well as educators did not seem to know what was important for helping or teaching.

HUMAN TECHNOLOGY:

TARGETS, STRUCTURE, FUNCTIONS

STRUCTURE

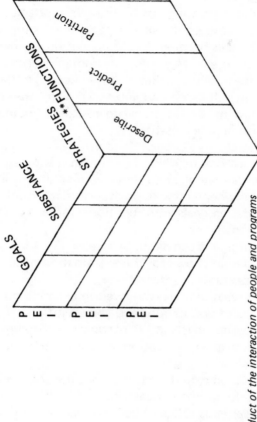

T
A * PEOPLE
R
G PROGRAMS
E
T MATERIALS
S

*Organization is a product of the interaction of people and programs

**Functions of research (control):

Describe	**Predict**	**Partition Variance**
What Is	Cues to Where Need to Be	Cues to What Is Needed to Achieve Goals

Figure 12-3. The Targets, Structure and Functions of Human Technology

Second, the question of rigor vs. meaning confused methodology with substance and goals. This issue is resolved simply when we meet both criteria: rigor and meaning.

For those pressing for more rigor, strategies become the goals and the substance. For those pressing for more meaning, goals become the substance and the method.

We can break free because human technology will a) determine what makes a difference; b) differentiate goals from substance and substance from strategies; and c) develop means to translate research findings effectively into people benefits.

1. The design is a program and can be entered at any cell (see Figure 12-3). The human technology investigators may elect to move vertically and/or horizontally depending upon their initial hypotheses.

2. The design deals with functional rather than theoretical constructs.

3. The design is behaviorally based.

4. The design allows for the examination of simple as well as complex interactions.

5. The design may be employed to examine the widest variety of populations and communities.

6. The design assists in the production of naturalistic, predictive, generalization, extension and application studies.

7. The design can, if need be, meet the assumptions of powerful mathematical models.

8. The design is efficient because traditional variables drop out when impact variables (people + programs) are introduced. With appropriate impact variables, human technology research comes to involve demonstration projects rather than experimental projects.

9. The **major** activities of life become the subject matter for hypotheses.

10. The design gives systematic direction along with flexibility.

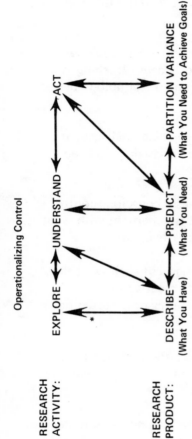

HUMAN TECHNOLOGY:

Operationalizing Control

RESEARCH
ACTIVITY:

EXPLORE — UNDERSTAND — ACT

RESEARCH
PRODUCT:

DESCRIBE — PREDICT — PARTITION VARIANCE
(What You Have) (What You Need) (What You Need to Achieve Goals)

*

DESCRIPTION + PREDICTION + PARTITIONING VARIANCE

EFFECTIVE GOAL ORIENTED PROGRAMS

EFFECTIVE PEOPLE

EFFECTIVE PEOPLE + EFFECTIVE PROGRAMS

*Two-Way vectors: Recycled process shaped by feedback
Description increases understanding
Understanding increases description
Prediction → Action → Increases accuracy of prediction

Figure 12-4. Operationalyzing Control in Human Technology

268

In Figure 12-4 the objectives of human technology become a reflection of the values and the methods of human technology. This is possible because Figure 12-4 equates efficiency with effectiveness and learning. The design also identifies some of the basic ingredients for effective delivery (research product) and ties the delivery to the learning process.

Because the research product is tied to the fundamental behaviors related to learning and because learning is equated with research activity, human technology personalizes its deliveries.

Because human technology personalizes delivery, it increases conscious control by emphasizing goals and skills.

Because human technology increases conscious control by emphasizing goals and skills, it is congruent with what the individual needs to experience life creatively.

Because human technology is congruent with what the individual needs to experience life creatively, the individual becomes the object and the agent of teaching and learning.

Because human technology makes the individual the object and the agent of teaching and learning, it eliminates non-functional dichotomies.

Because human technology eliminates non-functional dichotomies, it can facilitate the determination of the goals, substance and strategies for human technology products.

Because human technology determines the goals, substance and strategies for human technology projects, it integrates people, goals and the means to achieve goals.

Because human technology integrates people, goals and the means to achieve goals, it renders issues like rigor vs. meaning academic.

Because human technology renders issues like rigor vs. meaning academic, human technology strategies are inseparable from human benefit.

Human Technology and Human Nourishment

The choice is ours. We may choose to commit ourselves to a lifetime of learning, secure in the knowledge that life and learning are one and the same. Or we may choose to commit ourselves to a lifetime of defending the fruitless attitudes and efforts in which we have engaged. In the latter case, we make conscious our choice to move from victim to killer.

Life or death—however slow! These are the only choices.

Not familiarity! Or comfort! Or tradition!

Outcome is what outcome produces. If we can increase our prospects for producing over a 90% success rate (against a base rate of 20% or less) by learning to attend physically to another human being, then let us, for the helpee's sake, do so.

It matters not that we feel initially like automatons if we facilitate the growth of those whom we are paid to serve. Our disposition toward being comfortable in standing or sitting are at best irrelevant. Our disposition toward 'hearing' better when we are not observing is at worst retarding. If we can only help when we learn to face the helpee squarely, leaning forward or toward and making eye contact, then let us make our choice. Between our own personal freedom, spontaneity and creativity or the human benefits of those whom we serve. And, in context, let us remind ourselves that there are millions of little children who never make it to adulthood—physically, emotionally or intellectually—because no one in their developing years has ever attended physically to them except in moments of anger and punishment.

Let us choose between ourselves and these children if we must. If we must write ourselves off in order to choose life for others, than let us do so. But let us choose! The time grows late.

Growth or deterioration!

Skills alone determine growth. There is no growth without skills. Physical skills! Emotional skills! Intellectual skills!

Deterioration is reflected in all of the other irrelevancies in which we engage in order to avoid the hard work and discipline of learning and teaching skills.

And remember, when we choose, we choose for all mankind. Not just ourselves but our families. Our friends! Our communities! Our countries! Our world! For the fundamental rule of man is that no one else can have more than he can have.

Yes, the choice is a real one. To invest in the development of a Construct System that will change not just the face of the world but the substance of its people. Or to trigger the Destruct System which has been poised for so long in anticipation of its final moment.

A Big Bomb from little bombs is made.

(Carkhuff, 1976)

"An insane society indulges the indolence of extremists while negatively reinforcing the productive. We must blend objective technology with human experience so that we may·cope with the **unknown** implications of being the best we can be; we cannot afford to be resigned to the certainty that will follow being less than we can be.''* (Berenson, 1976)

Several decades ago, we left an era when simple and essentially good people had simple and good goals they understood, sacrificed for and, in sacrificing, experienced deprivation as a privilege. Then we entered an era of self-indulgence with no standards, full of temper tantrums and tragic contempt for old and new learning. Now, for the sake of survival as well as growth, we must create an era of teaching and learning that has no plateau.

References

Berenson, B. G.   **Belly-to-belly and back-to-back: The militant humanism of Robert R. Carkhuff.** Amherst, Mass.: Human Resource Development Press, 1975.

Berenson, B. G.   A human technology for human effectiveness. Chapter in **Toward excellence in education** (R. R. Carkhuff, Ed.) Amherst, Mass.: Human Resource Development Press, in preparation, 1976.

Berenson, B. G.   Toward a humane human technology. **L'orientation professionnelle, vocational guidance.** Summer 1973, **9** No. 2.

Carkhuff, R. R.   **The promise of America. Keynote address, 1974, A.P.G.A. Convention.** Amherst, Mass.: Human Resource Development Press, 1976.

Carkhuff, R. R. and Berenson, B. G.   **Beyond counseling and therapy. Second edition.** New York: Holt, Rinehart and Winston, 1976.

Hughes, T. P.   **The development of western technology since 1500.** New York: MacMillan Company, 1964.

Singer, C.   **A short history of scientific ideas to 1900.** New York: Oxford University Press, 1959.

Section 6—Conclusions

Chapter Thirteen

Upstream

Fortunately and unfortunately, human systems are not necessarily functionally or constructively related.

Fortunately, because the tyrants of history and the forces of physical deterioration could have been even more devastating than they were.

Unfortunately, because the technology needed to link human systems constructively may require more efficiency, precision and wisdom than is required by other technologies.

Human technology is far behind on all accounts when compared to mechanical or other technologies. For example, social planning could replace political expediency if a human technology for human resource development were fully developed (Berenson, 1975). Historically, politics has been employed in the service of pathology with few exceptions. One tyranny has invariably been replaced by another tyranny. The relationship between politics and human benefit was positive only on those rare moments when power was employed to substitute constructive and achievable goals for the pathology of power for its own sake.

Until now, there has been no potent human technology capable of training people to understand one another and to employ that understanding in developing a higher-order technology: a technology of human resource development. The promise of human technology is that, for the first time, human beings can control the functional integration of people and programs.

There are profound implications in accepting technology as man's greatest achievement. One of the most important implications is that we must cease to treat technology as an entity outside the sphere of ordinary historical experience. In the past, technology has not been subject to mature moral-political judgments. The human value system has been, and often still is, missing, just as technical considerations are often missing in humanistic movements. Today we must recognize that a technology divorced from values can be devastating; and that values without technology are important.

Perhaps we have treated the tide of technological advance as a life force all its own, independent of human purpose and judgment, because such a treatment has allowed us to gain wealth while being less than we can be. Man has yet to learn that he will always be the victim until he becomes all he can be.

An effective human and humane technology must enable us to: 1) effectively communicate our personal experience as well as our technology; 2) systematically select and create constructive solutions to our problems; and 3) systematically implement those preferred solutions so that our increased responsibility, gained through increased skills, will translate to human resource development.

In recent decades we have done things simply because we have had the technology to do them.

Now we must do things because they must be done.

Helping Is Teaching

Today many of us in the helping professions, when we explore it, find anti-technological roots. We saw our evolution as having stemmed from a need to aid the victims of a very crude and wasteful, technologically-based social system. Now we are being asked to accept the same technology to prevent the human waste in the first place. This is a difficult choice for many of us.

Indeed, the choice is compounded for many within education. Many of them have chosen guidance and counseling as a profession in order to individualize and personalize the learning experiences and problem-solving activities of students who have become lost or excluded by a very cold and impersonal educational system that services our crude and wasteful social system.

But choose we must.

For many of us, the choice is between our livelihoods and the outcomes that our professions were designed to deliver.

What this all boils down to is a choice between becoming victims of the same system which produces the victims we are supposed to help or freeing ourselves of such a system to produce a new and better one that, at worst, minimizes the victims and, at best, saves them.

In this regard, there is no answer other than technology.

Only the systematic step-by-step process that put a man on the moon can put a child fully in control of his or her world.

In addition, there is no answer other than education for the educator who wishes to glean from his or her experience that which is meaningful in the world and then transmit it in the most efficient and effective manner to the learner; who, in turn, explores it, experiences it, experiments with it, understands it, adapts it, refines it and modifies or rejects it for his or her purposes in his or her own world.

In this context, all helping is teaching.

It does not matter what the setting, who the population.

If we are helping people, we are teaching them.

When Kaye Jeter counsels a child in Michigan, she teaches the child the skills which the child needs to live, learn and work effectively in his or her world. In addition, she enters the classroom to teach the teacher how to do likewise because each teacher comes in more direct contact with the student than she herself does.

When William Anthony counsels physically or psychiatrically disabled patients in Massachusetts, he teaches the patients all of the skills which they need to live, learn and work effectively in their world. In addition, he teaches the nurses and psychiatric aides how to do likewise because they come in more direct contact with the patient than he himself does.

When Tom Keeling counsels inmates in the Illinois

Correctional System, he teaches the inmates all of the skills which they need to live, learn and work effectively in their world. In addition, he teaches the correctional officers how to do likewise because they come in more direct contact with the inmates than he himself does.

It is all education.

Life skills education! Rehabilitative education! Correctional education!

It is the same process by which each generation organizes and passes on the wisdom of the last in order to make the next generation wiser.

It is the same process by which the next generation reorganizes and provides feedback to the previous one in order that the previous one may become more useful and effective.

Teaching is Focused

Three learnings force us to move beyond counseling and therapy.

The first of these is that learning styles and cognitive processes are almost entirely formed by the time a child goes to school.

Still, of all the years that a human lives, these are the most neglected in terms of preparation for learning.

This learning comes hard for people who spent much of their lives downstream and who have gradually been working their way upstream. Again, this is not to say that we cannot guide or rehabilitate or correct at a later age. It is to say that we can accomplish our purposes most efficiently and effectively at a younger age. And, in that context, understand that our function in guiding, rehabilitating and correcting at a later age is just that: helping the distressed to re-learn and re-use the skills which they have unlearned, misused or abused.

Here is Karen Danley, a counselor in Pontiac, teaching her children how to learn in her learning-to-learn center and dramatically increasing the learning of the children involved. She maximizes the effect of the human environment upon the children's naturally endowed neurological systems by stimulating, organizing and reinforcing learning.

Here is the future of helping. Whether in a guidance, rehabilitative or correctional setting, the chain reaches back to the child's early years and helpers must do likewise.

The second of these learnings is that parents are the main source of learning for the child. Certainly, through modeling and imitation, the principle source of learning. But also through the direct didactic teaching which they offer, or fail to offer, as well as through the experiential base which they provide in support of learning.

Yet of all people, the parents are almost totally excluded from the formal learning process. Independently, the schools contribute essentially nothing to the learning achievement of children. Alone or in interaction with the schools, parents account for almost all learning. And still they have little to teach because no one ever taught them.

Here is Richard Pierce, a counselor in Amherst, teaching parents how to teach their children how to learn and dramatically reducing the child-rearing problems of the families involved. He maximizes the effect of the environmental impact equation by delivering the skills to the source of the delivery system.

The third of these learnings is that youth who have learning skills tend to stay in school and become contributing citizens while youth who do not have learning skills tend to leave school and tend to become delinquent, unemployed, dependent and, perhaps later on, criminal.

Still, we continue not to teach the children the learning skills that they need to stay in school. We lower standards to converge on performance instead of raising performance to converge on standards.

Here is Tom Collingwood, a counselor running a youth diversion program in Dallas, teaching the youth how to learn effectively and the police how to teach effectively and producing a delinquency recidivism rate below 10% compared to a base rate of over 50%. He maximizes the effect of the environmental impact equation by doing the things that make a difference.

The equation referred to is a simple equation emphasizing the ingredients of environmental impact that maximize the growth of the learner.

Cutting to the heart of the helper's contribution, we must organize our delivery systems to **deliver the products which make the greatest difference (skills) into the hands of the people who make the greatest difference (parents) at the point in the child's development which makes the greatest difference (the early childhood years).**

Reversed, the equation means that if we continue to neglect the skills development of children in early childhood and parents in early parenthood, we can continue to look forward to dramatic increases in crime and unemployment and welfare and all of the other symptoms of a system that does not service its people.

We can no longer afford to continue this pattern of neglect, for financial reasons if not for human reasons.

The Helping Mission

It is time for the helping professions to move on, to make a difference, to grow. We have been mired in the muck of questionable personality theories and dubious therapeutic practices for so long that we have lost sight of our mission: to help individuals and groups to maximize the development of their human resources.

We now know what we need to know to fulfill our role. We can move upstream to develop the preventative mental health and learning-to-learn programs that insure the success of HRD. We need no longer wait hopelessly downstream to fish the hapless victims out of the river, giving the living ones artificial respiration and shipping them back upstream only to have them thrown in once again by a system which neglected them (Chapter One).

We now know that all helping and human relationships can be helpful or they can be harmful. It all depends upon the skills which we have. The skills which we have to responsively enter our helpees' frames of reference. The skills which we have to initiate to help our helpees to achieve goals that are meaningful for them in their worlds. We know that when we fail ourselves or others, we do so by choice because there was a successful way. We simply chose to practice losing instead of learning how to win (Chapters Two and Three).

To be effective helpers we must also unlearn a great deal of what we have learned. To put it succinctly, we have replaced one set of myths about human functionality with another.

An effective helper brings only three useful things from the traditional therapeutic orientations. From client-centered approaches, he or she brings an appreciation for feeling and the skill of reflection. From trait-and-factor approaches, he or she brings the skills for goal definition. And from behavioristic approaches, he or she brings the skills for developing steps to achieve particular goals. Each of these contributions has a function within the more generic category of program development. The rest is irrelevant (Chapter Four).

We conclude that the most efficient and effective way to transmit skills is through teaching. Teaching is the preferred mode of helping. To be effective helpers, then, we need not only learn the specialty skills which we would deliver to our helpees but also the teaching skills which we need to make this delivery (Chapter Five).

The Teaching Goal

What an effective helper does bring to the helping process is full appreciation for the outcomes which he or she wishes to effect. These outcomes define human resource development. They are physical, emotional and intellectual. They guide all of our helping efforts, for if our helpees do not grow in the quantity and quality of skill responses in each of these areas, they have not grown at all (Chapter Six).

The process by which these outcomes are accomplished is learning. The learning process involves all the skills which our helpees need in order to: explore where they are in relation to their worlds; understand where they are in relation to where they want to be; and act to get from where they are to where they want or need to be. The learning process must be recycled. The feedback from acting stimulates more extensive exploration, more accurate understanding and more effective action. This is the cycle of learning. This is the cycle of growing (Chapter Seven).

We are able to involve our learner-helpees in the process of learning which leads to physical, emotional and intellectual outcomes through use of our skills. Our skills fall into three categories of teaching. We teach living skills through our helping or human achievement skills. We teach learning skills through our teaching or educational achievement skills. We teach working skills through our planning or career achievement skills. We use all of these skills simultaneously to facilitate the learner's movement through exploration, understanding and action to living, learning and working skills development (Chapter Eight).

We acquire skills through our own training. We concede to persons more functional than us in order to acquire the specialty skills necessary to discharge our responsibilities. The most efficient modality is training. In order to become teachers, then, we must first become learners (Chapter Nine).

The helping system is the means by which we organize our people and programs to deliver our skills to the learner. For the effective helper, a functional delivery system involves becoming a teacher-trainer and a parent-trainer in the living, learning and working skills specialty areas. In addition, with regard to working with learners, a delivery system involves the increased use of groups for skills training, the increased movement into the environment to offer skills training in the real life situations and the increased monitoring of the learner's development of human resources (Chapter Ten).

To this end, the teaching goal necessitates a human technology that bridges the gap from our concepts of helping to our delivery of human benefits. A human technology promises the development of all of the steps which we need to achieve our human values and offers the means to predict and influence human behavior. It offers the means to break down our teaching goal into objectives in order to achieve our helping mission (Chapters Eleven and Twelve).

The Learning Goal

Every creature struggles fully to stay alive; some struggle to grow. Only humanity thinks it can do less.

We now know what and who we want to be. We also know who our products are and what we want them to look like. Most of all, we know that we can acquire the skills to get where we want and need to be.

Understand fully that the learning goal is to fill in the missing ingredients. Each new human goal demands a new technology—drawn from the old and refined perhaps, but with new steps developed where the old falls short. We throw out a "sky hook" to our goals and bridge the gap from our current technology to our goals with whatever it takes to get us there. And we refine our methods to become increasingly more efficient and effective.

To do this, we must commit ourselves personally to understanding what is missing in ourselves and our system as well as what is present and to fill in the part that is missing, demanding of ourselves and our system no less than we can be and using any means available to achieve our goals.

This is the place to end as well as begin. In every moment of every day, we make life-and-death decisions. Some are small, some are large, but each leads inevitably to its final culmination.

This book was written to gain your attention and consideration as well as to teach. Your attention may now be focused on what might be modern man's only real opportunity to acquire control of his own circumstances: a human and humane technology. This may well be his first and, at the same time, last chance to do so. Technology's triumph over humanity and the former's steady growth will not wait for human technology to catch up. Human technology must capitalize on other technologies as well as overcome man's reluctance to employ fully his own personal resources. This new combination of technology and human values must be precise and efficient yet dynamic, self-regulating and balanced if it is to be truly effective.

This book could be the beginning of an ethic (Berenson, 1976; Carkhuff, 1976). An ethic that guides the applications of a technology even as that same technology regulates applied human psychology.

The danger in developing a human technology is identical to the dangers involved in the initial growth of any technology. The promise of a high-level technology and fantasies of power have inevitably led to the corruption of the potentially constructive use of the technology. There are, however, a few differences in a truly human technology which offer built-in checks: 1) like biological systems, human technology can be self-regulatory; 2) human technology requires specific achievable goals that emerge from what is missing in the response repertoire of people; 3) goals are evaluated and influenced by what is already operative for persons; 4) means to achieve goals are not only systematic but selected in terms of explicit value judgments. These points make it possible to study the implications of a technology as the means to social ends. The single and most important aspect of a human technology, however, is that it will distinguish itself from the mechanical because the individual is both the tool and the goal. In this context, the complete delivery system, it must be emphasized, can never be free of mechanics any more than biological systems can function free of mechanics.

The "human" in human technology means explicit value judgments; and "technology" means efficient action upon those value judgments. In the very same sense the "militant" in "Militant Humanism" entails efficient and effective action and "humanism" entails explicit value judgments upon which the action (technology) is to be based.

A human technology can serve those who believe it is worthwhile to be fully human and even those who do not. In both instances, life itself may be the criterion: balanced, selective, purposeful, conditional, self-directed and regulated. At the very least, human technology can broaden awareness, lengthen memory, expand perspective, deepen feelings, sharpen communication, test understanding, render actions purposeful and create the possibility of a human community based upon respect and decency.

For those who insist that life itself is a myth and therefore a game, mechanical applications of human technology can produce an approximation of life. Those who pay the full price of growth will find the technology of human resource development a vehicle to expand life.

This is what we believe.

I Believe

I believe that the **goals** of human technology should be related to measurable people benefits.

I believe that the **substance** of human technology should include only those dimensions of people, programs and materials that make a difference.

I believe that the **strategies** of human technology, viewed in their ultimately cyclical form, should begin and end with responding.

I believe that **technology** alone becomes supercilious logic.

I believe that **humanism** alone is impotent.

I believe human technology will make a **difference** when we make a full effort.

I believe human technology will **interfere** with our ignorance and vanity.

I believe human technology **nourishes** expanding experience, responsibility, productivity and life.

I believe human technology supplies the means to **serve** and be served.

I believe human technology is the means and the **meaning.**

References

Berenson, B. G.   **Belly-to-belly and back-to-back: The militant humanism of Robert R. Carkhuff.** Amherst, Mass.: Human Resource Development Press, 1975.

Berenson, B. G.   A human technology for human effectiveness. Chapter in **Toward excellence in education** (R. R. Carkhuff, Ed.) Amherst, Mass.: Human Resource Development Press, in preparation, 1976.

Berenson, B. G.   Toward a humane human technology. **L'orientation professionnelle, vocational guidance.** Summer 1973, **9** No. 2.

Carkhuff, R. R.   **The promise of America. Keynote address, 1974, A.P.G.A. Convention.** Amherst, Mass.: Human Resource Development Press, 1976.

Hughes, T. P.   **The development of western technology since 1500.** New York: MacMillan Company, 1964.

Singer, C.   **A short history of scientific ideas to 1900.** New York: Oxford University Press, 1959.

other
publications
from Human
Resource
Development
Press

THE SKILLS OF TEACHING SERIES

Written by teachers for teachers and hailed as ". . . a landmark in educational technology". This series features INTERPERSONAL SKILLS to help you to improve your relationships with your students, CONTENT DEVELOPMENT SKILLS to help you organize and prepare what is to be taught and LESSON PLANNING SKILLS to help you plan how to teach the material to your students. Volumes to be released in 1979 will deal with TEACHING DELIVERY SKILLS and LEARNING MANAGEMENT SKILLS.

THE SKILLS OF TEACHING: CONTENT DEVELOPMENT SKILLS

By David Berenson, Sally Berenson and Robert Carkhuff. The second book in the acclaimed Skills of Teaching Series. Teaches you how to develop and organize your yearly and daily teaching content. Learn how to identify skills and the steps needed to do them, along with the facts, concepts and principles your students will need to perform these skills. Can be used in any content area and features pre-post tests for each chapter, exercises to insure mastery of the material and stimulating photographs. 216 pages, annotated bibliography, 40 illustrations, 11x8½", paper, $8.95.

THE SKILLS OF TEACHING: LESSON PLANNING SKILLS

By David Berenson, Sally Berenson and Robert Carkhuff. This third volume in the Skills of Teaching Series picks up where CONTENT DEVELOPMENT leaves off. Here's how to take a piece of your content and develop a lesson plan for delivering it, drawing from dozens of exciting teaching methods for reviewing, overviewing, presenting, practicing and summarizing. Features exercises to help you to acquire, practice and apply these skills in your teaching, pre-post tests for chapter-by-chapter feedback, plus an open format and easy-to-read style for maximum learning. 215 pages, annotated bibliography, 41 illus., 11x8½", paper, $8.95.

THE SKILLS OF TEACHING: INTERPERSONAL SKILLS

By Robert Carkhuff, David Berenson and Richard Pierce. This text is the most advanced book available to teach both education students and teachers the basic interpersonal skills they need to teach effectively. Covered are attending skills, responding skills, personalizing skills and initiating skills. This book features exercises to help the reader learn and apply the skills, pre-post tests for immediate feedback, a straightforward style and open format for easy reading; plus 60 photographs to illustrate the skills in actual use. Teachers love it! 206 pp., annotated bibliography, 60 illus., paper, $8.95.

THE SKILLS OF TEACHING: INTERPERSONAL SKILLS TEACHER'S GUIDE

By Robert Carkhuff, David Berenson, Richard Pierce, et al. A training manual that details how to teach interpersonal skills to teachers. Includes time-saving features like summaries of key concepts, exercises, lesson plans and examination questions. Written for college professors, inservice trainers and staff development personnel who want their teachers to relate more effectively to students. Based upon 15 years experience teaching interpersonal skills! 153 pages, annotated bibliography, 11x8½", paper, $11.95.

KIDS DON'T LEARN FROM PEOPLE THEY DON'T LIKE

By David Aspy and Flora Roebuck. A textbook presentation of the research evidence linking teacher interpersonal skills to student achievement and classroom control. KIDS describes the instruments, methodology, training techniques and research results, and then presents their implications for the future of teacher training. This text is written for educators, education students, researchers and administrators and features summaries and overviews in addition to the complete text of 15 research articles. 297 pages, tables, references, 6x9", paper, $11.95

LIVING SKILLS

THE ART OF HELPING III

By Robert Carkhuff, Richard Pierce and John Cannon. This best-selling interpersonal skills text is now even better. There's a new helping model, more skill steps, built-in pre-post tests, more realistic illustrations, new practice exercises and examples of actual helping interviews. It's clean format and straightforward style make for easy reading. And it still breaks this complex subject into easy-to-learn steps. Designed for anyone interested in relating more helpfully to people. 196 pp., annotated bibliography, 190 illus., 8½ x 5½", spiral bound, $6.95.

THE ART OF PROBLEM SOLVING

By Robert Carkhuff. A manual for developing decision-making skills. Includes sections on defining problems, defining goals, developing values, plus selecting and implementing courses of action. Uses a case study approach and clear step-by-step exercises to teach this skill. Designed for anyone who needs a simple, systematic technique for approaching complex decisions. 143 pp., 140 illus., 8½ x 5½", spiral bound, $6.95.

THE ART OF HELPING III TRAINER'S GUIDE

By Robert Carkhuff, Richard Pierce, et al. Contains training techniques for people who teach helpers. Based on over 15 years of experience teaching interpersonal skills. Includes tips on planning a training program, exercises for skill development, outside assignments for skill application and evaluation tools. Has The Art of Helping III reprinted inside for easy reference. A real time-saver! 170 pp., annotated bibliography, 8½ x 11", paper, $11.95.

HOW TO HELP YOURSELF

By Robert Carkhuff. A manual for building program development and implementation skills. For people who need to learn how to systematically plan and follow programs. Chapters on self-diagnosis, defining goals, developing steps to reach goals and implementing action plans. Features scales to assess physical, emotional and intellectual human functioning, plus case study examples. 173 pp., 160 illus., 8½ x 5½", spiral bound, $6.95.

FITNESS SKILLS

GET FIT FOR LIVING

By Tom Collingwood and Robert Carkhuff. A text designed to teach you how to develop individualized physical fitness programs based upon your present physical condition and your unique goals. Includes skills for self-assessment, setting goals, plus developing and implementing fitness programs to increase your endurance, strength and flexibility. Written for helpers, parents, teachers and everyone who needs a high level of physical energy. 100 pp., 6 x 9", paper, $6.95.

GET FIT FOR LIVING TRAINER'S GUIDE

By Tom Collingwood and Robert Carkhuff. This is a training manual that details methods for teaching fitness skills. To help save you time in preparation it includes: complete lesson plans, how to develop personalized fitness programs and what you need to know about exercise and the body. 272 pp., bibliography, 6 x 9", $11.95.

GETAJOB!

By Robert Carkhuff, Richard Pierce, Ted Friel and David Willis. This is a handbook for anyone who wants to land a job. GETAJOB! teaches you the skills you need to identify assets from both your school and work experiences, find job openings before they're advertised, write powerful resumes and personal cover letters and control the job interview. It features step-by-step instructions, with examples, case studies and room to write in the book for permanent reference. After reading GETAJOB!, you'll never need help in finding a job again! 178 pp., 7 x 10'', paper, $6.95.

CAREER STUDENT'S GUIDE

By Robert Carkhuff and Ted Friel. This workbook teaches you exactly how to develop your career. Chapters on Career Expanding, Narrowing and Planning Skills give you the tools. Hundreds of exercises, examples of each step, plus thousands of job titles insure that you won't need outside help to plan your path through life. 229 pp., 8½ x 11'', paper, $6.95.

CAREER HELPER'S GUIDE

By Ted Friel and Robert Carkhuff. This guide is a collection of techniques that helpers, counselors and teachers can use to teach career skills to students. Included are methods you can use to involve students in exploring, understanding and acting upon their careers. The entire book will save you time when teaching students how to plan their lives, 323 pp., 8½ x 11'', paper, $11

JUNIOR HIGH CAREER COMIC

By Ted Friel and Robert Carkhuff. Scaled-down version of the above career books designed especially for Jr. High students. Helps make school work more relevant for students. 63 pp., illus. 8½ x 11'', $3.95.

ELEMENTARY CAREER COMIC

By Robert Carkhuff and Ted Friel. Scaled-down version of the above career books designed especially for elementary school students, grades 4-6. 48 pp., illus., 8½ x 11'', $3.45.

TEACHING AS TREATMENT

By Robert Carkhuff and Bernard Berenson. A textbook presentation of the research evidence and rationale for operationalizing "teaching as the preferred mode of helping." Written for teaching and helping personnel who want to stay on the cutting edge of their field. Offers research evidence for living, learning and working skills development with resulting physical, emotional and intellectual outcomes. Concludes with a comprehensive design for educational delivery systems. 286 pp., references, 50 illus. and 36 tables, 6 x 9'', paper, $11.95.

BELLY-TO-BELLY, BACK-TO-BACK:

By Bernard Berenson. A collection of essays, stories and poetry by Robert Carkhuff with commentaries by Dr. Berenson. These writings (some previously unpublished) provide an intimate look inside "Carkhuff the person." Written for anyone interested in the ethic, values and assumptions of Carkhuff and the emerging Human Technology movement. 102 pp., 6 x 9'', paper, $9.95.

CONFRONTATION: FOR BETTER OR WORSE!

By Bernard Berenson and Kevin Mitchell. This text provides you with a summary of a decade of research on confrontation, an in-depth view of its uses and abuses, and the perspective necessary to use the skill constructively. This is the definitive work on this subject to date! 106 pp., references, 15 tables, 6 x 9'', paper, $9.95.

CRY TWICE!
The Story of Operation Changeover

By Robert Carkhuff, et al. This is an in-depth case study of the process and ingredients of successful institutional change. It details the people, program and organizational variables that needed to be changed to transform an institution from a custodial to a treatment orientation. All this and a good story too! 128 pp., 15 illus., 6 x 9'', paper, $9.95.

THE ART OF HEALTH CARE

By William Anthony and Robert Cark-huff. Teaches the kind of interpersonal skills health care professionals need to do their job well. This text-workbook uses the vocabulary and discusses the unique problems that face nurses, physical and occupational therapists and doctors each day. Also overviews decision-making and planning skills to provide the ideal training manual for both in-service and pre-service training. 104 pp., 6 x 9", paper, $6.95.

HELPING BEGINS AT HOME

By Robert Carkhuff and Richard Pierce. This handbook of basic parenting skills is designed to be used with parents who want to learn how to make their families more effective. The physical, emotional and intellectual skills covered will lead to increased energy levels, improved interpersonal relationships and better planned lives. It features an enjoyable story of a typical family that needs and uses these easily learned and effective skills. 121 pp., 6 x 9", paper, $.6.95.

TEACHER AS PERSON

By Robert Carkhuff and Richard Pierce. This manual is designed to teach inter-personal skills to teachers who wish to avoid the ill effects of racism and sexism in their classrooms. Discusses the multicultural implications of these skills and shows how their use prevents racism and sexism. 64 pp., 9 x 10", paper, $5.95.

IPC: INTERPERSONAL COMMUNICATION SKILLS FOR CORRECTIONAL MANAGEMENT

By Jack Blakeman, Tom Keeling, Richard Pierce and Robert Carkhuff. A new train-ing manual-workbook written expressly for correctional officers who need human man-agement skills to supervise and control inmates. Teaches officers the skills they must have to size up prison situations, com-municate with inmates, control inmate behavior and prevent tragedies from happening. Features a step-by-step teach-ing process that tells the officer about the skill and why it is important, shows him how to use the skill and then allows him to try it out for himself. 116 pages, 6x9", paper, $5.95.

IPC: TRAINER'S GUIDE

By Jack Blakeman, Tom Keeling, Richard Pierce and Robert Carkhuff. This trainer's version of the IPC manual is written for the staff developer or correctional officer trainer who wants to understand the re-search base behind IPC and use proven teaching steps to deliver these skills to correctional officers. Its step-by-step in-structions, lesson plans, examples, exer-cises and homework assignments will save the trainer time, while increasing his effectiveness. 160 pages, 8½x11", paper, spiral bound, $11.95.

Mix and match titles for a discount
on **prepaid** orders only:
2-4 books 10%; 5 or more 15%.

THE HRD VIDEOTAPE SERIES

By Robert Carkhuff. Includes two levels of training videotapes produced to be used with any population above the 10th grade level. Each tape is in black and white and features Dr. Carkhuff as a model for effective helping and training. Each module has built-in pre-post tests and a lecture-demonstration-practice delivery format. As a series, they will add to any trainer's understanding of training techniques and principles, plus offer a non-threatening means for introducing the Carkhuff Model in your skills training. Finally, they allow you to stop the action to discuss key points and can save you time by allowing your trainees to independently review and preview specific skills.

THE LIFE SKILLS MODEL VIDEOTAPES

include three basic training modules to introduce the Carkhuff Model:

Helping Model Module

introduces the basic interpersonal skills of the Carkhuff model including Attending, Responding, Personalizing and Initiating. 1 hour, $250.00.

Problem Solving Model Module

reviews the Carkhuff Model and teaches the skills involved in decision-making. 1 hour, $250.00

Program Development Model Module

reviews the Carkhuff Model and then teaches the skills involved in program development. 1 hour, $250.00

THE ART OF HELPING DEMONSTRATION VIDEOTAPE

includes a taped interview with Dr. Carkhuff demonstrating the use of all of the above skills:

The Case of Jerry

involves a young man who must make an important life decision. Dr. Carkhuff utilizes interpersonal, decision-making and program development skills in this interview. 1 hour, $250.00

The above videotapes are available for purchase only. Write for our Videotape Brochure for more information on previewing, discount policy and other uses for these tapes.

THE HRD AUDIOTAPE SERIES

By Robert Carkhuff. Each of the following tape packages is a set of recorded tests to be used to measure an individual's ability to communicate and discriminate effective interpersonal skills. These packages can be used by trainers to evaluate skill gains due to training; by researchers to measure levels of interpersonal skills in different populations; and by graudate students as a valid measure for masters or doctoral level applied research. Each of the four packages contains 16 helpee stimulus problems with 5 helper responses to each problem. The items have been grouped for ease of use when pre-post testing. The problems have been chosen from a range of problems typical to each setting. Also included is a booklet with a complete transcript of the tape, directions for its use and a summary of the research behind the tapes and the Carkhuff Scales. These tapes will save time by providing you with a readily available measure of interpersonal skills functioning.

COUNSELOR-COUNSELEE PACKAGE

is designed to be used in settings concerned with counseling and guidance activities like high schools, colleges, community mental health centers and paraprofessional training programs. $25.00.

TEACHER-STUDENT PACKAGE

is designed to be used with individuals involved with students like: teachers, teacher's aides, school nurses, coaches, administrators, principals and anyone else whose work involves student contact. $25.00.

CORRECTIONAL HELPER-INMATE PACKAGE

is designed to be used with correctional officers, counselors, administrators and others whose work centers on inmates in either juvenile or adult correctional settings. $25.00.

HUMAN RELATIONS PACKAGE

is designed to be used in any of the above settings where either racism or sexism issues are of particular concern. $25.00.

ORDERING INFORMATION

1. **TO ORDER** Send list of titles and payment (check or money order) to:
   HRD PRESS
   Box 863 Dept M31
   Amherst, MA 01002

2. **TERMS:** Payment with order unless accompanied by official institutional purchase order. Books shipped BOOK RATE unless otherwise specified and paid for. We pay book rate postage on all pre-paid orders.

3. **DISCOUNTS** for prepaid orders of more than one book; mix and match titles as you wish!
1 book	0%
2-4 books	10%
5 or more	15%

4. **FOR EXTRA FAST DELIVERY** enclose 35¢ per book for UPS or 75¢ per book for 1ST CLASS MAIL. When using a purchase order full postage will be charged.

5. **WHEN ORDERING VIDEOTAPES** please specify make and model number of your machine and tape size (½" EIAJ, ¾" UMATIC CASSETTES, 1" AMPEX). Please write for our Videotape Brochure for information on previewing these tapes.

6. **BOOKSTORES ONLY:** 20% discount on all titles, shipped prepaid, FOB Lawrence, MA. Returns must be made within 90 days of invoice date and must be authorized in advance. No cash refunds permitted. All credits must be used within 1 year of date on credit memo. Invoices not paid within 30 days of end of month billed will lose discount. See NACS Trade-Text Manual for complete policy.

7. **DESK COPIES** or Teacher's Guides (when available) are sent only to adopting professors upon receipt of a photocopy of their class order for 20 or more copies of a title.

8. **COMPLIMENTARY EXAMINATION COPIES** for the purpose of review for possible adoption will be sent if you are currently teaching, or within the next year, plan to teach a course for which one of our texts is appropriate. Requests for complimentary examination copies must be on letterhead and include course title and number, current text, adoption decision date and approximate enrollment.

9. **PRICES EFFECTIVE UNTIL JANUARY 1, 1978. SEND FOR OUR LATEST CATALOG.**

order form

Please send the materials I have checked below.

	Unit Price	Quantity	Price
TEACHING SKILLS			
☐ The Skills of Teaching: Content Development Skills	$ 8.95		
☐ The Skills of Teaching: Lesson Planning Skills	$ 8.95		
☐ The Skills of Teaching: Interpersonal Skills	$ 8.95		
☐ Teacher's Guide to The Skills of Teaching: Interpersonal Skills	$ 11.95		
☐ KIDS Don't Learn from People They Don't Like	$ 11.95		
LIVING SKILLS			
☐ The Art of Helping III	$ 6.95		
☐ The Art of Helping III - Trainer's Guide	$ 11.95		
☐ The Art of Problem Solving	$ 6.95		
☐ How to Help Yourself: The Art of Program Development	$ 6.95		
RESEARCH AND PERSPECTIVE			
☐ Teaching As Treatment	$ 11.95		
☐ Belly-to-Belly, Back-to-Back	$ 9.95		
☐ Confrontation: For Better or Worse	$ 9.95		
☐ Cry Twice!	$ 9.95		
WORKING SKILLS			
☐ GET A JOB	$ 6.95		
☐ The Art of Developing A Career — Student's Guide	$ 6.95		
☐ The Art of Developing a Career — Helper's Guide	$ 11.95		
☐ Junior High School Career Comic	$ 3.95		
☐ Elementary School Career Comic	$ 3.45		
FITNESS SKILLS			
☐ Get Fit for Living	$ 6.95		
☐ Get Fit for Living — Trainer's Guide	$ 11.95		
APPLICATIONS			
☐ The Art of Health Care	$ 6.95		
☐ Helping Begins at Home	$ 6.95		
☐ Teacher As Person	$ 5.95		
☐ IPC: Skills for Correctional Management	$ 6.95		
☐ IPC: Trainer's Guide	$ 11.95		
☐ **HRD AUDIOTAPE SERIES** (following 4 packages)	$ 75.00		
☐ Counselor-Counselee Audiotape Package	$ 25.00		
☐ Teacher-Student Audiotape Package	$ 25.00		
☐ Correctional Helper-Inmate Audiotape Package	$ 25.00		
☐ Human Relations Audiotape Package	$ 25.00		
☐ **LIFE SKILLS MODEL VIDEOTAPES** (following 3 tapes)	$635.00		
☐ Helping Model Module	$250.00		
☐ Problem Solving Model Module	$250.00		
☐ Program Development Model Module	$250.00		
THE ART OF HELPING DEMONSTRATION VIDEOTAPES			
☐ The Case of Jerry	$250.00		
☐ **HRD PRESS CATALOG PACKAGE** (everything listed)	$999.95		

SUBTOTAL		
Minus Discount -		
Mass. Residents add 5% Sales Tax +		
Postage for Extra Fast delivery +		
Payment or purchase order must accompany this order. Amount enclosed $		

(check or money order)

Name_____
(please print)

Address_____

City_____ State_____ Zip_____

MAKE CHECK PAYABLE TO "HRD PRESS" AND SEND IT WITH THIS ORDER FORM TO:
HRD Press
Box 863, Dept. M31
Amherst, MA 01002

cut along this line